INTR

By
Mark Lassoff
with Julius Hernandez

LearnToProgram, LLC
129 Church Street #230
New Haven, CT 06510

To Collin

From Grandpa Lewis
2018

LearnToProgram.tv, Incorporated
129 Church Street #230
New Haven, CT 06510

contact@learntoprogram.tv

(860) 840-7090

ISBN: 9781980820574

©2018 by LearnToProgram.tv, Incorporated

All rights reserved. No part of this document may be reproduced or transmitted in any form or by any means, electronic, mechanical, photocopying, recording, or otherwise, without prior written permission of LearnToProgram.tv, Incorporated.

Limit of Liability/Disclaimer of Warranty: While the publisher and author have used their best efforts in preparing this book, they make no representations or warranties with respect to the accuracy or completeness of the contents of this book and specifically disclaim any implied warranties of merchantability or fitness for a particular purpose. No warranty may be created or extended by sales representatives or written sales materials. The advice and strategies contained herein may not be suitable for your situation. You should consult with a professional where appropriate. By following the instructions contained herein, the reader willingly assumes all risks in connection with such instructions. Neither the publisher nor author shall be liable for any loss of profit or any other commercial damages, including but not limited to special, incidental, consequential, exemplary, or other damages resulting in whole or part, from the readers' use of, or reliance upon, this material.

Dedication

For my family, friends and colleagues who supported
the development of LearnToProgram.tv and this book.

and

To my niece who is the best ten-year-old programmer I know!

Table of Contents

Chapter 1 – Introduction	10
Intended Audience	10
What Does the Book Cover?	11
Important Things to Remember	18
Chapter 2 – Getting Started	19
Downloading and Installing Python	19
Running IDLE	21
Writing Your First Python Program	22
Running the Program	23
Editing your First Program	25
Using the Shell Window	26
To Change the Editor's Various Font-Related Features	27
To Change the Editor's Highlighted Text Colors	29
To Use the Shell in Interactive Mode	32
Writing Code in the Editor Window	35
Executing Python on the Command Line	38
Coding Exercise: Writing, Running and Debugging	40
Chapter 3 – Output	44
The print() Function	44
Separators and Newlines	47
Coding Exercise: Using the print() Function	50
Chapter 4 – Variables	53
Variable Assignment	53

Number Variables (int , float, and complex)	59
String Variables	63
Substrings and Concatenation	65
Variables with Lists, Tuples, and Dictionaries	69
Coding Exercise: Using Variables	73
Chapter 5 – Operators	75
Mathematical Operators	75
Order of Operations	82
Comparison Operators	85
Logical Operators	89
Coding Exercise: Operators Practice	91
Chapter 6 – Code Branching	93
Simple If Statements	93
If…Else Statements	97
Nested If Statements	103
The Ternary Operator	105
Coding Exercise: Operators Practice	107
Chapter 7 – Loops	109
The While Loop	109
The For Loop	117
Nested Loops	121
Break and Continue Statements	124
Coding Exercise: Loops	128
Chapter 8 – Math Functions	132
Casting Functions	132

Mathematical Functions	136
Random Functions	140
Coding Exercise: Math Functions	143
Chapter 9 – String Functions	146
The capitalize (), center (), and count () functions	146
The find (), isalpha (), and isdigit () functions	150
The join (), len (), and split () functions	152
Coding Exercise: String Functions	154
Chapter 10 – Tuples and Dictionaries	157
Creating Tuples	157
Accessing Values in Tuples	158
Printing specific values from a tuple	159
Looping through a Tuple	159
Tuple Functions	161
What are lists?	161
The len() Function	162
Using the len() Function to Loop through a Tuple	163
The min() and max() Functions	163
Converting a List to a Tuple	163
Declaring a Dictionary	165
Accessing and Editing Values in Dictionaries	165
Printing specific values from a dictionary	166
Changing the elements in a dictionary	166
print("Change:", player["Position"])	166
Deleting an element in a dictionary	166

Dictionary Functions	167
The len() Function	168
The str() Function	168
The clear() Function	168
The get function	168
The items function	168
The values function	169
The keys function	169
Getting the Elements and Key-Value Pairs in a Dictionary	169
Coding Exercise: String Functions	170
Chapter 11 – Time and Date	**173**
The Time Tuple	173
time.asctime(time.localtime(time.time()))	175
The Calendar	176
The Time and Calendar Functions	177
Coding Exercise: Functions	179
Chapter 12 – Python Functions	**182**
Defining and Calling a Simple Function	182
Required Argument Functions	185
Keyword Argument Functions	187
Default Function Arguments	191
Return Statement	196
Creating and Consuming Python Modules	198
Coding Exercise: Functions	200
Chapter 13 – Input and Output	**202**

Reading Keyboard Input	202
Reading an External Text File	205
Writing an External Text File	209
Coding Exercise: File I/O	212
Chapter 14 – More with Python	214
Handling Exceptions	214
Web Server Coding with Python	218
Processing Form Data with Python	221
Wrap Up and Goodbye	224

Chapter 1 – Introduction

Figure 1.1. The familiar Python logo. Python is a well-supported, open-sourced language. It is freely-available for both personal and commercial use.

Welcome to Python for Beginners! With this book, you will learn the basics of Python, a powerful high-level and object-oriented programming language that is suitable for both beginners and experienced programmers. The goal of Python is to make programming easy to learn. It is open-source and is free to use and distribute, even commercially.

Intended Audience

Prior knowledge of Python is not required to learn from this book. Whether you are new to programming or you are someone who has programmed before using another language, you will find this book to be the ideal resource for learning Python.

For beginners who are new to Python, computer science knowledge would be helpful. However, it is not required. It is important to spend time understanding the concepts and doing the coding exercises. This is a sure-fire way to retain knowledge gained from this book.

The concepts discussed in the book will be familiar to someone with prior programming experience. For those readers, it is expected that the book will fast-track their understanding of Python programming concepts and how they differ from the language/s they have used before.

At the end of the course, you will have the basic skills necessary to take your Python programming skills to the next level. Learn to Program's Python for Game Development courses are perfect for that.

Figure 1.2. Learning the basics of Python programming has never been easier with the Python for Beginners video course on Learn to Program TV and this companion book. After you have completed this beginner's course, you can take your Python development skills to the next level with our Game Development for Python courses.

What Does the Book Cover?

This book has 12 chapters, including this introductory chapter. We will go through the next chapters briefly below.

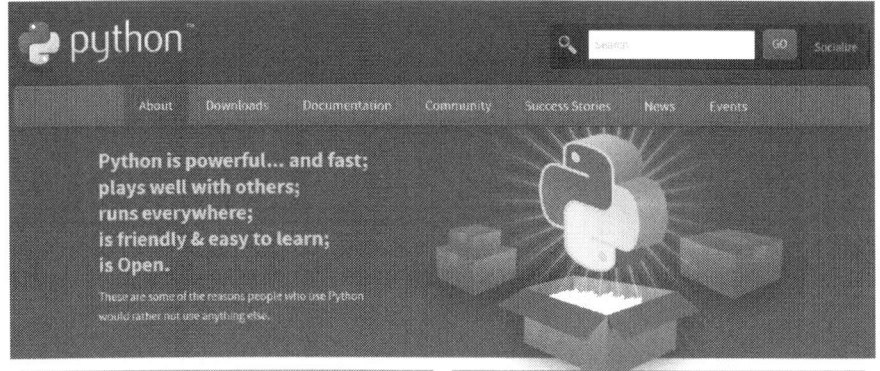

Figure 1.3. The home page of the Python.org website, where you can download installers and documentation on the Python programming language. The website also features the latest news and events about Python, and the robust Python user community.

In Chapter 2, you will start by downloading and installing Python (installation packages are available for Windows, Linux and other Unix-based platforms, and Mac OS X). You will then code your first Python program using **IDLE**, or the **Integrated Development and Learning Environment**, which is installed with Python. Your very first Python program would be a simple program. However, what better way is there to fire up the excitement of learning a programming language than writing your first program? You will then execute the program from the command line. In this chapter, you will also learn how to use the Python shell window interactively. You will be able to write and run programming commands directly from the shell window. You will then have a coding exercise at the end, that will reinforce the concepts discussed in the chapter.

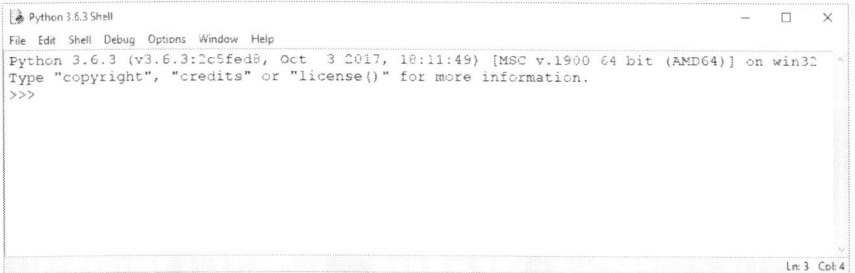

Figure 1.4. Python includes a cross-platform IDE known as IDLE, for Integrated Development and Learning Environment. IDLE was coded entirely in Python and can be configured to your liking.

In Chapter 3, you will learn how the first program you wrote in Chapter 1 works. This chapter will teach you how to output the results from your program onto the screen, by using the Print function. You will also learn about the proper usage of separators and newlines, which allow a finer grain of control on displaying output on the command line. At the end, you will tie this all together with a coding exercise on the Print function.

Figure 1.5. IDLE has built-in syntax highlighting, and code indentation, among other features, commonly found in commercial IDEs.

Chapter 4 discusses the use of variables in Python. You might remember variables from your algebra class, such as in the expression x + 10 = 15, what is the value of the variable *x*? Variables play an important role in Python, as well as other programming languages. You will learn how to assign variables, and then review the different types of variables you can use in your programs, including numbers, strings, and substrings and how to concatenate them. You will also learn about the different variables that you can use in lists, tuples, and dictionaries (we will discuss these data structures in greater detail in Chapter 10). Finally, you will tie together everything you learned about variables in another coding exercise.

Chapter 5 focuses on the use of operators, which are used to complete expressions made up of variables. For example, in the expression x + 10 = 15, the symbols + and = are operators (the + sign is a mathematical operator, denoting that the number *10* should be added to the variable *x*, while the = sign is an assignment operator, which means it assigns the number *15* to the expression *x+10*). The order in which these operators are evaluated works is the same way as in math – given an expression, you should solve it in the following order:

parentheses, exponents, multiplication, division, addition, and subtraction. In addition to mathematical operators, you will also learn about comparison and logical operators. As the name implies, a comparison operator *compares* two variables or values, while a logical operator allows you to join expressions. A coding exercise will be given at the end to test your newly-acquired knowledge.

In Chapter 6, you will learn about code branching, or decision making, in Python. Given a condition, which path should your program take? Does it go this way, or that? You will learn about various conditional statements, ranging from simple *If* to nested *If-Else* statements, and how to implement them properly in your Python programs. You will also learn about Python's ternary, or conditional, operator, which works differently than similar operators in other programming languages. You will also have an opportunity to again test your understanding of the skills you learned in the chapter with another coding exercise.

Chapter 7 is all about loops. They perform an operation repeatedly, until all its conditions are met. You will learn about Python's implementation of different kinds of loops. **While** loops are the simplest. **For** loops are implemented differently in Python, compared to other programming languages. **Nested** loops are contained within another loop, while break and continue statements allow greater control over an operation. In this chapter's coding exercise, you will be asked to code a program that will compute interest on an investment. Your output will result in the first useful program in the course.

Chapter 7 is the midpoint of the course. Chapter 8 discusses Python's powerful math functions, which are a strong suit of the language. It is one of the reasons why data analysts prefer Python to other programming languages. You will learn about casting functions, more advanced math functions and randomization functions. Casting functions are used to convert one variable type to another, such as by using int(), you can convert a floating-point number to an integer. Python's advanced math functions allow increasingly complex calculations to be performed, while the random functions allow random number generation. This is useful for programs where random numbers are required. The sheer number of functions in Python's Math library makes it impossible to cover all of them in the book. However, you will learn the most essential and important functions and how they can be used. Chapter 8 is similar to other functions, since it ends with a coding exercise that will test your knowledge about Python math functions.

Chapter 9 teaches you about the functions that you can use for string manipulation and processing in your Python programs. Like its math functions, the Python String library is so large that it is impossible to discuss them all in an introductory book on Python programming (the material may be enough to fill a book or two of its own). You will, therefore, only learn a few string functions that are essential to make you a competent Python programmer. As you continue on your coding journey, you will discover the other string functions on your own. Another coding exercise awaits you at the end.

Chapter 10 discusses lists, tuples, and dictionaries. These are data structures that allow you to store more complex data for your programs. There are many functions available for manipulating data stored in these structures. First, you will learn how to create lists and tuples and access the values available in them, by using the various tuple functions. Lists are like tuples, except that, once created, you can still edit them. By contrast, you cannot edit a tuple once it is created. You will learn the same things with dictionaries, which are like lists, except that the objects contained in a dictionary are accessed via keys (you access objects in a list via their position within the list). You will then learn how to manipulate data within these data structures yourself through another coding exercise.

In Chapter 11, you will learn about some of the time and date functions available in Python. This includes how to access data in a Time tuple, advance to the Calendar object and then learn about the time and calendar functions. You will apply what you have learned via a coding exercise involving these functions.

Chapter 12 builds upon your knowledge of the various built-in Python functions by teaching you how to write your own custom functions. The information contained in this chapter will allow you to start taking your programming skills to the next level. You will learn how to define and call a simple function, required argument functions, keyword argument functions, as well as the default arguments available to your functions. You will also learn how to use return statements with your functions. This allows them to return a value when called. You will also learn how to consume existing Python modules. The last part of this chapter teaches you how to create your own custom Python module. You will have the opportunity to apply all this critical information in a coding exercise.

By this time, you will nearly be at the end of your coding journey using Python. In the previous chapters, you did all your programming on the Python shell. In Chapter 13, input and output (I/O, as it is called in programming) from outside the shell will be the focus. You will learn how to let your programs read input from the keyboard and external files. You will then write to an external file using your program. Your coding exercise will be on file I/O.

Chapter 14 will present other topics that are designed to prepare you for more advanced Python programming skills. You will learn how to handle exceptions, or run-time errors in your program. You will then learn about web server coding with Python. You will learn how to run Python on a web server and use it to serve HTML pages to users. Finally, you will learn about processing form data from a website using Python. There will not be a coding exercise in Chapter 14.

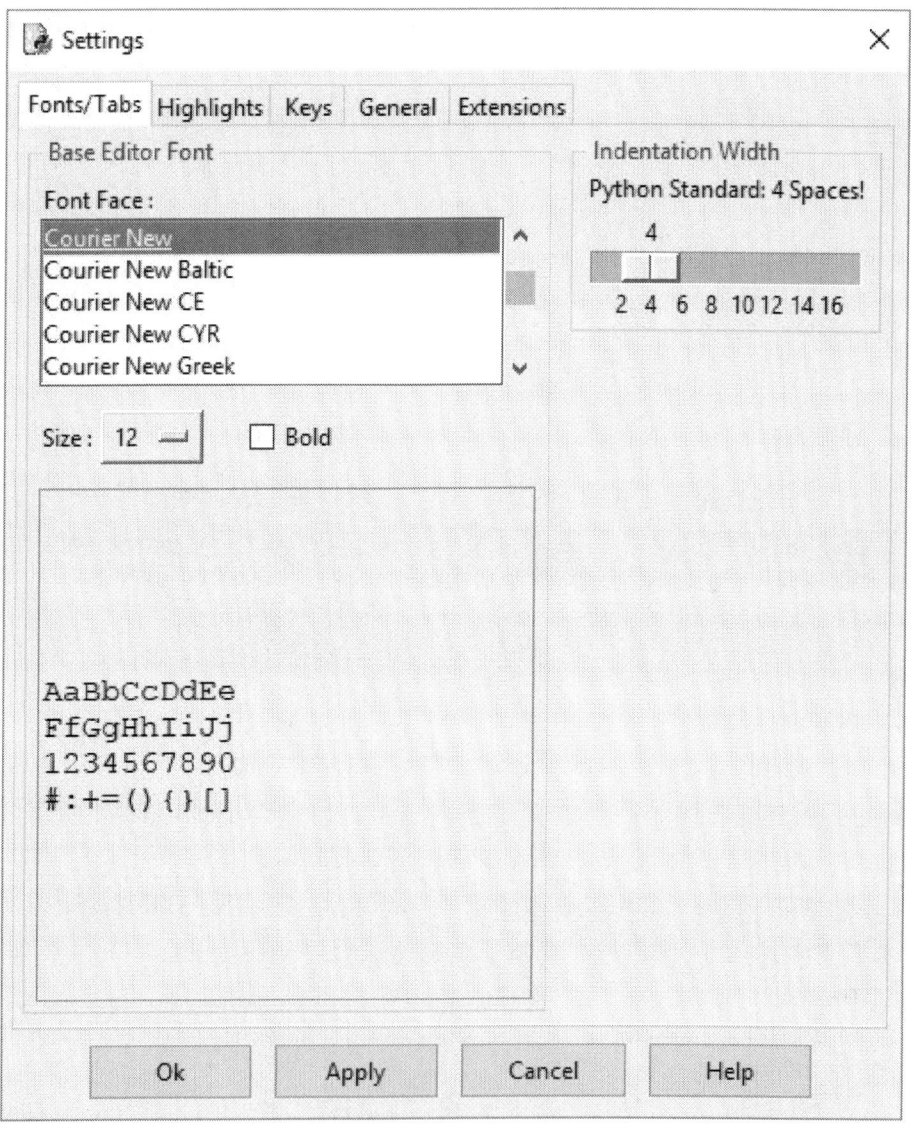

Figure 1.6. IDLE is easy to configure. You can change font faces and sizes, customize the foreground and background colors used in syntax highlighting, use built-in highlighting themes, customize keyboard shortcuts (useful if you are accustomed to working on another platform), start it up when you boot into your OS, and use extensions.

Important Things to Remember

One of the advantages of Python is that it is platform-independent. For any preferred coding platform, the chances of modifying your code so that, as an example, your Windows program would run on Macs, *are* minimal. Moreover, IDLE (which is entirely coded in Python) operates in a similar way across platforms. If you change platforms midway through a project, you can proceed seamlessly and pick up from where you left off.

Other than IDLE, you can also use your trusty text editor for coding Python programs. There are IDEs that specifically target or support Python. If you like to use other IDEs as you go through the book, feel free to do so. You can expect minimal modification of the coding exercises to suit your preferred IDE.

For the sake of readability, this book primarily uses Windows keyboard shortcuts in its instructions. As Mac users probably know, Mac shortcuts are generally the same. However, the Command key is used in place of Ctrl and Option instead of Alt. Please refer to the table below for a full list of shortcuts for both Mac and Windows. You don't have to memorize it, but feel free to use it as a reference. We will cover more specific shortcuts as they come up in this book. However, some basic shortcuts to keep in mind are Undo (Ctrl+Z), Step Backward (Ctrl+Alt+Z), Step Forward (Shift+Ctrl+Z), Copy (Ctrl+C), and Paste (Ctrl+V). If you are working on a Mac, simply replace Ctrl with Command and Alt with Option.

The Linux equivalents to Windows shortcuts depend on your desktop environment. On Gnome and KDE, two of the more popular Linux desktop environments, shortcuts are generally the same as in Windows.

There is one last thing to mention before proceeding to the next chapter. Many Linux distributions have Python installed by default. If you are using Linux and you cannot see Python among its installed packages, you can often just use your package manager to install Python.

With that out of the way, let's proceed to the next chapter, where you will code your first Python program!

Chapter 2 – Getting Started

This chapter will teach you how to download and install Python on your computer, run its built-in programming environment, and create your very first Python program. In the process of learning these things, you will also learn about executing your program on the command line, and using the Python shell for coding interactive programs. At the end of this chapter, you will have a coding exercise where you will apply the concepts of writing, running, and debugging Python programs.

Before you start on your coding journey, you should have already installed Python on your computer. If you have not yet installed Python, go through the next section first. If you have Python installed already, you can skip to the next section.

Downloading and Installing Python

The easiest way to install Python is to download an installer for your computer from the official Python website, https://www.python.org.

Python 3.6.3 is the latest version, as of December 2017. The coding exercises in this book assume that you are using this version, or at least a version close to it. It is recommended that beginners to the language, or any programming language for that matter, start learning with the latest version to avoid any problems with older, legacy versions.

Python has official releases for Windows, Linux/Unix, and Mac OS X, as well as other platforms, including iOS (yes, you can write Python scripts on your favorite iPad or iPhone). If you are using Linux or Unix, Python is probably already available on your favorite package manager, ready for installation at any time. You can also try compiling Python from tarball sources, which are also available for download on the website.

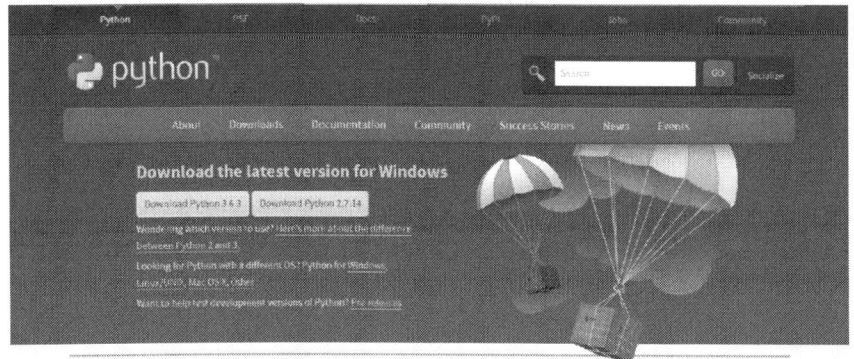

Figure 2.1. Python installers for Windows, Linux, MacOS, and other platforms are available for download from the Python.org website.

Installing Python is relatively straightforward, and should proceed without any hassle.

Figure 2.2. After downloading an installer for your platform, you can then install Python. The process is relatively straightforward, and should run without a hitch.

A short note before we start coding: Python is a popular language. It has a robust, active user community that you might want to join. A supportive community comprising both fellow newbies and veteran coders is always a welcome ally, as you march towards Python mastery.

As mentioned in Chapter 1, the book uses Windows keyboard shortcuts for its instructions. Whatever platform you are using, you should still be able to follow the instructions.

Running IDLE

Any text editor should suffice for writing Python programs. However, in this book, you will be using Python's integrated text editor named IDLE, for Integrated Development and Learning Environment.

To run IDLE:
1. Press ⊞ on your keyboard, and enter the phrase "Python."
2. Select **IDLE (Python 3.x 32-/64-bit)** from among the results, then click or press **Enter** on your keyboard. IDLE should run soon after.

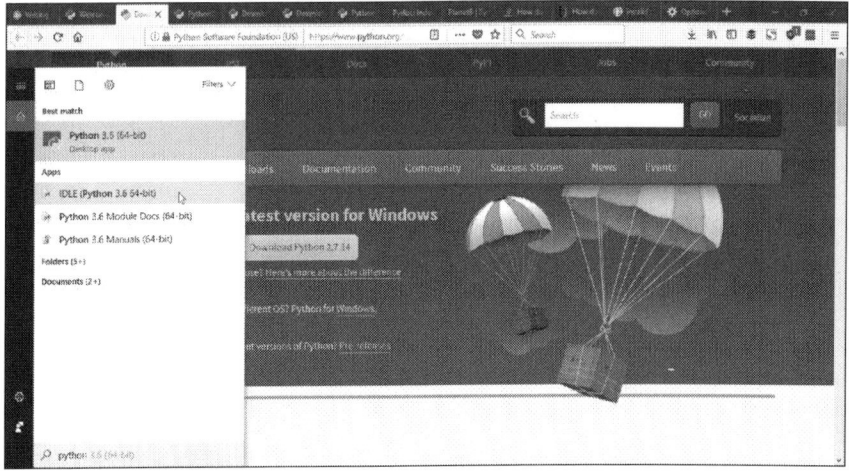

Figure 2.3. Python's Integrated and Development Learning Environment, or IDLE, is used to show code samples throughout the book. Built entirely in Python, IDLE is also open source.

You will notice that the IDLE's Python Shell is similar to your Windows command line, or your Linux and Mac OS terminal, at least in appearance. It also operates in much the same way.

```
 Python 3.6.3 Shell                                              — □ ×
File Edit Shell Debug Options Window Help
Python 3.6.3 (v3.6.3:2c5fed8, Oct  3 2017, 18:11:49) [MSC v.1900 64 bit (AMD64)]
on win32
Type "copyright", "credits" or "license()" for more information.
>>>
                                                                    Ln: 3 Col: 4
```

Figure 2.4. IDLE's Python Shell is similar in many ways to the Windows command prompt, or the terminal on Linux and Mac OS.

Writing Your First Python Program

As is customary among first-time programmers, your first program will output the phrase "Hello World" on your computer. To do this, the program uses the Print() command.

With IDLE now open, it is time to start writing your first Python program.
1. Click **File,** then **New File**. Alternatively, press **Ctrl+N** on your keyboard.

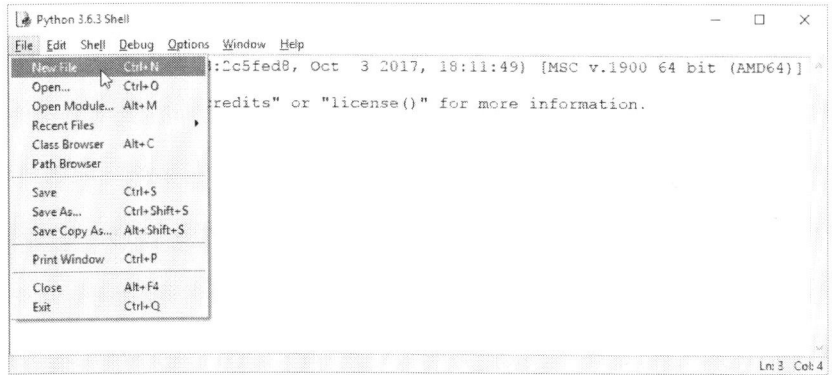

Figure 2.5. Click **File**, then **New File**, or press **Ctrl+N** on your keyboard to open a blank Editor window, which you will use to write your code.

2. A blank *editor* window opens. You will write your code here. Enter the following commands on separate lines:

print("Hello World")

print("Welcome to Python for Beginners 2017!")

3. To save the file, click **File**, then **Save**, or press **Ctrl+S** on your keyboard.

Page 21

4. On the **Save As** window, enter **Hello** as the file name, then click **Save**. The file can be saved to any location on your computer. For example, all the code in this book are saved to a Python 2017 folder on our desktop.

You have just created a program that will print, or output, the lines *Hello World* and *Welcome to Python for Beginners 2017* to your screen.

Running the Program

There are two ways to run a Python program. The first one involves opening a command prompt (or terminal, on Linux and Mac), then running the program from there. The second one involves running the program from the IDLE.

Let's try the first method.
1. On your PC, bring up a command prompt window, or press ⊞ on your keyboard, and enter the phrase **Command Prompt**.
2. On the command prompt, navigate to the folder where you saved your file.
3. Enter the following command to call the program:

python hello.py
4. The program then outputs the following on the command prompt.

Hello World

Welcome to Python for Beginners 2017!

Figure 2.6. Navigate to the folder where you saved your program, then run the program. The command to run a Python program is in the form *python+filename*. In this screenshot of the command prompt, the program is called by python hello.py. Note the lines that appear right after the command are entered on the window.

From Fig. 2.6, we can see the following:

* The command to call Python programs is **python**, followed by the complete file name, in this case, **hello.py**. Thus, to run the program, you enter **python hello.py** on the command prompt.
* All Python programs have a **.py** file suffix. You need to include the suffix every time you run a program this way. Otherwise, you will get an error.
* The program output, **Hello World**, and **Welcome to Python for Beginners 2017**, on two separate lines, correspond to the two lines enclosed in parentheses we asked our Hello World program to output, or **print**, on screen.

The second, more direct way to run the program involves using IDLE.
1. Click **File**, then **Open**, and navigate to the folder where you saved your program to open the file in a new window.

2. Click **Run**, then **Run Module**, or press **F5** on your keyboard.

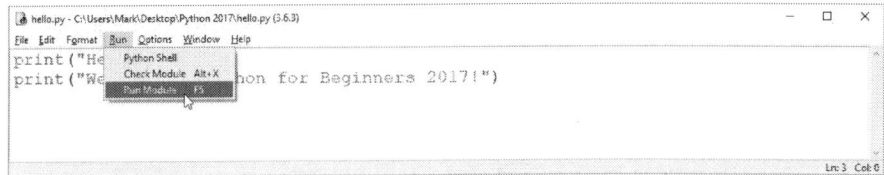

Figure 2.7. Click **Run**, then **Run Module**, to run the program. Alternatively, press **F5** on your keyboard.

3. The Python shell then runs the program by *printing* the phrases "Hello World" and "Welcome to Python for Beginners 2017."

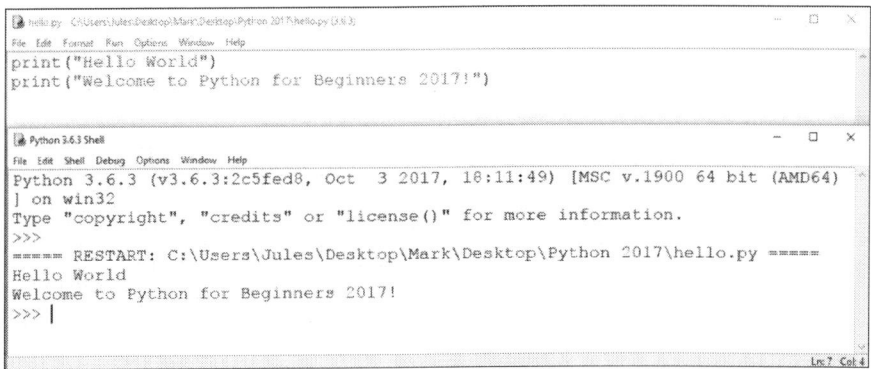

Figure 2.8. When the program is run, it prints the output (the lines highlighted in blue) to the Python shell window. The color of the output text can be customized by clicking **Options**, then **Configure IDLE**. You will learn more about this later in this section.

Editing your First Program

Let's see what happens, if you add another line of code to your program.
1. Click **File**, then **Open**, then navigate to the folder where you saved your program to open the file in a new window.

Add the following line to your program:

print("I'm Mark Lassoff, your instructor")

2. Click **Run**, then **Run Module**, or press **F5** on your keyboard, to run the program again, the output of which is shown below.

Hello World

Welcome to Python for Beginners 2017!

I'm Mark Lassoff, your instructor

That's it for your first program! You started out with just a couple of lines, then added another line at the end. The final output might just be three lines long. However, it's your very first Python program, so clap yourself on the back and congratulate yourself on your achievement.

Using the Shell Window

This next section teaches you how to use the Python shell. You will learn to customize its appearance to suit your tastes, and then learn about its other features. It will also teach you to code interactively using the shell. This means that you enter code on the shell, then also run it directly from within the shell. This is a great way to learn Python, since it allows you to test out code without writing a formal program. At least, not yet. You can then try the same code within the context of a program, having learned how the code behaves using the shell window.

When you start IDLE, there is a line on top of the shell that advises you to enter *copyright(), credits(),* or *license()* to learn more about the software. If you enter *copyright()* on the shell, you will see the copyright terms for Python appear on screen. Entering *credits()* will display the organizations credited with developing Python, and *license()* will display Python's open-source license.

Let's look at the Shell window in more detail. Specifically, let's look at how you can change the font face, size, and color for the highlighted code in the Editor.

To Change the Editor's Various Font-Related Features

1. On your PC, press ⊞ on your keyboard, and enter **IDLE**. This will display **IDLE (Python 3.x 32-/64-bit)** on the Search results.

2. Click **IDLE (Python 3.x 32-/64-bit)**, or press **Enter**, to run the Python shell.
3. When the shell window appears, click **Options**, then **Configure IDLE**.

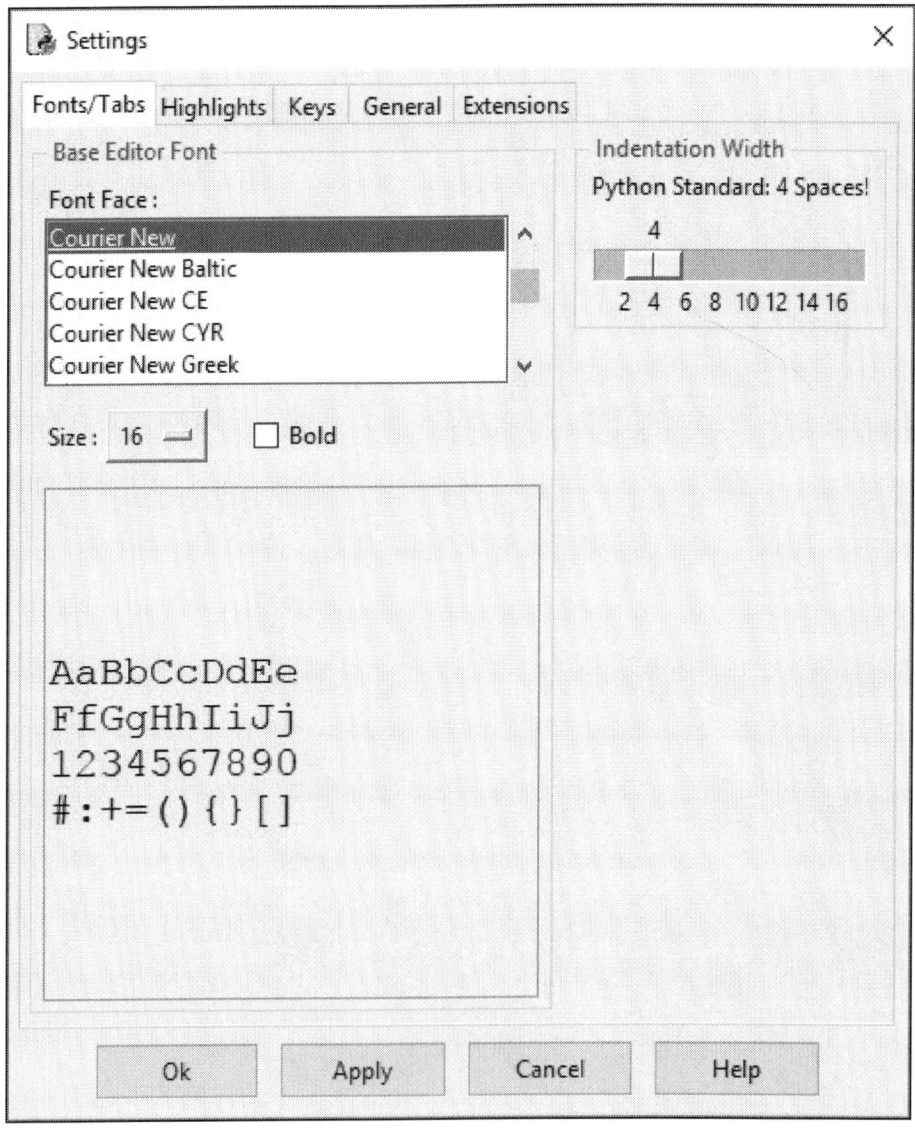

Figure 2.9. Click Options, then **Configure IDLE** to open the **Settings** window, where you can customize the font face, size, and colors of the highlighted text on the Editor.

4. On the **Settings** window, the **Fonts/Tabs** tab is selected by default. To customize the font used for various highlighted text in the Editor, select another one from the list.
5. To increase the font size for more readability and make the font bold by default, select a different size from the list, and check the **Bold** box.
6. To increase the indentation width from the standard four (4) spaces, drag the slider down to the minimum size 2 or up to size six and above. It is recommended, however, to stay with the standard size.
7. After you are done customizing the fonts used within IDLE, click **Apply** to have IDLE implement your changes.

To Change the Editor's Highlighted Text Colors

1. On the **Settings** window, click the **Highlights** tab.

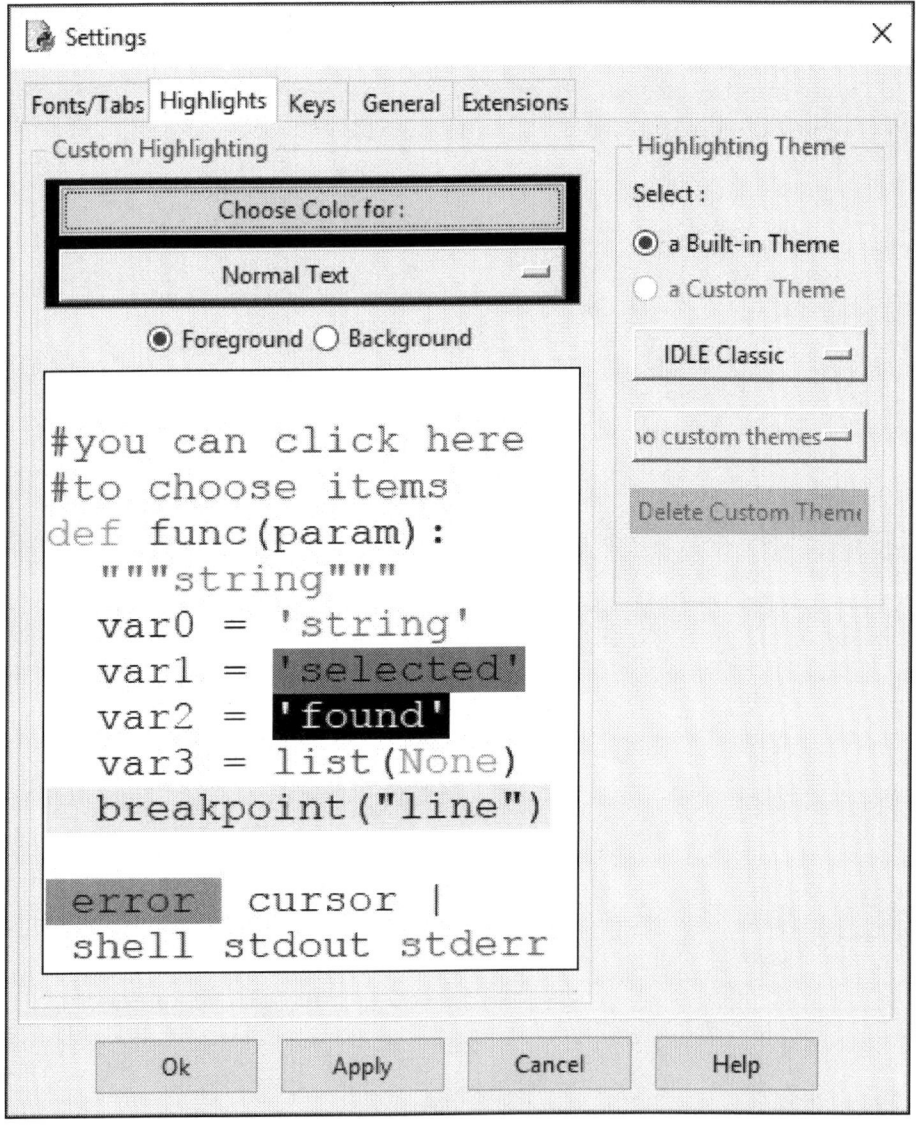

Figure 2.10. The Settings window's Highlights tab is where the foreground and background colors of highlighted text are customized. Here, highlight themes can also be applied to the Editor.

2. To change the foreground and background colors used for highlighting text within the shell, select the text type first by either clicking the **Normal Text** button and selecting another text type, for

example, **Python keywords**, from the list, or clicking the sample text in the box.
3. After selecting the text type, change the foreground color by clicking the **Choose Color for:** button, then selecting another color from the palette.
4. To change the highlighting theme, select another theme from the three available on the list.
5. After you are done customizing the text colors used within IDLE, click **Apply** to have IDLE implement your changes.

There are three other tabs on the **Settings** window. The **Keys** tab is where you can change the built-in key set available for your operating system (OS). This is useful, if you are coming from or are more familiar working with another OS.

The **General** tab allows you to set various other Window and Editor preferences, as well as set another Help source for when you are using the Editor. For example, you can set this book as a reference by pointing the shell to a PDF copy on your computer.

The **Extensions** tab shows you IDLE's extensions, with zzdummy the only current default extension. Zzdummy is used for testing.

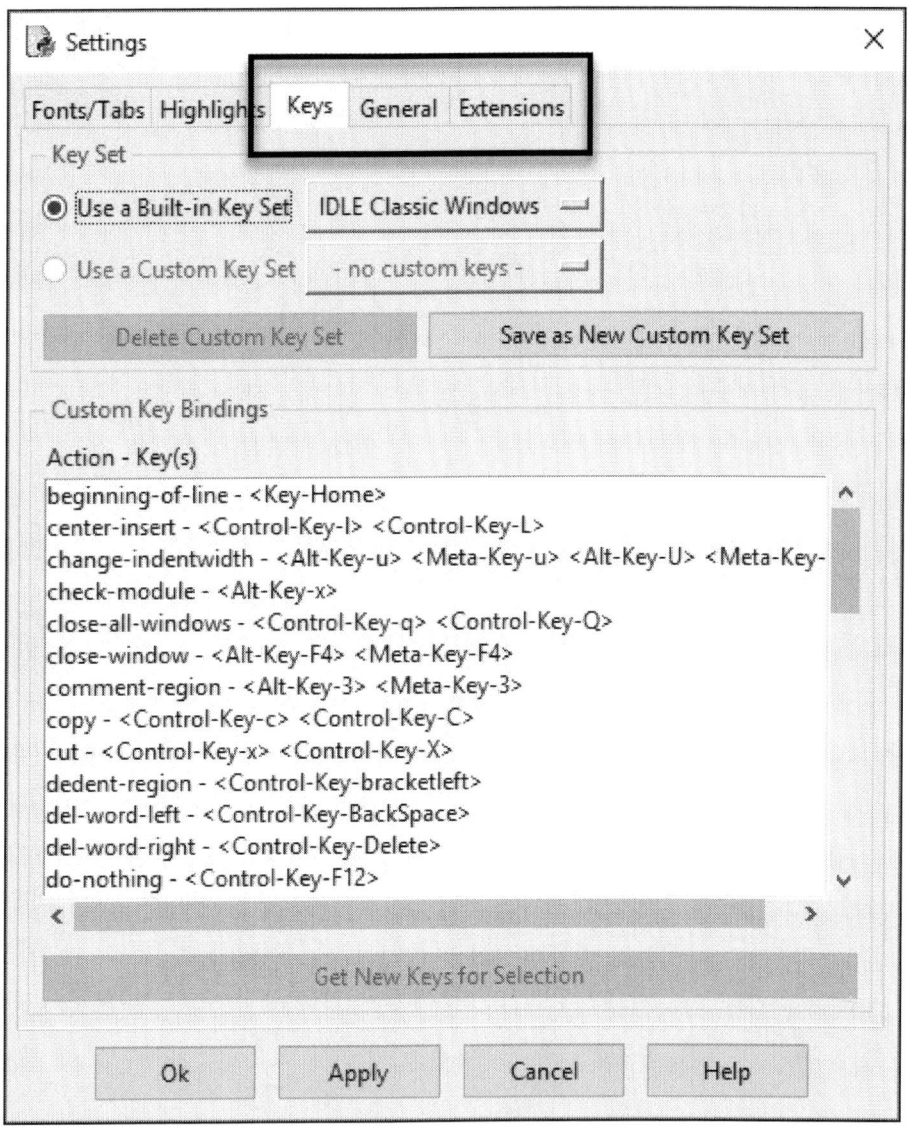

Figure 2.11. The **Keys**, **General**, and **Extensions** tabs on the **Settings** window contain the other settings in the IDLE that you can customize. Experiment with the settings, until you feel comfortable with how your program code and output looks when displayed on the Editor.

To Use the Shell in Interactive Mode

Let's now look at running code interactively on the shell.

1. Run IDLE.

On the shell, where the >> is, enter the following command:

print("I'm Mark Lassoff, your instructor")

2. Press **Enter**. This prints **Mark Lassoff, your instructor** on the next line.

As you can see from the above example, Python processed the code you entered in the shell window.

Let's try out other commands.

Enter **2 + 2** on the shell, then press **Enter**.

The answer to our short, simple addition problem, **4**, then appears on the next line.

Let's enter a more complex expression.

Enter **26874/2.5*8-.076+3**, then press **Enter**.

Python solves the problem for us, by showing the answer on the next line.

So far, we have shown that mathematical expressions, simple and complex, are processed interactively by the shell.

Let's have the shell solve for variants next.

Enter the following code on the shell, press **Enter** after each line.

x = 10

print (x)

What happens? That's right, the answer, **0**, appears on the next line. The code assigns **10** to x, then prints the value of **x** to the screen.

Let's try out another example.

Enter the following code:

name = "Mark Lassoff, your instructor"

print (name)

Pressing **Enter** prints the following on the next line:

Mark Lassoff, your instructor

Let's have Python solve for x again.

print (x)

What happens? **10**, the value we gave x previously, appears on screen.

So far, you have seen that Python interprets what we enter on the shell interactively. Python retains all these in memory, at least until you restart the shell.

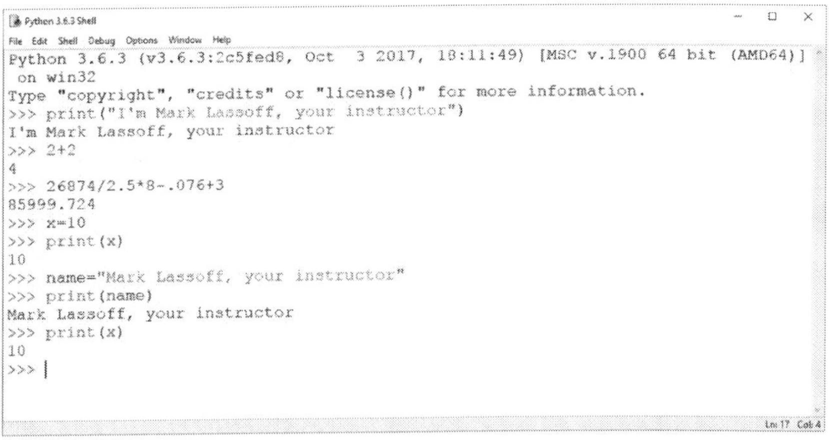

```
Python 3.6.3 Shell
File Edit Shell Debug Options Window Help
Python 3.6.3 (v3.6.3:2c5fed8, Oct  3 2017, 18:11:49) [MSC v.1900 64 bit (AMD64)]
on win32
Type "copyright", "credits" or "license()" for more information.
>>> print("I'm Mark Lassoff, your instructor")
I'm Mark Lassoff, your instructor
>>> 2+2
4
>>> 26874/2.5*8-.076+3
85999.724
>>> x=10
>>> print(x)
10
>>> name="Mark Lassoff, your instructor"
>>> print(name)
Mark Lassoff, your instructor
>>> print(x)
10
>>>
```

Figure 2.12. This screenshot shows the interactive Python commands you entered and their results displayed on the Python shell window.

Let's try that next.

Restart the shell by clicking **Shell**, then **Restart Shell**, or pressing **Ctrl+F6**.

Then enter:

print (x)

This time, an error occurs. From the last line on that technical gobbledygook, we can see the cause of the error: name 'x' is not defined.

Let's try the same thing with the **name** variable we defined earlier.

print (name)

The same type of error occurs.

```
Python 3.6.3 Shell
File Edit Shell Debug Options Window Help
Pytho  View Last Restart  F6      :2c5fed8, Oct  3 2017, 18:11:49) [MSC v.1900 64 bit (AMD64)]
on w   Restart Shell    Ctrl+F6
Type   Interrupt Execution Ctrl+C   redits" or "license()" for more information.
>>> print("I'm Mark Lassoff, your instructor")
I'm Mark Lassoff, your instructor
>>> 2+2
4
>>> 26874/2.5*8-.076+3
85999.724
>>> x=10
>>> print(x)
10
>>> name="Mark Lassoff, your instructor"
>>> print(name)
Mark Lassoff, your instructor
>>> print(x)
10
>>>
```

Figure 2.13. Restarting the shell by clicking **Shell**, then **Restart Shell**, or pressing **Ctrl+F6**, effectively refreshes the Python shell and clears it of the interactive commands you entered earlier.

As you can see from the above examples, restarting the shell tells Python to start from scratch, erasing from its memory the values that you have previously associated with the variables **x** and **name**.

You can see from the example above, how easy it is to play around with code on the shell. While learning to code, you can adopt the shell as a training tool, experimenting with code segments that you can use in your programs.

Writing Code in the Editor Window

Let us take a more detailed look at how the Editor works in this section.

1. Run IDLE.
2. Click **File**, then **New** File, or press **Ctrl+N**, to open a new Editor window.
3. Define the following variables:

name = "Python for Beginners 2017"

age = 42

instructor = "Mark Lassoff"

4. Add the following commands:

print (name)

print (age)

print (instructor)

Note that as you type, the Editor shows *calltips* to guide you as you write your program.

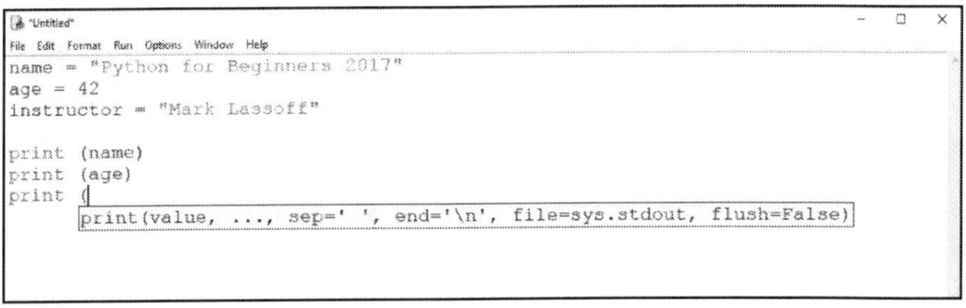

```
name = "Python for Beginners 2017"
age = 42
instructor = "Mark Lassoff"

print (name)
print (age)
print (
      print(value, ..., sep=' ', end='\n', file=sys.stdout, flush=False)
```

Figure 2.14. The Editor window shows *calltips* as you enter your code. These serve as guides as you go about creating your programs.

5. Before saving the program, add the following comments on top.

#Python Course

#Mark Lassoff

#LearnToProgram.tv

Comments are preceded by ampersands and are not interpreted, or are disregarded by Python when it runs the program. They explain what the program is all about, as a guide to readers or other developers who might need to study the program later. Comments will be essential, as you learn to code more complex programs. They will make your life easier, and serve to document your code.

6. Add separate comments for the variables and commands. Your code now looks like the following:

#Python Course

#Mark Lassoff

#LearnToProgram.tv

#Set Variables

name = "Python for Beginners 2017"

age = 42

instructor = "Mark Lassoff"

#Output

print (name)

print (age)

print (instructor)

7. Before saving, you can try experimenting with formatting your code by clicking **Format**, then going through the available options under that menu. For example, to indent your code, highlight the code you want to indent, then click **Format**, then **Indent Region**. Commenting out code blocks is another option. It makes commenting easier, since you can comment out several lines of code at the same time, rather than appending an ampersand at the beginning of each line to be commented out one at a time.
8. Click **File**, then **Save**, or press **Ctrl+S** to save the program.
9. Run the program by clicking **Run**, then **Run Module**, or pressing **F5**. The output will look like the following:

You wrote a longer program in this section while, at the same time, learning more about the Editor, including its formatting features. As your programs become more complex, you will find that proper formatting will make your codes more readable.

Executing Python on the Command Line

So far, you have been using IDLE's Python shell and editor window to run and create your programs. Note that you can still use Python, even outside the shell and the editor window. This is because Python resides on the operating system and does not require the Python shell to run. You will see how this works in this section.

In addition, as this section demonstrates, you can use another text editor to code your Python program before running it on the command line. If you are on Windows, you can use Notepad. If you are on Linux or Mac, you may use your preferred text editor to code your program.

Let's proceed.

1. Open Notepad. As mentioned, you may use any text editor you prefer.

Figure 2.15. Notepad, or any text editor, can be used for writing your Python programs

2. Enter the following lines on Notepad:

x = 45

y = 115

print("X times Y is: ")

print(x*y)

3. Save the file to any folder on your computer.
4. Open a command prompt, or press ⊞ on your keyboard, and enter the phrase **Command Prompt**.
5. On the command prompt, if you enter **Python**, an interactive **Python** window opens. However, you will not be running the program interactively, so navigate to the folder where you saved your file, then enter the following command:

python commandline.py
6. The program then outputs the following on the command prompt.

X times Y is:

5175

7. Let's edit the program by changing the values of **x** and **y**.

x = 2015.55

y = 8.79

8. Save the file, then run it again. You will get a different result this time, because of the changes to **x** and **y**.

X times Y is:

17716.6845

That is it for executing Python on the command line. Though this is not typical of the way programmers use Python, we showed this to you so that you can see that Python can be executed on the command line, if needed.

Coding Exercise: Writing, Running and Debugging

You will review the process of writing and executing a complete program in this exercise. You will also cause an error condition in the program, correct it, and execute the corrected code.

1. Open IDLE, then click **File**, then **New**, to open a new editor window.

Enter the following code on the editor window. As you can see, the code uses the print() command, assigns values to the variables **age**, **band**, **food**, **and state**, then prints out the strings and variable values.

```
#Code Exercise 1
#Python for Beginners 2017

print("Mark Lassoff")
print("Born: February 21")
age=42
print("I am", age, "years old")

band="Journey"
food="Spaghetti"
state="Connecticut"

print("My favorite band is", band)
print("I like to eat", food)
print("My favorite state is", state)
```

```
# exercise 1.py - C:/Users/Mark/Desktop/Python 2017/exercise 1.py (3.6.3)
File  Edit  Format  Run  Options  Window  Help
#Code Exercise 1
#Python for Beginners 2017

print("Mark Lassoff")
print("Born: February 21")
age=42
print("I am", age, "years old")

band="Journey"
food="Spaghetti"
state="Connecticut"

print("My favorite band is", band)
print("I like to eat", food)
print("My favorite state is", state)
```

Figure 2.16. The code from the exercise, as seen on the editor window. Note that the color coding makes the code elements stand out.

1. Run the code using the **Run Module** option within your editor window. You will see that Python asks that you save the file first before running it. Verify the output and make sure your code runs as expected. Otherwise, look for errors in your code and correct them. Go, or step, through each line if you are having trouble finding the error.

Figure 2.17. Before you can run your program, you will be asked to save it first.

2. Let's now generate an error when running our code. Edit the last line to make it appear like the following:

print "My favorite state is", state

3. Click Run Module again, or press F5. As you can see, the editor points out a syntax error with your code. This is because Python expects the parenthesis with the print command.

Figure 2.18. A syntax error is raised, if your code violates Python syntax conventions.

4. Correct your code back to what it was before, except make the word **state** plural so that your code reads like the following:

print("My favorite state is", states)

5. Click Run Module again, or press F5. This time, your code runs, and prints the first two lines to the screen. However, it does not print the last line in your program. This is because the code is logically incorrect, as the variable **states** does not exist. The error, highlighted in red, says NameError: name 'states' is not defined.

Figure 2.19. The screen showing the logical error raised because of the undefined variable **states** included in your program. The error is highlighted in red.

6. Correct the code so that it compiles and runs correctly one last time. Run the code in the shell to be sure everything is correct.

Chapter 3 – Output

This chapter will teach you about output, or what the user sees from your program. Remember in Chapter 2, when you coded your first Python program and worked on a coding exercise that showed the output of your program on the screen? In both instances, you used the print() function to *output* your program's inputs.

As you may have guessed by now, print() is the primary function used for displaying your output. You will learn more about the print() function in this chapter.

You will also learn about newlines and separators, characters which act as formatting tools for your screen output. With the help of these characters, you can show exactly how you want your program output to look on screen.

At the end of this chapter, you will also complete another coding exercise designed to reinforce the concepts you learned while going through the chapter's sections.

The print() Function

You first encountered the print() function in Chapter 2. It is now time to take a closer look at the function. To help you understand the function better, follow along with the instructions below.

Before anything else, run IDLE.

Enter the following on the command line:

print "Mark"

What happens?

The shell displays a syntax error regarding the missing parenthesis in the command. This is because you will need to enclose anything you want to output in parentheses.

If you revise your program to include the parentheses:

print("Mark")

the error disappears.

Add "Lassoff" to the expected output:

print("Mark Lassoff")

Remember that anything that lies between the quotation marks and the parenthesis gets printed. Thus, you will see:

Mark Lassoff

appear on your screen.

Next, enter the following:

print("Mark Lassoff", "instructor")

This displays the following to the screen:

Mark Lassoff instructor

This example shows that if you want to output different values in a single line, you may also enter them separately, each enclosed in quotation marks, with a comma separating each value. This improves the readability.

Next, enter the following commands:

course="Python for Beginners (2017)"

print("course")

Here, you define the string variable *course* as having a value = *Python for Beginners (2017)*, then you output the value of the variable *course* to the screen. Thus, the following string is printed to the screen:

Python for Beginners (2017)

Now, combine the variable *course* with another string, using a comma to separate the values.

print(course, "Mark Lassoff")

This outputs the following:

Python for Beginners (2017) Mark Lassoff

Let's try integers next. Entering:

print(17)

gives you the following:

17

If you enter a floating-point number and then press **Enter**:

print(255.6987)

Python will spew out

255.6987

to the screen.

So far, you have seen how Python handles strings, numbers, and floating-point numbers. Let's try a mathematical expression next.

Enter

print(255/76*2+9-18)

In the case of mathematical expressions, Python evaluates the expression, then prints out the results.

-2.2894736842105274

If you look closely at how these values are displayed on your screen, you will notice a difference in how Python treats strings and numbers when using the print() function. Can you tell what it is?

Numbers, regardless of whether they are integers or floating-points, can be entered without quotation marks. In contrast, you can only use the print() function on a string without quotation marks, if the string is a variable. That is if you have previously assigned a value to the string.

```
Python 3.6.1 Shell                                              □ ×
File Edit Shell Debug Options Window Help
Python 3.6.3 (v3.6.3:2c5fed8, Oct  3 2017, 18:11:49) [MSC v.1900 64 bit (AMD64)] on win32
Type "copyright", "credits" or "license()" for more information.
>>> print "Mark"
SyntaxError: Missing parentheses in call to 'print'. Did you mean print("Mark")?
>>> print("Mark")
Mark
>>> print("Mark Lassoff")
Mark Lassoff
>>> print ("Mark Lassoff","Instructor")
Mark Lassoff instructor
>>> course="Python for Beginners (2017)"
>>> print (course)
Python for Beginners (2017)
>>> print("course")
course
>>> print(course, "Mark Lassoff")
Python for Beginners (2017) Mark Lassoff
>>> print(17)
17
>>> print(255.6987)
255.6987
>>> print(255/76*2+9-18)
-2.2894736842105274
>>>
```

Figure 3.3. This section's examples as they appear on the IDLE Python shell.

You have now learned how to use the print() function with strings, variables, integers, floating-point numbers, and mathematical expressions. In the next section, you will learn how to use newlines and separators with the print() function to format the output shown on your screen.

Separators and Newlines

In the previous section, you used a comma to separate a variable from another string, while using the print() function.

print(course, "Mark Lassoff")

This was after you defined a variable **course** as:

course = Python for Beginners (2017)

The commands above resulted in the following output:

Python for Beginners (2017) Mark Lassoff

```
>>> course="Python for Beginners (2017)"
>>> print(course, "Mark Lassoff")
Python for Beginners (2017) Mark Lassoff
```

Figure 3.2. Lines of code from the previous section, where a comma was used to separate two values in the Print statement. The code's output is seen at the bottom.

You will learn more about separators, as well as newlines, in this section.

Let's show this through another round of examples.

First, Open IDLE, then on the Python shell, select **File**, then **New File**.

Enter the following commands, then save and run the file.

print("Mark","Brett","Joan","Rick","Kerri", sep="|")

Instead of a comma, the command above uses the pipe character | to separate the values shown on the screen.

The output will be:

Mark|Brett|Joan|Rick|Kerri

You can use any character, or even none, to separate values printed to the screen.

Let's show this through another example. If we use four stars, ****, the following will be shown on the screen instead.

Mark****Brett****Joan****Rick****Kerri

NOTE: To be able to generate the required output, you need to save the file before running each command in this section.

You can also choose not to have a separator between the values. To do this, enter the following:

print("Mark","Brett","Joan","Rick","Kerri", sep="")

This will print the following to the screen:

MarkBrettJoanRickKerri

The same principle applies to numbers. If you enter the following:

print(10,15,20,25, sep="***")

the output will be:

10***15***20***25

Now that you have learned what separators are, it is time to go to newlines.

The character entity for a newline is \n.

If you use \n between the values in your print command, the values will be displayed on separate lines. To illustrate this, enter the following command to display the three rock band names on separate lines on your screen:

print("Journey", "\n", "REO Speedwagon", "\n", "Foreigner", "\n")

After saving and running the file, you will get the result shown in Figure 3.3.

If you look more closely at Figure 3.3, although the three bands appear on separate lines, you will see that the last two lines each had a space to the left. What happened in this case, is that Python also interpreted the comma between the three values.

```
print("Mark","Brett","Joan","Rick","Kerri", sep="")
print(10,15,20,25,sep="***")
print("Journey", "\n", "REO Speedwagon","\n","Foreigner")
```

```
============ RESTART: C:/Users/Mark/Desktop/Python 2017/separators.py ============
MarkBrettJoanRickKerri
10***15***20***25
Journey
 REO Speedwagon
 Foreigner
>>>
```

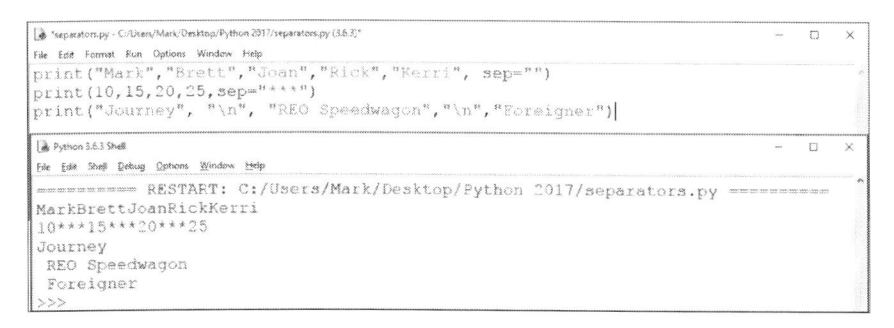

Figure 3.3. The output of inserting the newline character, \n, between the values in the 3rd line of code on the editor window on top, is shown on the last three lines of the shell window at the bottom. Note the spaces in the last two lines.

Although there is nothing wrong syntactically with your code, to avoid the spaces appearing in the output, you need to define \n as a separator just once in the code, like in the previous examples.

print("Journey","REO Speedwagon","Foreigner", sep="\n")

This results in the following output:

Journey

REO Speedwagon

Foreigner

As seen in Figure 3.4, the output is left-aligned and much cleaner, compared to the last two lines, with their spaces in Figure 3.3.

```
print("Mark","Brett","Joan","Rick","Kerri", sep="")
print(10,15,20,25,sep="***")
print("Journey","REO Speedwagon","Foreigner",sep="\n")
```

```
============ RESTART: C:/Users/Mark/Desktop/Python 2017/separators.py ============
MarkBrettJoanRickKerri
10***15***20***25
Journey
REO Speedwagon
Foreigner
>>>
```

Figure 3.4. Defining the newline character, \n, once as a separator, instead of inserting \n after every value in the last line of code as seen on the editor window on top, results in a left-aligned and cleaner output, as seen on the shell window at the bottom.

This is the end of the line for separators and newlines. You will have a fun exercise in the next section to test your new knowledge.

Coding Exercise: Using the print() Function

You will work more with the print() function in this exercise.
1. Open IDLE, then use the interactive mode to print the following:
a. The result of 2*5
b. A string that includes your name and age
c. The name of the book

```
Python 3.6.3 Shell
File Edit Shell Debug Options Window Help
Python 3.6.3 (v3.6.3:2c5fed8, Oct  3 2017, 18:11:49) [MSC v.1900 64 bit (AMD64)]
on win32
Type "copyright", "credits" or "license()" for more information.
>>> print(2*5)
10
>>> print("Mark Lassoff, 42")
Mark Lassoff, 42
>>> print("Mark Lassoff",42)
Mark Lassoff 42
>>> print("Python for Beginners 2017")
Python for Beginners 2017
>>> |
```

Figure 3.5. Th expected output for Step 1.

From Figure 3.5 above, note that the instructor's name and age is printed twice. Try using both styles with your own name and age. Your code should appear like the lines below.

print("Mark Lassoff, 42")

print("Mark Lassoff",42)

Both lines of code work, but yield slightly different results. Why do you think that is?

2. The character entity \t is used to output a tab to the command line. Using \t as a separator, output the following names with a tab between each name.

Bob, March, Larry, Lynda, Natalia, Woody, Wendy, Brett, Connie

Figure 3.6 shows the expected output from your code.

```
Bob       Marcy     Larry     Lynda     Natalia Woody     Brett     Connie
>>> |
```

Figure 3.6 The expected output for Step 2.

3. Look at Figure 3.7. Make a slight change to your code to output the list of names in Step 2 in this manner.

```
Bob$$$Marcy$$$Larry$$$Lynda$$$Natalia$$$Woody$$$Brett$$$Connie
>>> |
```

Figure 3.7. The expected output for Step 3.

4. Rewrite the following code, so that the poem inside the string is displayed on four separate lines.

```
print("With rue my hear it laden. For golden friends I had. For many a rose-lipped maiden. For many a light foot lad.")
```

Figure 3.8. The code to be rewritten in Step 4.

The output should look like what is displayed in Figure 3.9.

```
With rue my hear it laden.
For golden friends I had.
For many a rose-lipped maiden.
For many a light foot lad.
>>>
```

Figure 4.9. The expected output for Step 4.

Chapter 4 – Variables

This chapter will teach you about variables in Python programming. You might remember variables from your Algebra class, when you were told to solve for *x* and *y*, and topics in previous chapters where you encountered them.

In this chapter, you will learn about variable assignments and the different variable types, including numbers and strings.

Other topics covered in this chapter include: integers, floating-points, and complex number variables. It will also discuss variables that carry string values, as well as substrings and concatenation. You will also learn about variables in lists, tuples, and dictionaries.

At the end of the chapter, you will need to complete a coding exercise that is designed to let you apply the principles you learned about variables while going through the chapter.

Variable Assignment

Before going into the main topic of discussion in this section, you must have a clear view of what variables are. It is easiest to think of variables as boxes that have stored values located in your computer's memory. For example, a box *x* with the number **5** in it. Translated in terms of our topic, this means that we are assigning the integer **5** to x.

Let's take the above concept a bit further. If you need to know the value of *x* because you need to add it to another number, for example, you simply retrieve it from where it is stored in memory.

Variables are widely used in programming. For example, you can assign variables to track game scores and record positions in chess matches.

In this section, we will first look at simple variable assignments and then go on to increasingly complex ones. As with our previous topics, to really understand variable assignments, you will need to have your Python editor open, and follow along with the examples below.

Let's start by opening IDLE, then an editor window by either clicking **File** and then **New File** on the menu, or pressing **CTRL+N** on the keyboard.

On the editor window, enter the following:

name="Mark Lassoff"
company="LearnToProgram.tv"
age=42

If you remember this from the discussions in previous chapters, it means that we are *assigning* the **name** variable to Mark Lassoff, the **company** variable to LearnToProgram.tv, and the **age** variable to 42. In this case, the equal sign (**=**) acts as the assignment operator. It assigns values to the variables.

When you assign values to variables, it means that you have allocated spaces for those variables in your computer's memory. It would be easy to retrieve them at any time, since they are already stored somewhere in system memory. You performed this retrieving process in the previous chapter, when you printed variables on to your screen.

Python can have several variables pointing to the same storage spot within a computer's memory, which is a rare trait among programming languages. Let us show you an example.

On your editor window, enter the following:

x = 2

y = 2

z = 2

print (x, y, z)

Save and run the file to allow the file to print the values of x, y, z to the screen.

As you might have expected, the output of the above is:

2, 2, 2

```
name="Mark Lassoff"
company="LearnToProgram.tv"
age=42

x = 2
y = 2
z = 2
print(x,y,z)
```

```
Python 3.6.3 (v3.6.3:2c5fed8, Oct  3 2017, 18:11:49) [MSC v.1900 64 bit (AMD64)]
on win32
Type "copyright", "credits" or "license()" for more information.
>>>
============ RESTART: C:/Users/Mark/Desktop/Python 2017/variables.py ============
2 2 2
>>>
```

Figure 4.5. The shell window at the bottom shows the output of the print function on the editor window at the bottom. The first three lines on the editor window were not printed, because they were left out of the print () function.

Go back, and review what you have written on the editor so far.

name="Mark Lassoff"

company="LearnToProgram.tv"

age=42

x = 2

y =2

z = 2

print (x, y, z)

On the shell window, the output of the last line of code on the editor window, the print statement, should be displayed.

2 2 2

The first three variables in your program code were not printed to the screen because, as you might know, they were left out of the print statement.

Let us revise the variable assignments for x, y, and z. Delete lines 4-6 of the code on your editor window, and replace them with the single line of code below.

x = y = z = 5

If you have used another programming language before, this line might seem strange (there are very few languages that have the same capability).

Save, then run the file again to see what the revised variable assignment looks like.

5 5 5

```
name="Mark Lassoff"
company="LearnToProgram.tv"
age=42

x = y = z = 5

print(x, y, z)
```

```
Python 3.6.3 (v3.6.3:2c5fed8, Oct  3 2017, 18:11:49) [MSC v.1900 64 bit (AMD64)]
on win32
Type "copyright", "credits" or "license()" for more information.
>>>
============ RESTART: C:/Users/Mark/Desktop/Python 2017/variables.py ============
2 2 2
>>>
============ RESTART: C:/Users/Mark/Desktop/Python 2017/variables.py ============
5 5 5
>>>
```

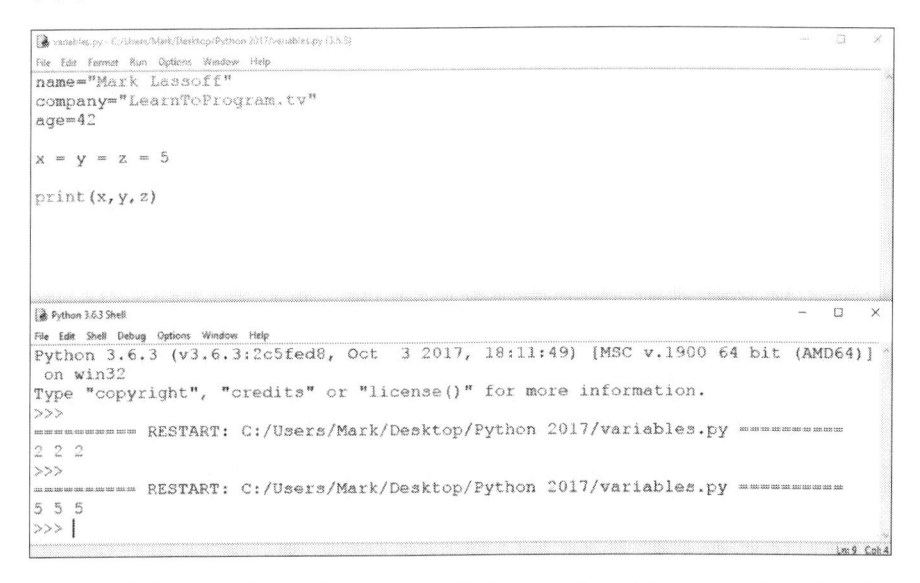

Figure 4.6. Python allows signing of multiple variables at the same time. In this example, the statement x = y = z = 5 assigns the value 5 to the variables x, y, and z.

At first glance, this above output seems to be the same as our earlier output. However, it is different because the three variables point to the same spot in your computer's memory. Why is it important to know this? You will understand from the additional examples below.

On the editor window, enter the following line right below the variable assignment x=y=z=5.

x = x + 2

Run, then save the file, and you should see the following result on the shell window:

7 5 5

From the result, you will see that the addition of the new line, x = x + 2, moves the memory location of x, while retaining the existing memory locations for y and z, respectively.

```
name="Mark Lassoff"
company="LearnToProgram.tv"
age=42

x = y = z = 5
x = x + 2
print(x,y,z)
```

```
Python 3.6.3 (v3.6.3:2c5fed8, Oct  3 2017, 18:11:49) [MSC v.1900 64 bit (AMD64)]
on win32
Type "copyright", "credits" or "license()" for more information.
>>>
============ RESTART: C:/Users/Mark/Desktop/Python 2017/variables.py ============
2 2 2
>>>
============ RESTART: C:/Users/Mark/Desktop/Python 2017/variables.py ============
5 5 5
>>>
============ RESTART: C:/Users/Mark/Desktop/Python 2017/variables.py ============
7 5 5
>>>
```

Figure 4.7. The 2nd to the last line on the editor window at the bottom, assigns a new memory location for the variable x. This is reflected in the results shown on the shell window at the top, where the value of x has become **7**.

Returning to our earlier analogy about looking at variable assignments as storage locations in memory, this means that x now has its own box **7**, while y and z still point to the same box **5**.

You can also assign values to different variables at the same time. Let us try this next.

On the editor window, enter the following:

age, weight, height = 42, 200, 70

In addition, comment out the first three lines of your program. Note that the 3rd line also assigns **42** to the variable **age**. To comment out the lines, highlight them, then click **Format > Comment Out Region**, or press **ALT+3**.

Page 55

Lastly, print both weight and height on separate lines on your screen. To do this, enter the following at the bottom of your program:

print (weight)
print (height)

Save, then run the program again. As you might have expected, **200** and **70** are then displayed on the shell window.

To make the output for weight and height clearer and more readable, you can also label them. Revise your code as follows:

print ("Weight:", weight)
print ("Height:", height)

```
##name="Mark Lassoff"
##company="LearnToProgram.tv"
##age=42

x = y = z = 5
x = x + 2
print(x,y,z)

age, weight, height = 42, 200, 70
print("Weight:", weight)
print("Height:", height)
```

```
2 2 2
>>>
========== RESTART: C:/Users/Mark/Desktop/Python 2017/variables.py ==========
5 5 5
>>>
========== RESTART: C:/Users/Mark/Desktop/Python 2017/variables.py ==========
7 5 5
>>>
========== RESTART: C:/Users/Mark/Desktop/Python 2017/variables.py ==========
7 5 5
Weight: 200
Height: 70
>>>
```

Figure 8.4. Variables can be assigned different values at the same time with Python. In this example, the variables **age**, **weight**, and **height** are each assigned a value in just a single line of code.

When you start coding more complex programs, assigning variables to the same memory location and labeling output are principles that you should keep in mind.

Thus far, you have assigned both strings and numbers to variables. You have also looked at various ways to assign variables, including assigning them to multiple values. In the next section, you will look at the different number variables – integers, floating points, and complex numbers.

Number Variables (int , float, and complex)

The ease with which Python performs numerical calculations is touted by many, as among the language's core strengths. Thus, it is important to understand how numerical variables work in Python.

In this section, you will learn about the three types of number variables in Python, which are:

- Integers or simply, int
- float
- complex

As you can see, Python has a limited set of number variables, unlike other languages. This makes Python a much simpler language and contributes to its popularity in mathematical programming.

Before proceeding with the rest of the section, run IDLE again, then click **File**, then **New File**, or simply press **CTRL+N**. You will again need an editor window for this section.

Integers are used for holding values that do not have any decimal points. Integers can be large or small, and positive or negative. For the latter, you should append a **minus sign** – before the number to make it negative.

If you are looking for a suitable variable for holding a game score, an integer would be ideal. Let's try this now.

On the editor window, enter the following:

#Integers
score = 1000
time = -42

Floating points, or simply float, are the next type of number variable, or numbers that have a decimal point. Numbers that begin with zero are floating point numbers. Let's add a couple of examples of floating point numbers, or simply float.

gpa = 3.44
battingAverage = 0.375

Complex, or scientific numbers are used for large numbers. Python's cmath method provides access to mathematical functions that can be used for computations involving complex numbers. You will not be adding complex numbers now, although you should keep in mind that any number that is not an integer nor a float, is a complex number.

Let's print the integers. Add the following to your code:

print(score)
print(time)

Save, then run the file. Score and time are then printed on the shell window.

Note that the output includes the negative sign in the variable **time** (see Figure 4.5).

```
#Integers

score = 1000
time = -42

#Floating Point
gpa = 3.44
battingAverage = 0.375

#Complex or scientific numbers

print(score)
print(time)
```

```
Python 3.6.3 (v3.6.3:2c5fed8, Oct  3 2017, 18:11:49) [MSC v.1900 64 bit (AMD64)] on win32
Type "copyright", "credits" or "license()" for more information.
>>>
======= RESTART: C:/Users/Mark/Desktop/Python 2017/numericalVariables.py =======
1000
-42
>>>
```

Figure 4. 9. Python prints negative integers as-is, with the negative sign -.

Let's see what happens if we print different types of variables, e.g.

Delete the last print statement in your code, then add gpa to the first print statement. Your print function should now look like this:

print (score, gpa)

Save, then run the file again. The output should be:

1000 3.44

Let's add another print function, this time allowing the integer and the float to interact mathematically.

print (score * gpa)

Save, then run the file. Observe what happens.

Perform another mathematical operation, this time adding the integer and the floating-point number.

print (score + gpa)

Save, then run the file again.

In both of these mathematical operations, the answers, 3440.0 and 1003.44, are floating-point numbers.

The reason lies in Python's respect for precision. Floating point numbers are more precise than integers. Therefore, the result of a mathematical operation involving a mix of integers and floating-point numbers will, in almost all cases, be another floating-point number. This is shown in the examples above.

```
#Integers

score = 1000
time = -42

#Floating Point
gpa = 3.44
battingAverage = 0.375

#Complex or scientific numbers

print(score, gpa)
print(score * gpa)
print(score + gpa)
```

```
======= RESTART: C:/Users/Mark/Desktop/Python 2017/numericalVariables.py =======
3440.0
>>>
======= RESTART: C:/Users/Mark/Desktop/Python 2017/numericalVariables.py =======
1000 3.44
3440.0
1003.44
>>>
```

Figure 4.6. Mathematical operations involving integers and floating-point numbers almost always result in another floating-point number.

You can also assign multiple types of values to different variables. For example, add the following to your program:

a = c = 1000.45
a = a - .45

In the first line above, you first assign the same floating-point number **1000.45** to variables **a** and **c**, then assign another value, **a-.45**, to **a**.

Add another line that prints the value of **a**.

When you save, then run the file, you will get the answer, as shown in Fig. 4.7.

```
# numericVariables.py - C:/Users/Mark/Desktop/Python 2017/numericalVariables.py (3.6.3)
File  Edit  Format  Run  Options  Window  Help
#Integers

score = 1000
time = -42

#Floating Point
gpa = 3.44
battingAverage = 0.375

#Complex or scientific numbers
a = c = 1000.45
a = a - .45
print(a)
print(score, gpa)
print(score * gpa)
print(score + gpa)
```

```
>>>
========= RESTART: C:/Users/Mark/Desktop/Python 2017/numericalVariables.py =========
1000.0
1000 3.44
3440.0
1003.44
>>>
```

Figure 4.10. As shown in this screenshot of the editor and shell windows, multiple floating-point values can be assigned to a variable. When you print the variable, the result is another floating-point number.

That wraps up our section on number variables. You will learn about string variables next.

String Variables

Another strength of Python is the unique way that it processes strings. To demonstrate, open IDLE. Do not open the editor window yet, since you will use the IDLE in interactive mode for the moment.

Write the following:

greeting = "Hello World"
activity = "Python Programming"

In these lines, using the assignment operator =, we assign the values **Hello World** and **Python Programming** to the string variables **greeting** and **activity**.

Next, print the variables.

print(greeting, activity)

As you can see, the combined values of the string variables, **Hello World Python Programming**, are printed to the screen.

Let's pause a moment, and dissect the way that Python interprets string variables.

Python treats string variables as separate characters that are strung together. Each character in a string is assigned a number, known as its index or position. For example, in the string **greeting**, each character in **Hello Word** has a corresponding index. This is illustrated in Table 1 below.

Index	0	1	2	3	4	5	6	7	8	9	10
Character	H	e	l	l	o		W	o	R	l	d

Table 1. Each character in a string variable has a corresponding number assigned to it. Therefore, to retrieve a character in a string variable, you enclose its corresponding number in a bracket.

Sample code will make this clearer. Write the following line on the shell window:

print(greeting[0])

This returns **H**, the character in position 0 in the string **greeting**.

Let's try another one.

print(greeting[1])

This time, the answer is **e**, the character in position 1 in the string **greeting**.

To access any character within the string, you print the variable name, and enclose the specific number corresponding to the character you want printed within a bracket.

To format strings, let's review our previous discussion on newlines and other separators, in particular, the newline, or **\n** character, and tab, or **\t**, character.

Enter the following lines one after the other on the shell window:

print(greeting,"\n",activity)
print(greeting,"t",activity)

print("Journey\nReo Speedwagon\nForeigner")
print("Journey\tReo Speedwagon\tForeigner")

If you recall, \n is the newline character and \t is the tab character in Python.

The results of the print function calls above are shown in Figure 4.8.

```
Python 3.6.3 (v3.6.3:2c5fed8, Oct  3 2017, 18:11:49) [MSC v.1900 64 bit (AMD64)]
on win32
Type "copyright", "credits" or "license()" for more information.
>>> greeting = "Hello World"
>>> activity = "Python Programming"
>>>
>>> print(greeting, activity)
Hello World Python Programming
>>> print(greeting[0])
H
>>> print(greeting[1])
e
>>> print (greeting,"\n",activity)
Hello World
 Python Programming
>>> print(greeting,"\t",activity)
Hello World 	 Python Programming
>>> print("Journey\nReo Speedwagon\nForeigner")
Journey
Reo Speedwagon
Foreigner
>>> print("Journey\tReo Speedwagon\tForeigner")
Journey	Reo Speedwagon	Foreigner
>>>
```

Figure 4.11. This section's examples as they appear on the shell window.

In this section, you learned how Python interprets string variables. You also reviewed the characters that you can use for formatting strings, the way you want them displayed on the screen. You will learn more about substrings and concatenation in the next section.

Substrings and Concatenation

In this section, you will learn about substrings, or taking part of a string, and concatenation, or merging two strings into one. This section builds upon what was discussed in the previous section on string variables.

You will again use IDLE in interactive mode in this section.

After firing up IDLE, enter the following on the shell window:

name = "Mark Lassoff"

course = "Python for Beginners (2017)"

In the previous section, you learned about calling characters by their index, or position, on the string. We'll try something similar in the next line.

print(name[6])

When you press enter, it returns **a**, the character corresponding to the 6th index in the string **name**.

On the next line, enter the following:

print("name[0:3]):", name[0:3])

When you press enter, the print statement returns the substring **Mar**, which corresponds to the characters in the range 0-3 in the string **name**.

If we change the earlier print function from print("name[0:3]:" name[0:3]) to print("name[0:4]:" name[0:4]), the substring **Mark** is returned instead.

Let us try using this with the string **course**. Enter the following:

print("course[4:12]:", course[4:12])

The output is:

course[4:12]: on for B

These examples are all substrings. Let us now look at concatenation. Enter the following:

total=name+course

print(total)

In the first line, you use the **+** sign to assign the concatenated strings **name** and **course** to another string, **total**. This results in the string **total** having the following value:

MarkLassoffPython for Beginners (2017)

Notice that there is no space between Lassoff and Python. This is because there is no space between the two strings when you concatenated them. To insert a space in between the strings **name** and **course** when you print them, your code should look like this:

total = name + " " + course

This will result in the following output:

Mark Lassoff Python for Beginners (2017)

You can also concatenate two substrings together. Enter the following:

partials=name[0:2] + course[5:12]

print (partials)

This line concatenates the characters with indices 0-2 in the string **name**, with the characters with indices 5-12 in the string **course**:

Man for B

Knowledge about dividing string variables into substrings and concatenating substrings together, will prove useful when you start coding programs which process text, such as email addresses and passwords.

```
Python 3.6.3 (v3.6.3:2c5fed8, Oct  3 2017, 18:11:49) [MSC v.1900 64 bit (AMD64)] on win32
Type "copyright", "credits" or "license()" for more information.
>>> name="Mark Lassoff"
>>> course="Python for Beginners(2017)"
>>>
>>> print(name[6])
a
>>> print("name[0:3]:", name[0:3])
name[0:3]: Mar
>>> print("name[0:4]:", name[0:4])
name[0:4]: Mark
>>> print("course[4:12]:", course[4:12])
course[4:12]: on for B
>>> total=name+course
>>> print(total)
Mark LassoffPython for Beginners(2017)
>>> partials=name[0:2]+course[5:12]
>>> print(partials)
Man for B
>>>
```

Figure 4.12. The substring and concatenation examples discussed in this section, as they appear on the shell window.

That wraps up our discussion on substrings and concatenation. Before we end this section, let's try a few more examples. This time we will show how string formatting is done.

Before working on the next examples, restart your shell so that you can clear up all the values you previously entered interactively on the shell window.

After restarting, enter the following:

print("My name is %s" % ("Mark"))

This line uses the % operator, which is used for formatting strings in Python. %s acts as a placeholder for a string, in this case, the string **Mark**. This line returns the following:

My name is Mark

You can also use string formatting with multiple values. On the shell window, enter the following:

print("My name is %s and I am %d years old" % ("Mark", 42))

This line uses %d, which is a placeholder for a number which, in this case, is **42**. The output of this print function is:

My name is Mark and I am 42 years old.

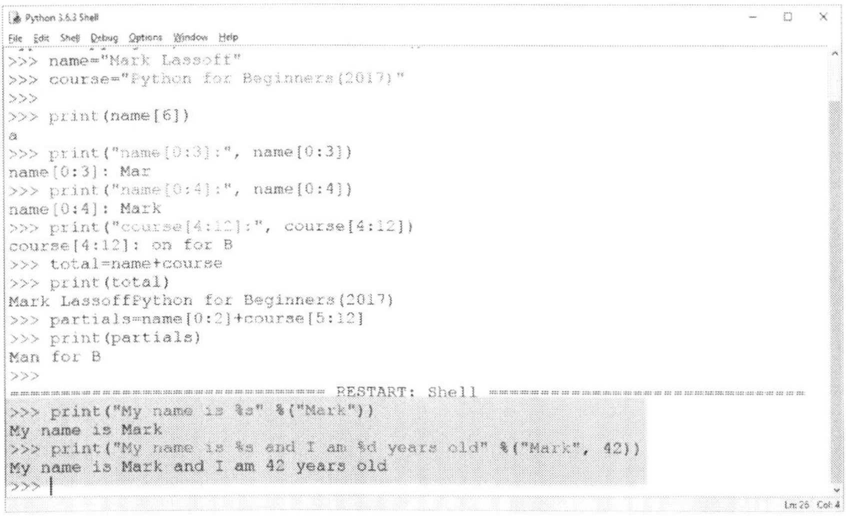

```
>>> name="Mark Lassoff"
>>> course="Python for Beginners(2017)"
>>>
>>> print(name[6])
a
>>> print("name[0:3]:", name[0:3])
name[0:3]: Mar
>>> print("name[0:4]:", name[0:4])
name[0:4]: Mark
>>> print("course[4:12]:", course[4:12])
course[4:12]: on for B
>>> total=name+course
>>> print(total)
Mark LassoffPython for Beginners(2017)
>>> partials=name[0:3]+course[5:12]
>>> print(partials)
Man for B
>>> ================= RESTART: Shell =================
>>> print("My name is %s" %("Mark"))
My name is Mark
>>> print("My name is %s and I am %d years old" %("Mark", 42))
My name is Mark and I am 42 years old
>>>
```

Figure 4.13. The highlighted part of the shell window in this screenshot shows the string formatting examples discussed in the section.

Now that we have discussed string formatting, let's sum up what you have learned so far. You learned how to divide strings into substrings, and concatenate two strings together to make them one. This section also showed a few examples of string formatting that you can use in your programs, as you progress through the rest of the book. It is now time to discuss how to use variables in data structures, particularly lists, tuples and dictionaries.

Variables with Lists, Tuples, and Dictionaries

In the previous sections, you learned how variables are used to store single values. In this section, you will build on concepts discussed previously and learn about using variables with data structures, specifically lists, tuples, and dictionaries. These topics will be discussed in more detail in Chapter 10.

For the exercises in this section, although you will still be using IDLE, you will open an editor window.

On the IDLE, click **File**, then **New File**, or press **CTRL+N** on your keyboard, to open a new editor window.

You will first create a list. A list is a data structure that is comprised of one or more elements. For example, it could be a list of your family members. On the editor window, enter the following:

family = ["Mark", "Brett", "Kerri", "Joan", "Rick", "Rose"]

In these lines of code, the first line is a comment that you are creating a list. On the next line, you assigned a list of family members to the variable **family**. Note that a list is enclosed in square brackets.

Let's print the variable.

print(family)

Click **File**, then **Save**, or press **CTRL+S**, then click **Run**, then **Run Module**, or press **F5**. The output is shown below:

['Mark', 'Brett', 'Kerri', 'Joan', 'Rick', 'Rose']

You probably guessed that the output will be as shown above.

Do you remember that you could output specific characters in a string variable to the screen in the previous section? This can also be done in a list, except that list members have specific numbers assigned to them. The following table illustrates this for our sample list.

0	1	2	3	4	5
Mark	Brett	Kerri	Joan	Rick	Rose

To output a list member to the screen, all you need to do is edit your print command by referencing, or enclosing in square brackets, its corresponding number after the variable name. To illustrate, let us output **Joan,** the third member on the list (see Table 1), to the screen.

Add another print command to the Python program you created earlier.

print(family**[3]**)

If you check the value of [3] on Table 2, you will know that the print command will output **Joan** to the shell window.

```
#List
family = ["Mark", "Brett", "Kerri", "Joan", "Rick", "Rose"]
print(family)
print(family[3])
```

```
Python 3.6.3 (v3.6.3:2c5fed8, Oct  3 2017, 18:11:49) [MSC v.1900 64 bit (AMD64)]
on win32
Type "copyright", "credits" or "license()" for more information.
>>>
========= RESTART: C:\Users\Mark\Desktop\Python 2017\variableLists.py =========
['Mark', 'Brett', 'Kerri', 'Joan', 'Rick', 'Rose']
>>>
========= RESTART: C:\Users\Mark\Desktop\Python 2017\variableLists.py =========
['Mark', 'Brett', 'Kerri', 'Joan', 'Rick', 'Rose']
Joan
>>>
```

Figure 4.14. List elements are enclosed in square brackets and can be printed through its index or position in the list.

Let us now discuss tuples, which are like lists, except that tuple members are enclosed in parentheses. Tuples are also immutable. This means that you cannot change nor delete a tuple's individual elements. However, you can take portions of existing tuples to create a new tuple, and even delete an entire tuple.

To see how tuples work, let us define a variable with several elements and print it to the screen. Remember that you should enclose the elements in a parenthesis. You should also separate each element with a comma.

numbers = (45, 47, 265, 13)
print (numbers)

Save, then run the file again to display the tuple on the screen.

(45, 47, 265, 13)

Try changing the value of the first element to 15.

numbers[0] = 15

As you can see, an error occurs. Comment out the erroneous line of code to avoid the error next time that you run the program.

Let us go back to our **family** list. Change its first element from **Brett** to **B-man**, then save and run the program again.

family[1] = "B-man"

print(family)

This time, the list is updated, as the new element **B-man** replaces the old element **Brett** in our list.

['Mark', 'Brett', 'Kerri', 'Joan', 'Rick', 'Rose']

As our example shows, list elements can be changed, unlike the immutable tuples.

```
#List
family = ["Mark", "Brett", "Kerri", "Joan", "Rick", "Rose"]
print(family)
print(family[3])

#Tuples
numbers = (45, 47, 265, 13)
print(numbers)
#numbers[0] = 15
family[1] = "B-man"
print(family)
```

```
(45, 47, 265, 13)
Traceback (most recent call last):
  File "C:\Users\Mark\Desktop\Python 2017\variableLists.py", line 8, in <module>
    numbers[0] = 15
TypeError: 'tuple' object does not support item assignment
>>>
========== RESTART: C:\Users\Mark\Desktop\Python 2017\variableLists.py ==========
['Mark', 'Brett', 'Kerri', 'Joan', 'Rick', 'Rose']
Joan
(45, 47, 265, 13)
['Mark', 'B-man', 'Kerri', 'Joan', 'Rick', 'Rose']
>>>
```

Figure 4.15. Tuple elements are immutable – their values cannot be changed. On the other hand, values of list elements can be changed.

Now that you have learned the main difference between lists and tuples, let us now look at dictionaries.

Dictionaries comprise elements that are related to each other. Each element has a key and associated value, with a colon between the key and its value;. The elements are separated by commas. Let us try this out with an example.

On the editor window, define, then print the following dictionary:

gpas = {"Name":"Mark", "GPA": 3.55}
print(gpas)

Note that the dictionary elements are enclosed in curly brackets.

Save, then run the file again. Your output should look like the following:

{'Name': 'Mark', 'GPA': 3.55}

As you can see, Python understands that the elements are related to each other.

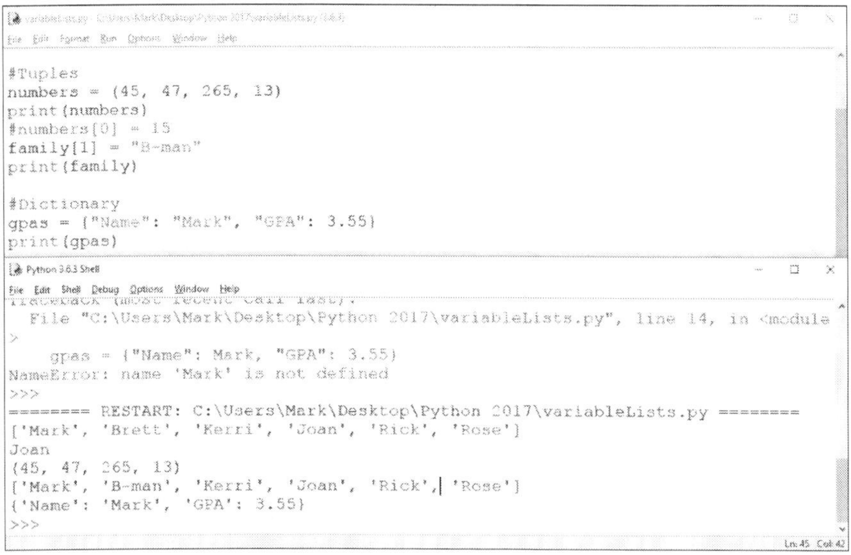

Figure 4.16. Dictionary elements are enclosed in curly brackets, allowing Python to recognize them as related to each other.

Thus far, you have learned about using variables with lists, tuples, and dictionaries. Later in the book, these data structures will be discussed in more detail. You will now have another coding exercise, so that you can check your understanding of the topics covered in the chapter.

Coding Exercise: Using Variables

You will get to practice what you learned about variables in this exercise.
2. Open IDLE, and click **File**, then **New**, to open a new editor window. Save the file as var_lab.py before going to Step 2.
3. Declare the following variables and assign them any value that makes sense to you.
GPA (should be a floating-point number)

studentName (should be a string)
studentNumber (should be a string)

4. Create print commands to output each variable's value on a separate line.

5. Using a single print command, your variables, and the string substitution technique discussed in the chapter, output a statement with the following format.

John Smith has the following student number: 0023452

6. Using a single print command, your variables, and the string substitution technique discussed in the chapter, output a statement with the following format.

John Smith has the following GPA: 3.15

Use the following to substitute for a floating-point number with two decimal places: 0.2f.

7. Create a variable named **places** with a list of five (5) places you would like to visit. Use the following example as a guide:

places = ["Hawaii", "Alaska", "Toronto", "London", "Greece"]

Using print statements, print out each member of the list on a separate line, when your program is run. Your final output should be as shown in Fig. 4.14.

```
============ RESTART: C:/Users/Mark/Desktop/Python 2017/var_lab.py ============
3.15
John Smith
0023452
John Smith has the following student number: 0023452
John Smith has the following GPA: 3.15
Hawaii
Alaska
Toronto
London
Greece
>>>
```

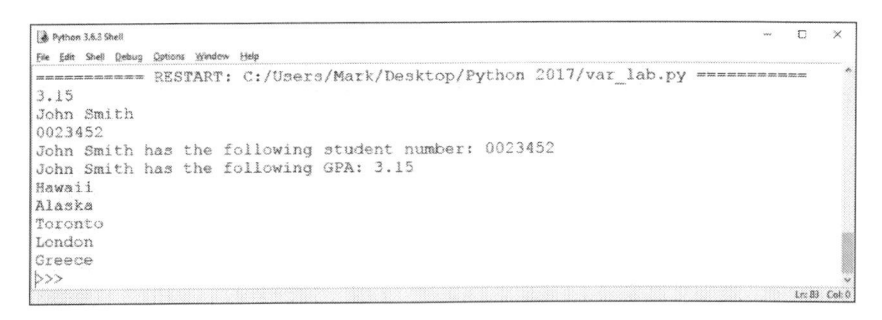

Figure 4.17. Sample expected output of this coding exercise.

Chapter 5 – Operators

This chapter will discuss operators in Python programming.

Operators are used to complete expressions that are made up of variables. They are symbols that allow you to carry out mathematical or logical operations, compare values, and make decisions. You have encountered, and used, most of these symbols in the previous chapters of this book.

The different types of operators used in Python include mathematical, comparison, and logical operators.

Similar to our previous topics, to really understand operators, you will need to have your Python editor open, and follow along with the examples that we provide in each section below.

At the end of the chapter, you will have another coding exercise that will allow you to reinforce what you learned in the earlier sections.

Mathematical Operators

In the expression **x + 10 = 15**, the symbol, the **+** sign is a mathematical operator, denoting that the number **10** should be added to the variable **x**. On the other hand, as discussed in previous chapters, the = sign is an assignment operator, meaning that it assigns the number **15** to the expression **x+10**.

In this section, you will learn more about mathematical operators. You have previously encountered mathematical operators. In this section, you will learn more about the four mathematical operators you might already be familiar with, based on our previous discussions (multiplication, division, addition, and subtraction).

You will also be taught three mathematical operators that we have not previously covered, including the modulus, exponent, and floor division. However, you might remember these being discussed in your mathematics subjects back in school.

Let's run IDLE again. Once IDLE is up and running, click either **File>New File** or **CTRL+N**. On the Editor window, click either **File>Save As** or

CTRL+Shift+S, and save the file as math.py. We will use this file to demonstrate the different mathematical operators.

On the Editor window, enter the following:

operand1 = 65
operand2 = 83.22

From previous chapters, you know that operand1 is an integer and operand2 is a floating-point number.

Let's add operand1 and operand2 together using the addition operator. Following the recommended practice, let's add a comment first before the line of code adding our operands.

#Addition

Now, let's insert the line of code that adds our two operands together.

print (operand1 + operand2)

Next, let's subtract operand1 and operand2 using the subtraction operator.

#Subtraction

print (operand1 – operand2)

Now that you have added the addition and subtraction operators, save the file, then run it by either clicking **Run>Run Module** or pressing **F5** on your keyboard.

On the shell window, you will get the following output:

148.22
-18.22

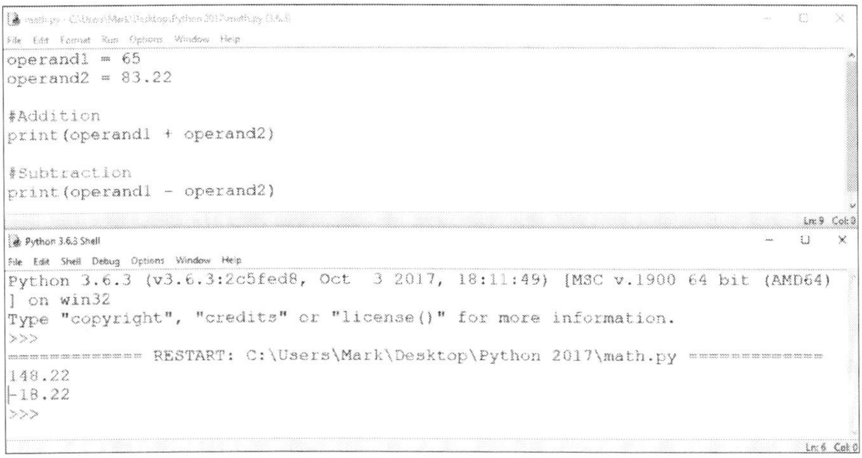

```
operand1 = 65
operand2 = 83.22

#Addition
print(operand1 + operand2)

#Subtraction
print(operand1 - operand2)
```

```
Python 3.6.3 (v3.6.3:2c5fed8, Oct  3 2017, 18:11:49) [MSC v.1900 64 bit (AMD64)] on win32
Type "copyright", "credits" or "license()" for more information.
>>> 
============ RESTART: C:\Users\Mark\Desktop\Python 2017\math.py ============
148.22
-18.22
>>> 
```

Figure 5.18. The shell window at the bottom shows the output of adding and subtracting the operands on the editor window at the top.

Let's go on to the other mathematical operations, multiplication and division.

#Multiplication
print (operand1 * operand2)

#Division
print (operand1 / operand2)

Save, then run the file again. You will get the following output:

148.22
-18.22
5409.3
0.7810622446527277

```
operand1 = 65
operand2 = 83.22

#Addition
print(operand1 + operand2)

#Subtraction
print(operand1 - operand2)

#Multiplication
print(operand1 * operand2)

#Division
print(operand1 / operand2)
```

```
Python 3.6.3 (v3.6.3:2c5fed8, Oct  3 2017, 18:11:49) [MSC v.1900 64 bit (AMD64)
] on win32
Type "copyright", "credits" or "license()" for more information.
>>>
============== RESTART: C:\Users\Mark\Desktop\Python 2017\math.py ==============
148.22
-18.22
5409.3
0.7810622446527277
>>>
```

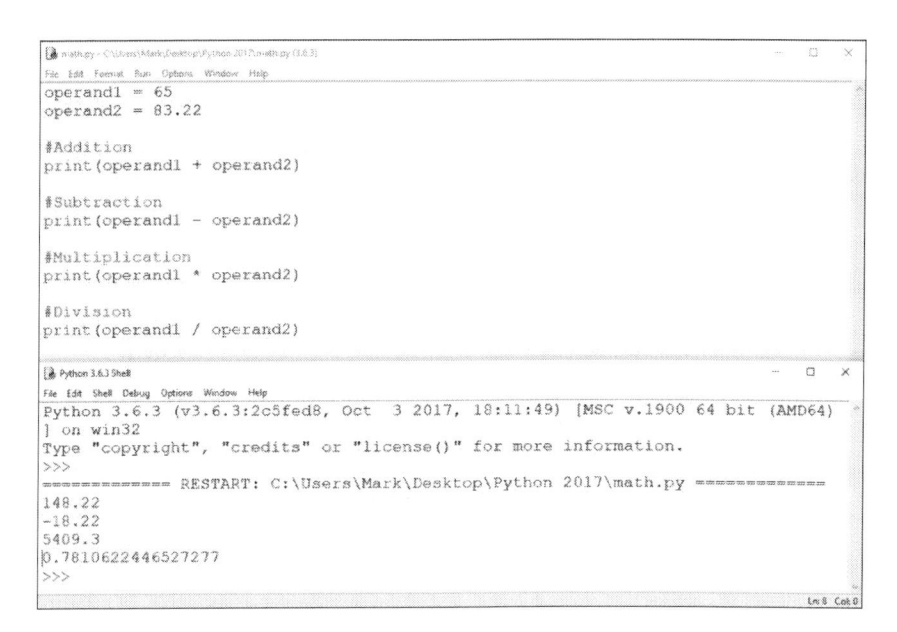

Figure 5.2. The shell window at the bottom shows the output of the four (4) mathematical operations on the editor window at the top.

It is not surprising that the output of the operations you performed above is similar to what you expected. These are the same mathematical operations you learned while you were growing up.

Let's go to the modulus operator, which is denoted by the % sign.

When used, the modulus operator displays the remainder of a division operation. To illustrate, let's go back to our math.py program file.

Enter the following on the editor window:

#Modulus
print (9 % 3)

If we save, then run the file again, we will see 0 displayed on the shell window. This is because 9 / 3 does not have a remainder.

Let's try a couple of other examples. Let's enter the following print statement on our editor window:

print (10 % 3)

After saving and running the file, 1 is displayed on the shell window. This is because 10 divided by 3 is 3 remainder 1.

Let's enter our next example.

print (15 % 6)

This will output 3 on the shell window, since the product of 15 divided by 6 is 2 remainder 3.

Fig. 5.3 shows the results of our modulus operations. Note that we commented out the other operations we had included earlier in our math.py file for brevity's sake. If you did not comment out the earlier operations, your output will display the results of all those other operations, plus the results of our sample modulus operations.

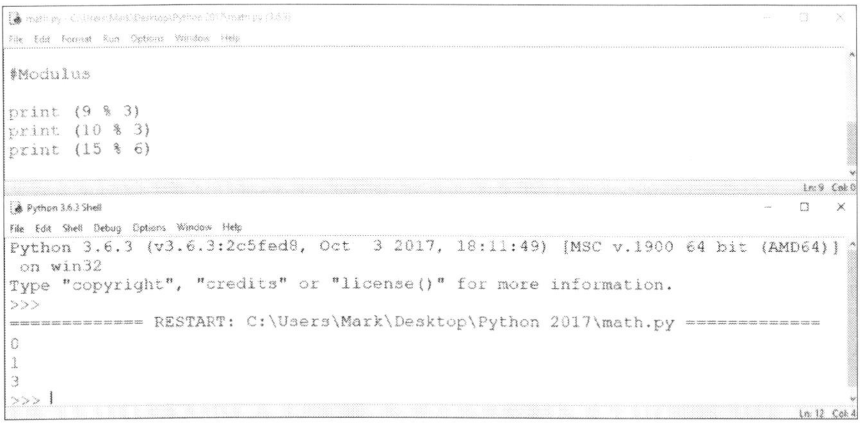

Figure 5.3. The results of the modulus operations on the editor window at the top is displayed on the shell window at the bottom. The modulus operation returns the remainder of one number being divided by another number.

You have now learned about multiplication, division, addition, subtraction, and modulus. We will discuss exponents next.

Exponentiation raises a number to the power of another number. The resulting number is known as the exponent. For example, 3 raised to the 3rd power, or 3 * 3 * 3, is 27.

In Python, we used two asterisks, **, to denote exponentiation. Therefore, to display the resulting number 9 in our above example, we used the following statement:

print (3 ** 3)

Let us try this now by entering this statement on our editor window, then saving and running our math.py file again. As you can see, the resulting number on the shell window is 27.

Let us enter another example.

On the editor window, enter the following:

print (10 ** 2)

After saving and running the program, the result, 100, is displayed on the shell window.

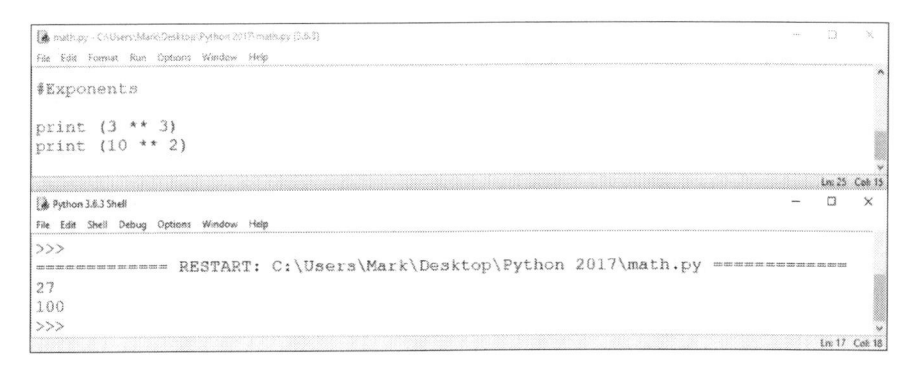

Figure 5.4. The results of the exponent operations on the editor window at the top, is displayed on the shell window at the bottom. The exponent operator, **, returns the result of a number raised to another number.

Let us now discuss Floor Division, or integer division, the last mathematical operator we will cover in this section. The symbols used for Floor Division are two forward slashes, //, in contrast to the single forward slash, /, used in division.

Floor Division displays the product of a division operation as a rounded down number. For example, 5 // 2 is 2. By contrast, if you divide 5 by 2, 5 / 2, the product would be 2.5.

Let us illustrate Floor Division using our math.py file.

On the editor window, enter the following statement:

print (10 // 3)

When you save, then run the file again, 3 will be the result. This is because 10 divided by 3 is 3, when rounded down.

Let us enter another example.

print (15 // 6)

After saving, then running the file, you will see 2 displayed on the shell window. This is again because 15 divided by 6 is 2, not counting the remainder.

```
# Floor Division
print (10 // 3)
print (15 // 6)
```

```
RESTART: C:\Users\Mark\Desktop\Python 2017\math.py
3
2
>>>
```

Figure 5.5. The results of the Floor Division operations on the editor window at the top, is displayed on the shell window at the bottom. Floor Division is denoted by the // operator, and displays the product of a division operation as a rounded down number.

Floor Division is the last of our mathematical operators. Prior to Floor Division, we discussed six other operators, including two other new ones, the Modulus and Exponent operators. These operators are explained in Table 1.

Mathematical Operator	Meaning
+	Add two operands
-	Subtract two operands
*	Multiply two operands
/	Divide left operand by right operand
%	Modulus, or the remainder of the division of the left operand with the right operand
**	Exponent, or the left operand

		raised to the power of the right operand
	//	Floor Division, or operation that results in a product with a rounded down number

Table 1. Mathematical operators and their meanings

In the next section, you will learn more about the order of operations in Python programming.

Order of Operations

The order in which operators are evaluated is the same as in mathematics – given an expression, you should solve it in the following order: parentheses, exponents, multiplication, division, addition, and subtraction, or PEMDAS (as in Please Excuse my Dear Aunt Sally, from your grade school days). Knowing the proper order in which mathematical operations are evaluated, is crucial for getting the correct answers when coding programs, where such operations are performed.

To illustrate the order of operations, we will again need our trusty IDLE. You will not need to open a new file yet. Instead, we will code interactively using the shell window.

Enter the following line on the shell window:

2 + 3 * 6

When you press **Enter**, the answer, 20, is displayed immediately below.

Let us dissect the above mathematical expression and determine why 20 is the answer we get.

Assume, for example, that we are using pen and paper to compute the result of this expression. Following the PEMDAS rule, since the statement does not contain any parentheses or exponents, we will start off by completing the multiplication part, 3 * 6, or 18, then adding 2 to 18 to get 20.

If we did not follow the PEMDAS rule to evaluate the statement, and instead evaluated starting from left to right, we would add 2 and 3 together, then multiply the result, 5, by 6. The answer we would get is 30, which would be incorrect.

Fortunately, Python knows the order in which to evaluate the statement and got the correct result. However, in the case of long, complex expressions, we should always use parentheses to ensure that Python will get the intended results. If we use parentheses, Python will be better able to determine the proper order for evaluating expressions.

Let us again open another new file from IDLE.

On the editor window, enter the following statements:

print (5 – 6 * 2)
print ((5-6) * 2)

What do you think is the result of these statements?

Assuming we are again computing the results manually, we will evaluate the first statement by multiplying 6 and 2 first, then subtracting 5 from the result. Thus, 6 * 2 = 12, then 5 - 12 = -7.

In the case of the 2nd print statement, we will subtract 6 from 5 first, then multiply the result by 2. Thus, 5 – 6 = -1 * 2 = -2.

Let us see if we computed for the results correctly. To do this, save, then run the file. What do you think the results are? Did you get the same results that we anticipated above?

The results of the two statements will be:

- 7

- 2

Let's try a couple more examples.

On the editor window, enter the following expressions:

print (3 ** 3 * 5)

print (3** (3 * 5))

Let's evaluate the first expression.

As we learned from the previous section on mathematical operators, 3 ** 3 means 3 raised to the 3rd power, or 3 * 3 * 3 = 27. Then 27 * 5 = 135.

The second statement is different since there is a parenthesis around 3 * 5. Thus, in this example, we will first evaluate the statement between the parentheses. Thus, 3 * 5 = 15. We then compute for 3 raised to 15.

Let's see if we got the answers correctly. Save, then run the file again. We then get the following result:

135

14348907

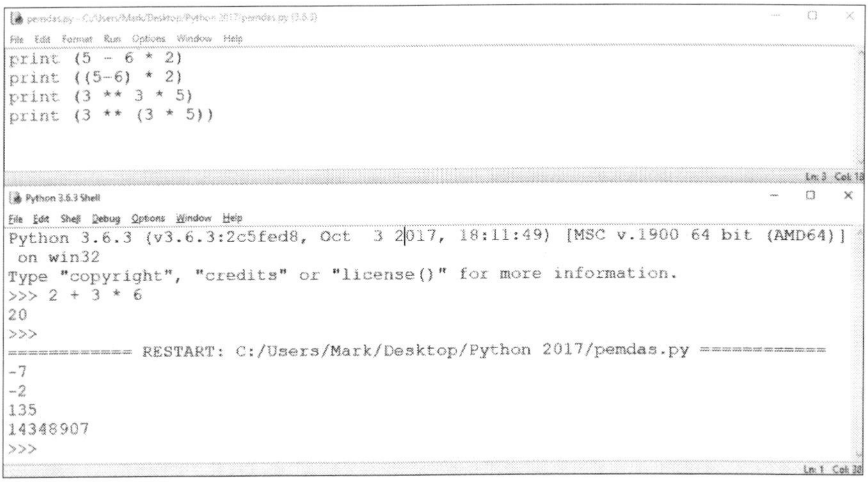

Figure 5.6. Python always computes mathematical expressions using the PEMDAS rule, which stands for Parentheses, Exponents, Multiplication, Division, Addition, and Subtraction.

This is it for the order of expressions. When working with mathematical expressions in Python, always keep PEMDAS in mind.

In the next section, you will learn more about comparison operators, or how we compare numbers in Python.

Comparison Operators

In this section, you are going to learn about comparison operators, or how to compare two values in Python.

We will use the interactive mode to demonstrate comparison operators.

Let's begin by running IDLE.

On the shell window, enter the following:

a = 5

b = 5

Let's then test for equality with the following statement:

a == b

Note that equality is denoted by two (2) equal signs joined together. As discussed previously, a single equal sign is the assignment operator.

When you press Enter, Python will return True, since the values of a and b are indeed the same, or equal.

Let's change the value of b to 6.

b = 6

If we test for equality again, a == b, will return false, since b = 6, whereas a = 5.

Let's test for equality between an integer and a floating-point number. Enter the following:

10 == 10.0.

Python returns True in this case, since Python, unlike other programming languages, treats these two numbers as equal.

```
Python 3.6.3 Shell
File Edit Shell Debug Options Window Help
Python 3.6.3 (v3.6.3:2c5fed8, Oct  3 2017, 18:11:49) [MSC v.1900 64 bit (AMD64)]
on win32
Type "copyright", "credits" or "license()" for more information.
>>> a = 5
>>> b = 5
>>> a == b
True
>>> b = 6
>>> a == b
False
>>> 10 == 10.0
True
```

Figure 5.7. Results of our operations involving ==, which tests for equality between two numbers.

To test if two numbers are non-equal, you can use the != operator.

Enter the following on the shell window:

a != b

Since a = 5 and b = 6, the answer here is True.

Note: The <> operator can be used in place of the != operator. These operators are essentially the same.

In addition to testing for equality, Python also allows a comparison of two numbers that are greater or less than each other, using the familiar > for greater than, and < for less than. Let's explore this more below.

On our shell window, enter 10 > 12, then press Enter. Since 10 is lesser than 12, the answer in this case is *False*.

Let's try another set of numbers. Enter 15 > 12. What is the answer? Of course, it is *True*.

Next, let's use the less than sign to compare two numbers.

Enter 6 < 10. The answer is *True.* If we enter 10 < 6, the answer is *False*.

We will now combine the less than and greater than signs with the equal sign, as in the following example:

10 <= 9

This equates to *False*, since 10 is neither less than 9 nor equal to 10.

Let's try another set of numbers as an example.

10 <= 10

As you can see, the answer is *True*, since 10 is equal to 10. Using another example,

10 <= 11, returns *True* again, since 10 is obviously less than 11.

You have seen how the combined less than and equal to operators work. Let's now combine the greater than and equal to operators.

On the shell window, let's enter the following:

12 >= 10

When you press **Enter** on your keyboard, it displays *True*, since 12 is obviously greater than 10.

You can also combine the assignment operator with addition and subtraction operators, by using the following symbols:

+=

-=

To better explain this, let's go back to the values for a and b, 5 and 6.

Given the value of b = 6, if we enter b += 4, it adds 4 to b, or 6 + 4, which means that b's new value = 10.

If you add a + b, or 5 + 10, the sum would be 15.

This can also be applied using a *minus* sign, denoting subtraction, rather than a *plus* sign. Given b = 10, if we enter b -= 7, then b's new value would be 10 - 7 = 3.

If you subtract a from b, or 5 - 3, the difference would be 2.

```
True
>>> a != b
True
>>> 10 > 12
False
>>> 15 > 12
True
>>> 6 < 10
True
>>> 10 < 6
False
>>> 10 <= 9
False
>>> 10 <= 10
True
>>> 10 <= 11
True
>>> 12 >= 10
True
>>> b += 4
>>> a + b
15
>>> b -= 7
>>> a - b
2
>>>
```

Figure 5.8. Results of the operations involving the other comparison operators, !=, >, <, <=, >=, +=, and -=.

Let's summarize what we have learned in this section.

The comparison operators are summarized in Table 5.

Comparison Operator	Meaning
==	Equal to
!=	Not equal to (the same as <>)
>	Greater than
<	Less than
>=	Greater than or equal to
<=	Less than or equal to

Table 2. Comparison operators and their meanings

That is all that we have for comparison operators. These operators will come in handy, in the next chapter on conditionals, or code branches.

Logical Operators

This section is easy, since there are only three logical operators in Python, namely, **and**, **or**, and **not**.

For our examples in this section, we will again be using IDLE's Interactive mode. Run IDLE, then enter the following:

(5 == 5 and 10 == 10)

When you press **Enter** on your keyboard, the operation will run and display the results.

In this case, since the two operands, 5 == 5 and 10 == 10, are true, the result will be True. The **and** operator requires that all operands, regardless of number, to be true to return True.

Let's try another example. Enter the following on the shell window:

(5 == 5 and 7 < 6)

In this example, 5 == 5 is true and 7 < 6 is false. Thus, the result will be False, since one of the two operands are false.

Let's enter another example:

(5 == 5 and 7 == 7 and 6 < 7)

As mentioned, since all operands are true, it will also result in True. Therefore, regardless of the number of operands, the **and** operator will always return True, if all the operands are true.

Let's go to the **Or** logical operator. On the shell window, enter the following:

(5 == 5 or 7 < 6)

In this case, 5 == 5 is true and 7 < 6 is false. Since only one operand is required to be true when using the **Or** operator, this statement is true.

Like the **and** operator, regardless of the number of operands, the **or** operator will always return True, as long as one of the operands is true.

Thus,

(5 == 5 or 7 < 6 or 5 > 10)

will return True.

Let's go to our third and last logical operator, **Not**, which goes before the operand. We will look at an example:

not (5 == 5)

This will return False because **not** negates the value of the operand. In this case, since 5 == 5 is true, putting **not** before the operand makes the operand false.

Let's try another example.

not (5 == 6)

will return True, since **not** negates the original value, False, of the operand 5 == 6.

That is all for logical operators.

So far, we have covered mathematical, comparison, and logical operators in this section. You have also learned about the order by which Python performs mathematical operations.

```
Python 3.6.3 (v3.6.3:2c5fed8, Oct  3 2017, 18:11:49) [MSC v.1900 64 bit (AMD64)]
on win32
Type "copyright", "credits" or "license()" for more information.
>>> ( 5 == 5 and 10 == 10)
True
>>> (5 == 5 and 7 < 6)
False
>>> (5 == 5 or 7 < 6)
True
>>> (5 == 5 and 7 == 7 and 6 < 7)
True
>>> not (5 == 5)
False
>>> not (5 == 6)
True
>>>
```

Figure 5.9. Results of the logical operator examples discussed in this section.

In the next section, you will be doing a coding exercise to help reinforce what you have learned in this chapter.

Coding Exercise: Operators Practice

This exercise will let you apply what you learned about operators in the chapter.

1. Load IDLE and choose **File>New File** to create a blank document, then declare two variables and assign to them the following initial values:

operand1 = 250.66

operand2 = 1008.2

2. Write code to generate the output shown on Fig. 5.10.

```
========== RESTART: C:/Users/Mark/Desktop/Python 2017/operators_lab.py ==========
250.66 + 1008.2 = 1258.8600000000001
250.66 - 1008.2 = -757.5400000000001
250.66 * 1008.2 = 252715.412
250.66 / 1008.2 = 0.24862130529656812
250.66 % 1008.2 = 250.66
>>>
```

Figure 5.10. Expected output from the program you will create in this exercise.

You should try not to use the following code, when you create the program. Otherwise, you will find the next step difficult to do.

```
operand1 = 250.66
operand2 = 1008.2

print("250.66 + 1008.2 =", (operand1 + operand2))
print("250.66 - 1008.2 =", (operand1 - operand2))
print("250.66 * 1008.2 =", (operand1 * operand2))
print("250.66 / 1008.2 =", (operand1 / operand2))
print("250.66 % 1008.2 =", (operand1 % operand2))
```

Figure 5.11. This is how beginning programmers would create the program being asked for in this exercise. Look for a better way to code this.

3. Change the values of operand1 and operand2 as follows:

operand1 = 12.722
operand2 = 33.8

4. Update your code so that the operands are referenced by their name, everywhere possible. This will allow your program to generate the correct output, regardless of the value of the operands.

For your reference, the correct code is shown below.

```
operand1 = 250.66
operand2 = 1008.2

print(operand1, "+", operand2, "=", (operand1 + operand2))
print(operand1, "-", operand2, "=", (operand1 - operand2))
print(operand1, "*", operand2, "=", (operand1 * operand2))
print(operand1, "/", operand2, "=", (operand1 / operand2))
print(operand1, "%", operand2, "=", (operand1 % operand2))
```

Figure 5.12. This is the correct code to use for the program that you are asked to create in this exercise.

Chapter 6 – Code Branching

This chapter will discuss conditionals in Python programming. After learning about operators in Chapter 5, it is now time to segue into conditionals. This is because operators are the building blocks for the conditional statements that we will cover in this chapter.

Conditional statements allow you to check conditions, then change your code's behavior, depending on how those conditions are met. In short, conditionals determine *program flow*.

The first conditional statement you will learn is the simple **If** statement, which basically states that *if x, then y*.

You will then be introduced to the ***if-else*** statement, which adds an **else** statement to the basic **If** statement, and follows the form *if x, do y; else do z*.

You will also learn about the **nested if** statement, which inserts an **If** statement within another **If** statement. For example, *if w, do x; if y, do z*, etc.

Another topic to be covered is the Python ternary operator, which is an abbreviated conditional form: ***a if condition else b***, which is read as *x if True, else y*.

Finally, there is another coding exercise at the end of the chapter. The exercise will require you to use the conditional statements discussed in the chapter.

Simple If Statements

This is the basic conditional statement. It follows the form *if x, then y*.

To demonstrate, let's create a program that will check your age and determine if you are legally allowed to buy and drink alcohol.

To create our demo program for this section, let's create a new Python file using IDLE, and name the Python file as conditionals.py.

On the editor window, enter the following:

age = 25

if age > 21:

Note that there is a colon, ":", at the end of our if statement. This is required – you should always end your if statements with a colon.

After entering the colon at the end of the *if* statement, press **Enter** on your keyboard. The editor then automatically indents the line immediately after the colon.

Next, let's enter a couple of statements that will get printed on the screen, if our *if* statement is determined to be true.

print ("You are legally allowed to purchase alcohol")
print ("What would you like?")

Finally, let's add a final print statement, this one *not* indented.

print ("End of program")

This final, un-indented line of code means that it is *not* considered as part of the *If* statement. Therefore, it will be printed, regardless of whether the *If* statement is evaluated to be true or not. The purpose of this statement will become apparent below.

To unindent, simply click **Backspace** on your keyboard.

If you save, then run the program, the indented statements "You are legally allowed to purchase alcohol." and "What would you like?" are displayed on your screen, since the program meets the condition imposed by the *If* statement, that *age > 25*. Since age is evaluated as 25, which is > 21, the print statements on lines 3 and 4 are displayed on the screen.

```
age = 25
if age > 21:
    print ("You are legally allowed to purchase alcohol.")
    print ("What would you like?")
print ("End of program")
```

```
Python 3.6.3 (v3.6.3:2c5fed8, Oct  3 2017, 18:11:49) [MSC v.1900 64 bit (AMD64)]
on win32
Type "copyright", "credits" or "license()" for more information.
>>>
========== RESTART: C:/Users/Mark/Desktop/Python 2017/conditional.py ==========
You are legally allowed to purchase alcohol.
What would you like?
End of program
>>>
```

Figure 6.19. The expected output of the sample program, where the value of age meets the condition of the If statement. Note the indented lines of code right after the If statement. The un-indented line of code at the end means that the line is not covered by the If statement.

Aside from the indented statements under the *If* statement, the un-indented last statement, **End of program**, is also printed to the screen.

Let's change the value of age and see what happens:

age = 18

We will now save and run the program.

As you can see, other than the final, un-indented line of code at the end, "End of program", nothing gets printed to the screen. This is because our *If* statement is evaluated as false, since age = 18 does not meet the age > 21 *If* condition.

```
age = 18
if age > 21:
    print ("You are legally allowed to purchase alcohol.")
    print ("What would you like?")
print ("End of program")
```

```
Python 3.6.3 (v3.6.3:2c5fed8, Oct  3 2017, 18:11:49) [MSC v.1900 64 bit (AMD64)]
on win32
Type "copyright", "credits" or "license()" for more information.
>>>
========= RESTART: C:/Users/Mark/Desktop/Python 2017/conditional.py =========
End of program
>>> 
```

Figure 6.20. The expected output of the revised sample program, where the value of age does not meet the condition of the If statement. Since the condition is not met, the 3rd and 4th lines of code are not printed. Only the un-indented line of code at the end is printed, since this line is not covered by the If statement.

Another example is where we create a program that checks for someone's eligibility to vote. We will create a new file and then save it as vote.py.

For someone to be eligible to vote, two things must be true: their age must be 18 and above, and the voter must be a citizen. Let's enter these as the parameters that we need our program to check using an *If* statement.

age = 18
citizen = "true"

We will then enter our *If* statement:

if (age >= 18 and citizen == "true"):

Note that our *If* statement, in this case, uses the logical operators, >= and ==, which were discussed in Chapter 5.

In addition, and more importantly, do not forget to enter the colon that goes after the condition.

After pressing **Enter** on our keyboard, let's enter what the program needs to do, once the *If* statement is evaluated as having met the conditions **age >= 18** and **citizen == "true"**.

print ("You are legally eligible to vote")

Saving, then running the program prints "You are legally eligible to vote" to your screen, since both our **age** and **citizen** parameters meet the conditions of the *If* statement.

```
age = 18
citizen = "true"

if (age >= 18 and citizen == "true"):
    print("You are eligible to vote")
```

```
RESTART: C:/Users/Mark/Desktop/Python 2017/vote.py
You are eligible to vote
>>>
```

Figure 6.21. The expected output of our sample program checking for a citizen's eligibility to vote.

If you change the value of **citizen** to *false*, then save and run your program, nothing gets displayed on your screen since the statement is evaluated as **not** having met the *If* condition.

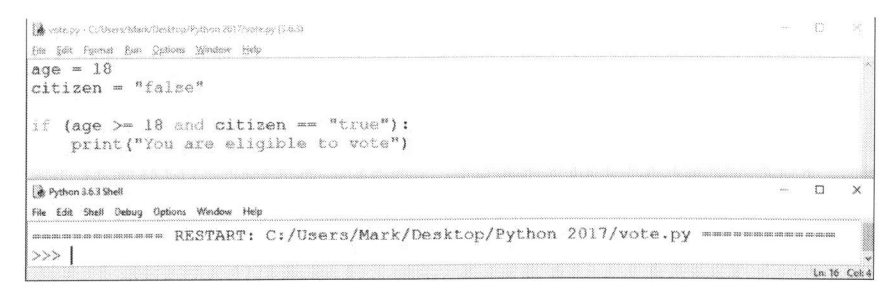

```
age = 18
citizen = "false"

if (age >= 18 and citizen == "true"):
    print("You are eligible to vote")
```

```
RESTART: C:/Users/Mark/Desktop/Python 2017/vote.py
>>>
```

Figure 6.22. The program does not do anything after the values of the parameters are changed, such that one or both conditions in the *If* statement are no longer applicable.

That is all for *If* statements. In the next section, you will learn about the *If-Else* conditional statement.

If...Else Statements

You learned about the simple *If* statement in the previous section. In this section, we will add an *Else* component to the *If* statement.

The *If...Else* statement is composed of two parts, the *If* clause, which is the same as the *If* statement discussed in the previous section, and the *Else* clause, which is performed in case our *If* condition is not met. This is a closer approximation of what happens in the real world, since we would want our programs to output something even if the condition tested is false.

To create our demo program for this section, let's create a new Python file using IDLE, and name the Python file as else.py.

On the editor window, enter the following:

score = 10000
highscore = 9000

Let's add our **If** statement:

if score > highscore:

Note from the above, the use of the colon at the end of the **If** statement. This was discussed in the previous section.

Let's now add a print statement to display the output, if the **If** statement is evaluated as true.

print ("You have achieved the new high score")

Note that your print statement is indented, since it falls under the **If** statement.

Save, then run the program. As you can see, since score > highscore is true, you will get the following output:

You have achieved the new high score.

```
score = 10000
highscore = 9000

if score > highscore:
    print ("You have achieved the new high score")
```

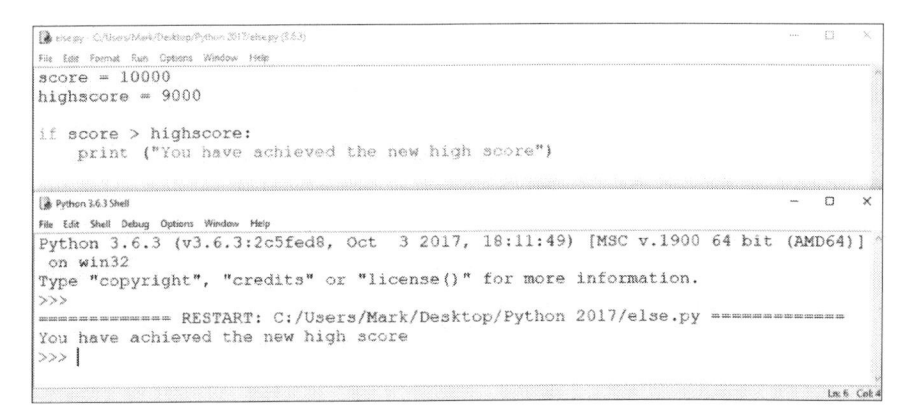

```
Python 3.6.3 (v3.6.3:2c5fed8, Oct  3 2017, 18:11:49) [MSC v.1900 64 bit (AMD64)]
on win32
Type "copyright", "credits" or "license()" for more information.
>>>
============ RESTART: C:/Users/Mark/Desktop/Python 2017/else.py ============
You have achieved the new high score
>>>
```

Figure 6.23. The expected output from our simple **If** statement, which was discussed in the previous section.

Let us change highscore from 9000 to 90,000, then save and run the program again. This time, you will not get an output, since score > highscore becomes false.

```
score = 10000
highscore = 90000

if score > highscore:
    print ("You have achieved the new high score")
```

```
Python 3.6.3 (v3.6.3:2c5fed8, Oct  3 2017, 18:11:49) [MSC v.1900 64 bit (AMD64)]
on win32
Type "copyright", "credits" or "license()" for more information.
>>>
============ RESTART: C:/Users/Mark/Desktop/Python 2017/else.py ============
>>>
```

Figure 5.24. If our **If** statement is false, our program does not output anything. Adding an **else** statement, that will get an output from our program, remedies the problem.

What you have here is a simple **If** statement, which, as is obvious in this case and the other examples that we discussed in the previous section, does not return any output, if our **If** statement is false. This is where our **Else** statement comes in.

Edit your else.py program by using an **Else** statement:

else:

Note that, like our **If** statement, we always end an **Else** statement with a colon.

You should also make sure to line up the **Else** statement with the **If** statement. Otherwise, you will get an error when you run your program.

Add the following print statements:

print ("Sorry. You did not achieve a new high score")
print ("Try again!")

The editor should automatically indent your **Print** statement, since it falls under our **Else** statement.

Save, then run the program again. This time, you will see the output of the **Else** statement displayed on your screen.

```
score = 10000
highscore = 90000

if score > highscore:
    print ("You have achieved the new high score")
else:
    print ("Sorry. You did not achieve a new high score")
    print ("Try again!")
```

```
=================== RESTART: C:/Users/Mark/Desktop/Python 2017/else.py ===================
Sorry. You did not achieve a new high score
Try again!
>>>
```

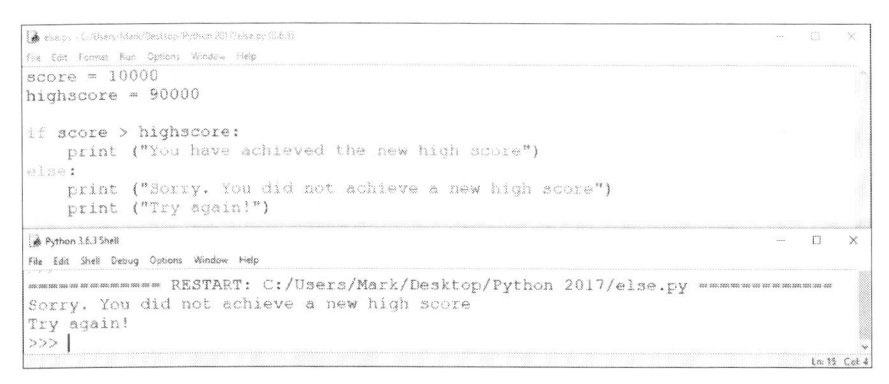

Figure 6.25. The expected output from our program using an **If...Else** statement. Our program displays the first print statement, if the **If** clause is true, and the second print statement if the **If** clause is false.

Let's try another example.

Open the editor window from IDLE, then enter the following:

grade = 92
if grade >= 90:
   letterGrade = "A"
if grade >=80:
   letterGrade = "B"
print (letterGrade)

Save your program as grades.py, then run it. What output did you get?

In this case, B is returned as the program output. Let us take a closer look at the answer.

The program checked for the value of grade using the first **If** clause, before checking the value of grade again through the second **If** clause. Since the program evaluated the second **If** clause last, and both **If** clauses were evaluated as true and the program returns B as the answer.

Therefore, we get an incorrect answer, if we use two **If** clauses simultaneously.

```
grade = 92

if grade >=90:
    letterGrade = "A"
if grade >=80:
    letterGrade = "B"

print (letterGrade)
```

```
Python 3.6.3 (v3.6.3:2c5fed8, Oct  3 2017, 18:11:49) [MSC v.1900 64 bit (AMD64)]
on win32
Type "copyright", "credits" or "license()" for more information.
>>>
============ RESTART: C:/Users/Mark/Desktop/Python 2017/grades.py ============
B
>>> 
```

Figure 6.26. The expected program output from using two If clauses that are both evaluated as true.

To get a correct answer, we use an **elif** statement in this case. Let's modify the grades.py program for an example.

On the editor window, edit the grades program accordingly:

grade = 72
if grade >= 90:
   letterGrade = "A"
elif grade >=80:
   letterGrade = "B"
elif grade >=70:
   letterGrade = "C"
elif grade >=60:
   letterGrade = "D"
else:

```
letterGrade = "E"
print (letterGrade)
```

Save the program, then run it again.

Your program should output C.

Let's look at our program again, this time in more detail.

When the program enters the **If** clause, it evaluates grade=72, and since grade >= 90 is false, it goes to the first **elif** statement. It then evaluates if grade >= 80. Again, the result is false, thus the program goes to the next **elif** statement. This time, since grade >= 70 is true, the program skips the rest of the **elif** clauses and prints the grade.

Note that we use an **Else** clause for the last letterGrade option, since any grade that returns *false* on the previous **elif** statements would already fall under "F."

```
grade = 72

if grade >=90:
    letterGrade = "A"
elif grade >=80:
    letterGrade = "B"
elif grade >=70:
    letterGrade = "C"
elif grade >=60:
    letterGrade = "D"
else:
    letterGrade = "F"

print (letterGrade)
```

```
============ RESTART: C:/Users/Mark/Desktop/Python 2017/grades.py ============
C
>>>
```

Figure 6.27. The expected program output from using a combination of If...Else clauses. The program evaluates grade = C since 72 is greater than 70.The **elif** clause stands for *else-if*. It allows the program to evaluate the value of each **elif** statement, then exit as soon as the statement returns true.

Still unclear? Play around with the program by changing the value of grade. You should have a better understanding of what an **elif** clause does once you finish.

That's it for **If...Else** statements. We will discuss nested **If** statements next.

Nested If Statements

Nested **If** statements arean **If** statement, or several **If** statements, contained within another **If** statement.

To demonstrate, let's write another program using IDLE. We will use several **If** statements within an **If** statement in this demo.

Once IDLE runs, on the editor window, enter the following:

```
value = 50
If value < 200:
   print ("Value is less than 200")
   if value < 150:
      print ("Value is less than 150")
      if value < 100:
         print ("Value is less than 100")
         if value == 50:
            print ("Value is 50")
```

Note that the program has several **If** statements within a single **If** statement. This is what we call *nested **If** statements*. We test for the value using these **If** statements.

Save the program as nested.py, then run the program.

Since value is 50, what do you think the output of the program will be? If you said that the program will return the four lines corresponding to the print statements, you are correct. This is shown in Fig. 6.10 below.

```
value = 50

if value < 200:
    print ("Value is less than 200")
    if value < 150:
        print ("Value is less than 150")
        if value < 100:
            print ("Value is less than 100")
            if value == 50:
                print ("Value is 50")
```

```
RESTART: C:/Users/Mark/Desktop/Python 2017/nested.py
Value is less than 200
Value is less than 150
Value is less than 100
Value is 50
>>>
```

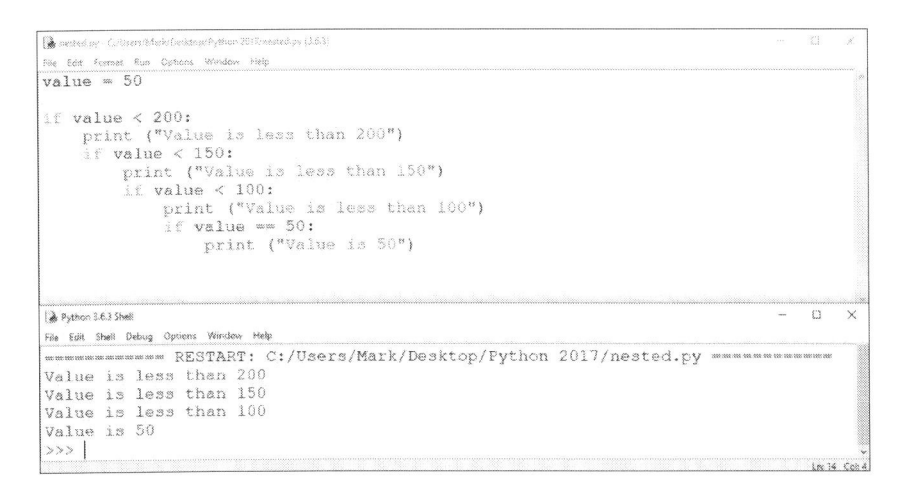

Figure 6.28. The expected output of our sample program named nested.py. With each **If** statement evaluated as true, the program outputs all four print statements in the nested **If** statements.

If we edit value to be 60, then save and run the program again, the program will only output the first three print statements. The program would skip the last print statement corresponding to the **If** statement *if value == 50,* since value == 50 is false. This is shown in Fig. 6.11.

```
value = 60

if value < 200:
    print ("Value is less than 200")
    if value < 150:
        print ("Value is less than 150")
        if value < 100:
            print ("Value is less than 100")
            if value == 50:
                print ("Value is 50")
```

```
Python 3.6.3 (v3.6.3:2c5fed8, Oct  3 2017, 18:11:49) [MSC v.1900 64 bit (AMD64)] on win32
Type "copyright", "credits" or "license()" for more information.
>>>
============ RESTART: C:/Users/Mark/Desktop/Python 2017/nested.py ============
Value is less than 200
Value is less than 150
Value is less than 100
>>>
```

Figure 6.29. The expected output of the program where value = 60, and the last **If** statement is evaluated as false. Therefore, only the first three print statements are displayed on screen, since the program skips the last print statement.

Let's add an **Else** clause after the last nested **If** statement in our program. First, let's change value to 3360. Our program would look like the one shown in Fig. 6.12.

```
value = 3360

if value < 200:
    print ("Value is less than 200")
    if value < 150:
        print ("Value is less than 150")
        if value < 100:
            print ("Value is less than 100")
            if value == 50:
                print ("Value is 50")
else:
    print ("value is not less than 200")
```

```
============ RESTART: C:/Users/Mark/Desktop/Python 2017/nested.py ============
value is not less than 200
>>>
```

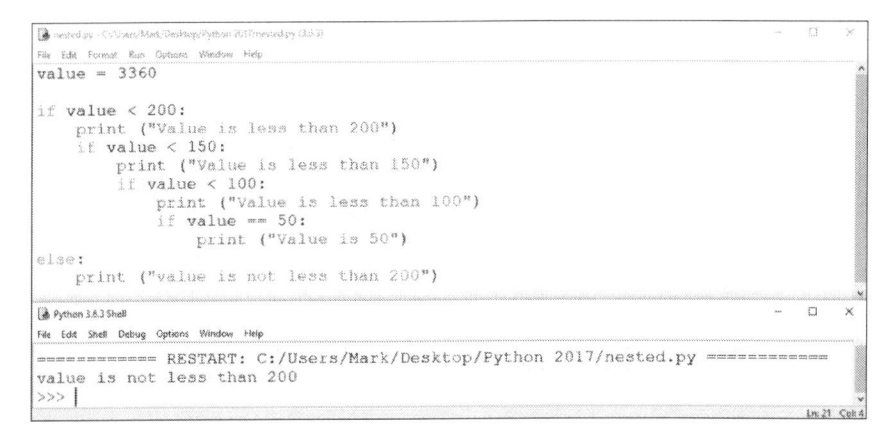

Figure 6.30. The expected output of our program with an **Else** clause. Since the nested **If** statements are all evaluated as false, the program skips to the **Else** clause, and prints the corresponding print statement.

This completes our discussion of nested **If** statements. To ensure that you understand how this type of conditional statement works, edit the program by changing value to any number. You should then run the program again. Once you are confident of your understanding of the subject, you may proceed to the next section, where you will learn about the *ternary operator* in Python.

The Ternary Operator

The simplest definition of a ternary operator is that it is a condensed **If** statement. Python's ternary operator is a source of confusion, even among experienced programmers. To make sure you understand this before we go into our coding exercise and then on to the next chapter of the book, let's code another program.

Run IDLE, then open a new file, and save the file as ternary.py. You should then enter the following on the editor window:

age = 23

print ('Eligible to buy alcohol' if age >=18 else 'Ineligible to buy alcohol')

Save, then run the program. What do you think the output will be? If you said **Eligible to buy alcohol** will be displayed onscreen, you are correct, since age is evaluated as true, since it meets the condition >=18.

```
age = 23
print ('Eligible to buy alcohol' if age >= 18 else 'Ineligible to buy alcohol')
```

```
Python 3.6.3 (v3.6.3:2c5fed8, Oct  3 2017, 18:11:49) [MSC v.1900 64 bit (AMD64)]
on win32
Type "copyright", "credits" or "license()" for more information.
>>>
============ RESTART: C:/Users/Mark/Desktop/Python 2017/ternary.py ============
Eligible to buy alcohol
>>>
```

Figure 6.31. The expected output from our sample program, where age = 23 is evaluated as true, since 23 >= 18.

If we change age = 17, then save

```
age = 17
print ('Eligible to buy alcohol' if age >= 18 else 'Ineligible to buy alcohol')
```

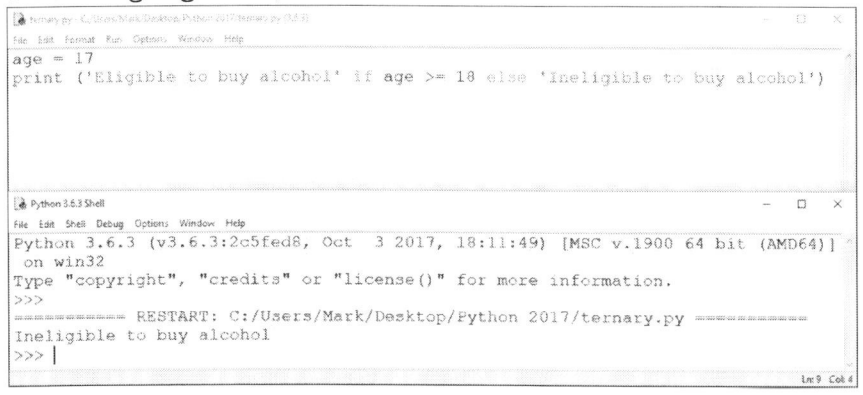

```
Python 3.6.3 (v3.6.3:2c5fed8, Oct  3 2017, 18:11:49) [MSC v.1900 64 bit (AMD64)]
on win32
Type "copyright", "credits" or "license()" for more information.
>>>
============ RESTART: C:/Users/Mark/Desktop/Python 2017/ternary.py ============
Ineligible to buy alcohol
>>>
```

Figure 6.32. The expected output from our sample program, where age = 17 is evaluated as false, since 17 >= 18.

and run the program again, we now get the **Ineligible to buy alcohol** output, since age=17 is evaluated as false, as it does not meet the age >= 18 condition.

As you can see from the above examples, the ternary operator puts the logic of the **If...Else** statements we discussed in the previous section all together in one line.

Let's add a couple of lines using the ternary operator to our program.

Enter the following on the editor window:

citizen = "true"

print ('You may vote' if citizen == "true" else 'You may not vote')

After saving and running the program, since citizen = "true", the output would be **You may vote**. If citizen = "false", the output would be **You may not vote** instead.

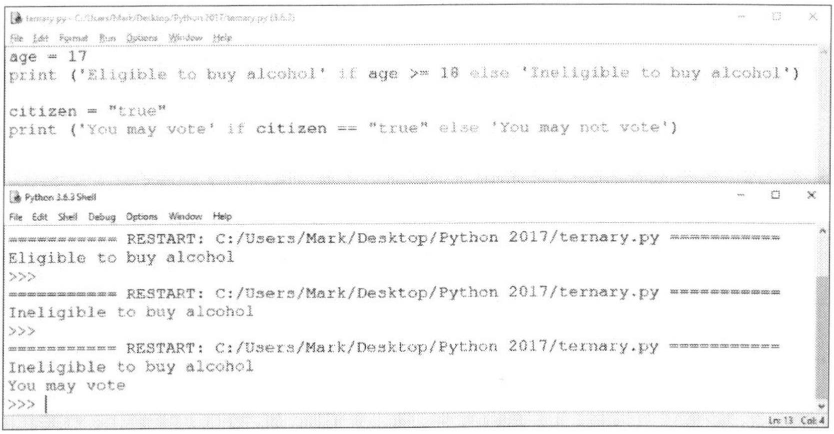

Figure 6.33. The expected output from our sample program, after evaluating for citizen = "true."

As you can see from our sample program, the ternary operator is simple. However, you should memorize it, if you want to use it in your program. It will allow you to save a couple of lines or more.

This concludes our discussion of the ternary operator in Python. In the next section, you will do a coding exercise to help you apply the conditional statements you learned about in the chapter.

Coding Exercise: Operators Practice

This exercise will allow you to reinforce your knowledge of the conditionals statements that you learned in the chapter.
1. Load IDLE and choose **File>New File** to create a blank document, then create the following list variables:

subjectList = ["English", "Spanish", "Algebra", "Geography", "Theater"]
gpas = [3.12, 3.45, 2.99]

Save the document as branching_lab.py.

2. Create a series of **If** statements that determine whether the subject "Geography" is on the list. If the subject "Geography" is on the list, the value of a Boolean variable called **takingGeography** should be set to True. If not, the **takingGeography** variable should be set to false.

3. Write an if statement that will determine whether the average of the GPAs is greater than or equal to 3.33. If it is, output the statement "Average is 3.33 or greater." If not, output the statement "Average is less than 3.33."

4. Check your answer against the code shown in Fig. 6.16.

```python
subjectList = ["English", "Spanish", "Algebra", "Geography", "Theater"]
gpas = [3.12, 3.45, 2.99]

if subjectList[0] == "Geography":
    takingGeography = True
elif subjectList[1] == "Geography":
    takingGeography = True
elif subjectList[2] == "Geography":
    takingGeography = True
elif subjectList[3] == "Geography":
    takingGeography = True
elif subjectList[4] == "Geography":
    takingGeography = True
else:
    takingGeography = False

print(takingGeography)

average = (gpas[0] + gpas[1] + gpas[2])/3

if average >= 3.33:
    print("Average is 3.33 or greater")
else:
    print("Average is less than 3.33")
```

Figure 6.16. After going through the steps in the exercise, this is what your code should look like.

Chapter 7 – Loops

This chapter will teach you how to use loops in Python programming. After learning about conditional statements, or code branching, in Chapter 6, you should now be ready to handle loops.

Along with conditional statements, loops are the most used statements in computer programming. This is also true for Python even if it handles certain loops differently from other programming languages.

In this chapter, you will learn about the different loops including: the *while* loop, the *for* loop, and the *nested* loop. The use of **break** and **continue** statements in loops will also be discussed.

The *while* loop is the simplest loop. Therefore, it is the easiest to understand loop. You will learn about this type of loop first. The basic structure of the *while* loop is **while (true), do this stuff**.

Some programming languages treat the *for* loop, the same as the *while* loop. This is not true with Python. You will know more about the differences, as you go through the rest of the section.

The next type of loop are *nested* loops. They are a loop, or loops, within another loop. These are just like the *nested* conditionals that were discussed in the previous section.

We then cover **break and continue** statements, which allow better control of operations within loops in our programs.

At the end of the chapter, is a coding exercise that computes the interest of an investment. Your output for this coding exercise is the first useful program that you will be coding in the course, although there will be others as you go through the rest of the book.

The While Loop

As mentioned previously, most things that happen in a computer program are part of a loop, which means that they occur repeatedly.

For example, let's say you need to write a program that involves a deck of playing cards in a card game. This program will go through the deck of cards and deal a card to each player, until everyone has the correct number of cards.

The act of dealing the cards is known as a loop in programming. In Python, there are several kinds of loops. This section will examine the *while* loop. As you will see in our next sample program, the *while* loop is the easiest to understand loop that you will learn about in this section. The other loops are not that difficult to learn. You just need to remember that constant practice is needed to ensure that you know how to use them within your programs.

Let's go to our usual sample program. Open **IDLE**, then click **File>New File**, or press **Ctrl+N**.

On the editor window, enter the following lines of code:

```
x = 0
while (x < 25):
    print ("The value of x: ", x)
    x = x+1
```

Let's pause for a moment and discuss these lines of code in more detail.

In Line 1 of our program, we have a value **x** which is initialized to **0**. In Line 2, we begin our *while* loop, as denoted in the **while** at the beginning of Line 2, then follow it with a **print** statement that prints the value of x, if x < 25 = true. Finally, in Line 3 of our program, we add (or increment, to use the correct term) 1 to the initial value of x. Therefore, **x** now becomes 2, after which it goes back to our **while** statement until x<25 is no longer true (x != 25).

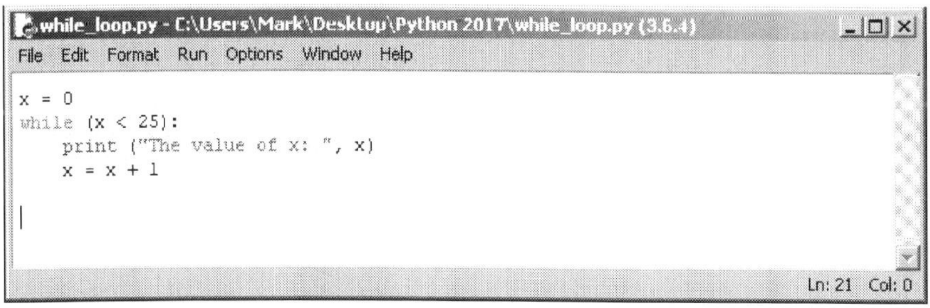

Figure 7.34 Sample program code using a *while* loop.

Let's now save and then run our program.

Since the initial value of x is 0, as we go through the **while** loop for the first time, 0 is printed to the screen. The program then continues running and displaying the value of x, until the statement x<25 is no longer true, or when x != 25. The program should output the numbers 0 through 24 on your screen.

```
Python 3.6.4 Shell
File Edit Shell Debug Options Window Help
Type "copyright", "credits" or "license()" for more information.
>>>
========== RESTART: C:\Users\Mark\Desktop\Python 2017\while_loop.py ==========
The value of x:  0
The value of x:  1
The value of x:  2
The value of x:  3
The value of x:  4
The value of x:  5
The value of x:  6
The value of x:  7
The value of x:  8
The value of x:  9
The value of x:  10
The value of x:  11
The value of x:  12
The value of x:  13
The value of x:  14
The value of x:  15
The value of x:  16
The value of x:  17
The value of x:  18
The value of x:  19
The value of x:  20
The value of x:  21
The value of x:  22
The value of x:  23
The value of x:  24
>>>
```

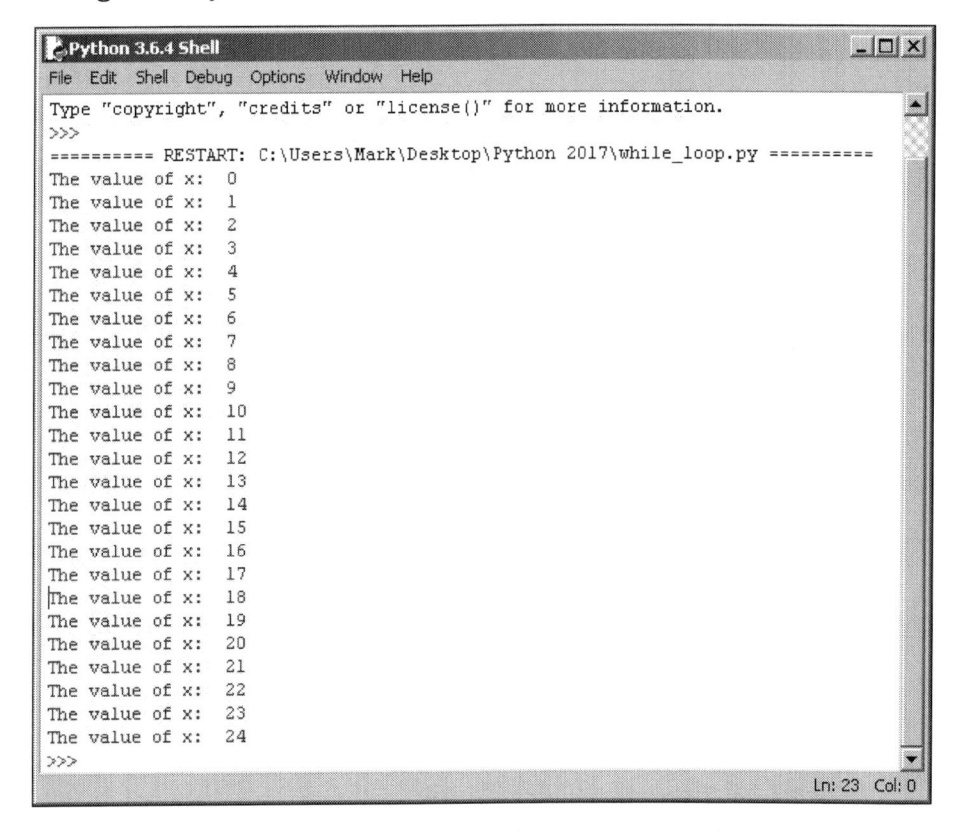

Figure 7.35. The program prints 1 through 24 on our screen, since this meets the condition of the **while** loop, x < 25. The program exits the **while** loop, once the condition no longer holds true.

Let's try another example using the same file we used for the above program.

counter=100
while (counter > 0):
  print (counter)
  counter=counter – 10

Let's again discuss what these lines of code mean.

In Line 1, we assign 100 to a **counter** variable. We then add our **while** loop, counter>0 in Line 2. On the next line of code, we print counter, after which we subtract 10 from counter in Line 4.

Let's save, then run our program again.

```
x = 0
while (x < 25):
    print ("The value of x: ", x)
    x = x + 1

counter = 100
while (counter > 0):
    print (counter)
    counter = counter - 10
```

Figure 7.36. The highlighted lines show our sample program code involving another while loop.

As shown, the program prints the numbers 100 down to 10 on your screen. This is because the program keeps running, until the condition counter > 0 becomes false, which happens after counter = 0.

```
100
90
80
70
60
50
40
30
20
10
>>>
```

Figure 7.37. The output of our 2nd sample program. Note that the program exits the loop, once the **counter** > 0 condition in the while loop becomes false.

There are a few things you should note when creating loops, including **while** loops. It might be possible that while coding your programs, you create what is called an *endless* loop. For example, if the operation in your **while** loops runs endlessly because its value is always true, then that is an endless loop.

This is generally bad coding practice. Your program can continue to run forever or generate an error due to your computer running out of memory. Your programs should always have a way to exit the loop. We will discuss how to avoid endless loops next.

Let's go back to the editor window of our IDLE. In this example, you will code an endless loop.

y = 0
while (y > 0):
   print (y)
   y = y+1

Take a closer look at our little program. Do you see anything wrong with it?

If you say that it will run forever, you are right. This is because the program is coded so that the condition y in out **while** loop is always true. It would always be y > 0. Our sample program above, is an example of an endless loop.

```
y = 1
while (y > 0):
    print (y)
    y = y + 1
```

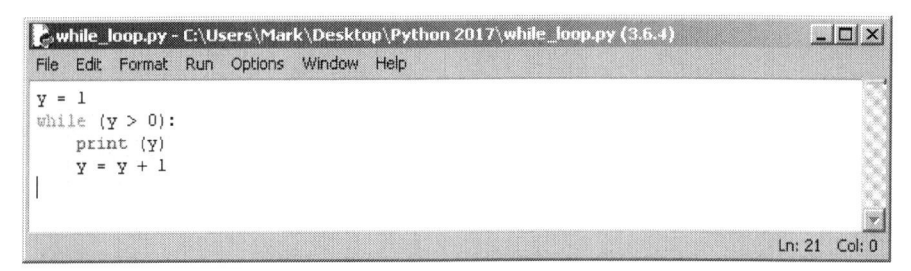

Figure 7.38. An example of an endless loop. Note that the y>0 condition of the **while** loop in this program code will always be true.

Let's save and run the program. You will see that the program will not end. It will continue to churn out numbers to your screen, until you force it to stop by pressing **Ctrl+C** on your keyboard (**Ctrl+C** intercepts the program via the keyboard, effectively stopping it from running).

```
577
578
579
580
581
582
583
584
585
586
587
588
589Traceback (most recent call last):
  File "C:\Users\Mark\Desktop\Python 2017\while_loop.py", line 19, in <module>
    print (y)
KeyboardInterrupt
>>>
```

Figure 7.39. Pressing **Ctrl+C** stops the output operation of the endless loop in the sample program.

Pressing a combination of keyboard buttons to stop a program is not how your Python programs are meant to be coded. Therefore, we will present a method to ensure that an endless loop would not occur in this case.

Let's go back to our program.

Since you do not want to run a program containing an endless loop, let's comment out the lines you added at the bottom of the program by manually entering a couple of #, or sharp, signs to the left of each line. You can also comment out the offending lines by either selecting them, then clicking **Format > Comment Out Region** from the menu, or pressing **Alt+3** on your keyboard.

Next, let's add an **else** statement right after the print operation for our original **while** statement.

else:
  print("Y is no longer greater than zero")

Our code should now look like the following:

counter = 100
while (counter > 0):
  print (counter)

```
        counter = counter – 10
    else:
        print("Y is no longer greater than zero")
```

Let's save and run the program again.

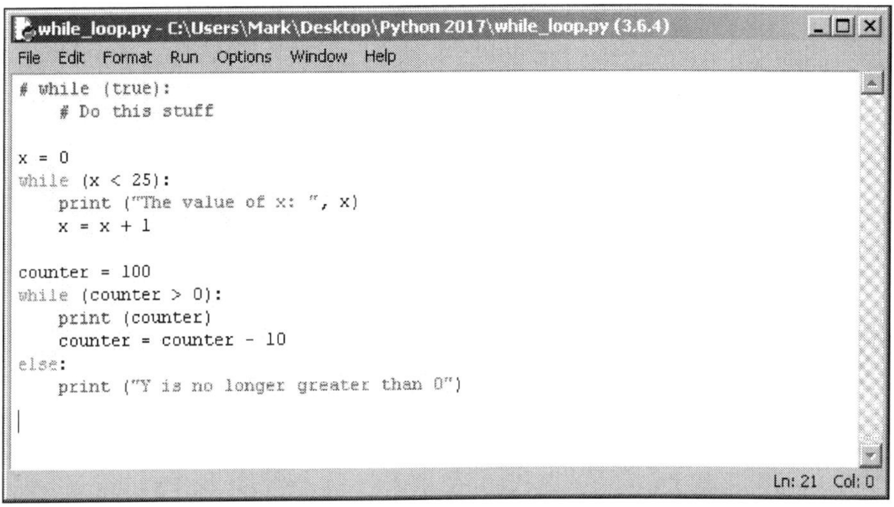

```
# while (true):
    # Do this stuff

x = 0
while (x < 25):
    print ("The value of x: ", x)
    x = x + 1

counter = 100
while (counter > 0):
    print (counter)
    counter = counter - 10
else:
    print ("Y is no longer greater than 0")
```

Figure 7.7. The complete sample program for this section. Note the **else** statement on the last two lines.

In addition to printing out the values of 100 down to 10 on your screen, the program should now display the statement "Y is no longer greater than zero" at the bottom. This is a sign that it has reached the end of the line, and that the value of Y is already 0.

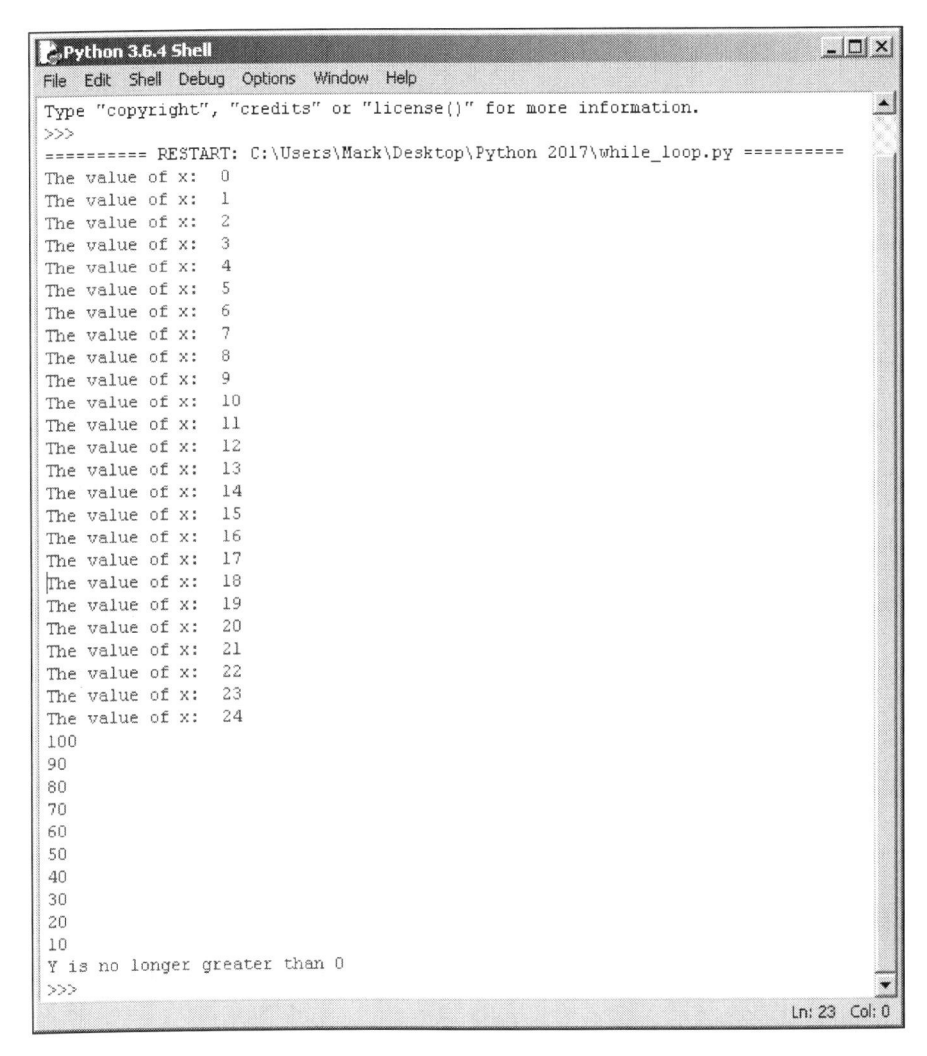

```
Python 3.6.4 Shell
File Edit Shell Debug Options Window Help
Type "copyright", "credits" or "license()" for more information.
>>>
========== RESTART: C:\Users\Mark\Desktop\Python 2017\while_loop.py ==========
The value of x:  0
The value of x:  1
The value of x:  2
The value of x:  3
The value of x:  4
The value of x:  5
The value of x:  6
The value of x:  7
The value of x:  8
The value of x:  9
The value of x:  10
The value of x:  11
The value of x:  12
The value of x:  13
The value of x:  14
The value of x:  15
The value of x:  16
The value of x:  17
The value of x:  18
The value of x:  19
The value of x:  20
The value of x:  21
The value of x:  22
The value of x:  23
The value of x:  24
100
90
80
70
60
50
40
30
20
10
Y is no longer greater than 0
>>>
```

Figure 7.8. The output from our sample program in this section. Note that the last printed value is the output of the else statement in the complete program that is shown on Fig. 7.7.

When coding **while** loops, you should have an **else** option, if possible, to ensure that your program exits the loop. As you can see from the final version of our sample program in this section, that is exactly what we did.

This is the end of the section. In the next section, you will learn more about **for** loops.

The For Loop

In many programming languages, the **For** loop is a shorter version of the **while** loop. This is not exactly true when it comes to Python, where a **For** loop allows us to iterate through objects, such as a string. You will learn how **for** loops work in this section.

Let's run **IDLE**, then open another editing window.

Enter the following on the editor window:

courseName = "Python for Beginners 2017"
for letter in courseName:
 print ("Current Letter is ", letter)

Let's save our program before running it.

```
courseName = "Python for Beginners 2017"
for letter in courseName:
    print ("Current Letter is ", letter)
```

Figure 7.9. Our sample program code showing a **for** loop.

When you run the program, you will see that the value of courseName, the string **Python for Beginners 2017**, is printed to the screen, with each letter in the string appearing on a separate line. This is shown in Fig. 7.10.

```
Python 3.6.4 (v3.6.4:d48eceb, Dec 19 2017, 06:54:40) [MSC v.1900 64 bit (AMD64)]
on win32
Type "copyright", "credits" or "license()" for more information.
>>>
============ RESTART: C:/Users/Mark/Desktop/Python 2017/for_loop.py ============
Current Letter is  P
Current Letter is  y
Current Letter is  t
Current Letter is  h
Current Letter is  o
Current Letter is  n
Current Letter is
Current Letter is  f
Current Letter is  o
Current Letter is  r
Current Letter is
Current Letter is  B
Current Letter is  e
Current Letter is  g
Current Letter is  i
Current Letter is  n
Current Letter is  n
Current Letter is  e
Current Letter is  r
Current Letter is  s
Current Letter is
Current Letter is  2
Current Letter is  0
Current Letter is  1
Current Letter is  7
>>>
```

Figure 7.10. The output of our sample program code, using a for loop.

Take a look at the output again. Note that the spaces between the words in our string are treated as empty characters. Let's change our program, so that it will display an output when it detects a space in the string.

Let's add the following to our code.

if (letter == " "):
  print ("This is a space character")

Let's save, then run our program again.

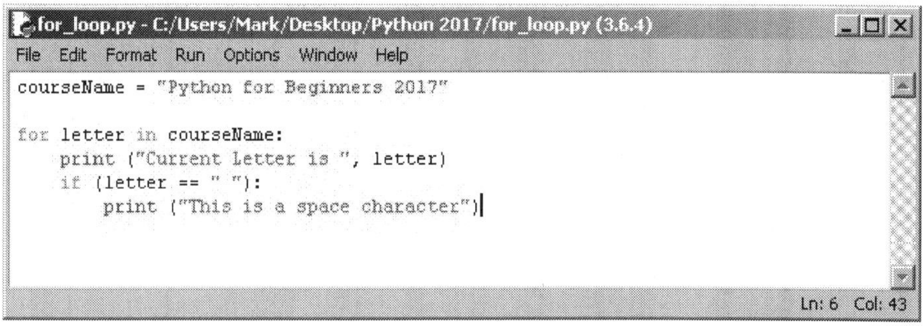
for_loop.py - C:/Users/Mark/Desktop/Python 2017/for_loop.py (3.6.4)
File Edit Format Run Options Window Help
courseName = "Python for Beginners 2017"
for letter in courseName:
print ("Current Letter is ", letter)
if (letter == " "):
print ("This is a space character")
Ln: 6 Col: 43

Figure 40.11. Our revised program code identifying the space characters in our string.

As you can see, the program now identifies where the space characters are in our string.

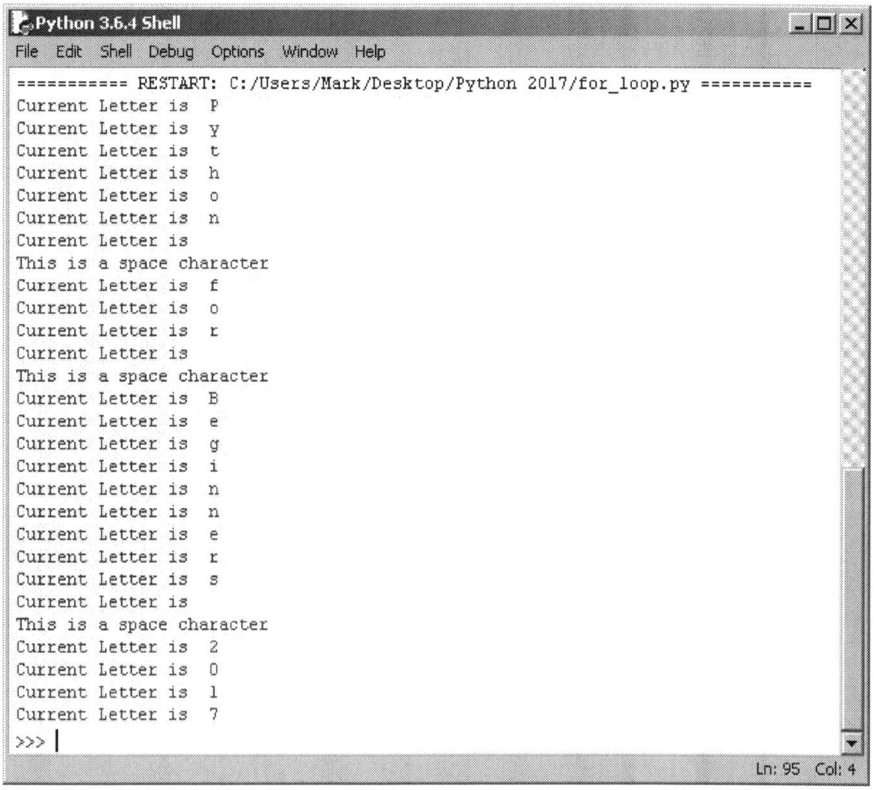
Python 3.6.4 Shell
File Edit Shell Debug Options Window Help
=========== RESTART: C:/Users/Mark/Desktop/Python 2017/for_loop.py ===========
Current Letter is P
Current Letter is y
Current Letter is t
Current Letter is h
Current Letter is o
Current Letter is n
Current Letter is
This is a space character
Current Letter is f
Current Letter is o
Current Letter is r
Current Letter is
This is a space character
Current Letter is B
Current Letter is e
Current Letter is g
Current Letter is i
Current Letter is n
Current Letter is n
Current Letter is e
Current Letter is r
Current Letter is s
Current Letter is
This is a space character
Current Letter is 2
Current Letter is 0
Current Letter is 1
Current Letter is 7
>>>
Ln: 95 Col: 4

Figure 7.12. The output of our revised program code, identifying the space characters in the string.

Therefore, in Python, a **for** loop is used for string processing. The ease with which you can perform string processing in Python can be traced to this use of the **for** loop.

Let's try another program using a **for** loop. Similar to our example in the previous section, we will use our existing file, and add to it the following lines of code.

Bands = ["Journey", "REO Speedwagon", "Foreigner", "Heart", "The Cure"]
for band in bands:
  print ("Current Band: ", x)

Save, then run the program again.

```
bands = ["Journey", "REO Speedwagon", "Foreigner", "Heart", "The Cure"]

for x in bands:
    print ("Current Band: ", x)
```

Figure 7.13. The program code showing another example of using a **for** loop.

The program then displays each band in our **Bands** list on a separate line.

```
=========== RESTART: C:/Users/Mark/Desktop/Python 2017/for_loop.py ===========
Current Band:  Journey
Current Band:  REO Speedwagon
Current Band:  Foreigner
Current Band:  Heart
Current Band:  The Cure
>>>
```

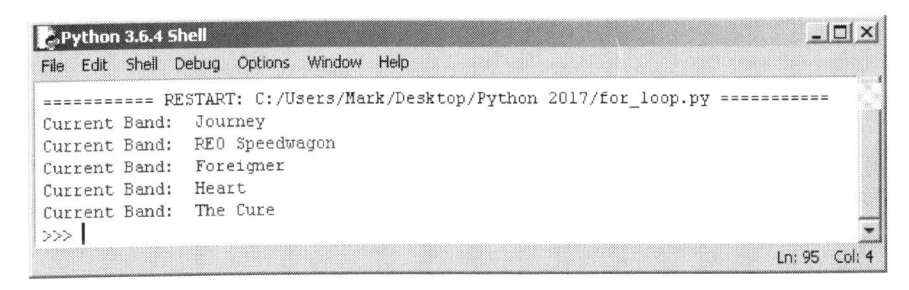

Figure 7.14. The output from the additional lines in our sample program code.

Note that **for** loops work for just about any objects in Python. As you go through the rest of the book, there are additional examples of **for** loops being used for string processing.

This wraps up our discussion of **for** loops. In the next section, you will learn about nested loops.

Nested Loops

A nested loop, as the name suggests, is a loop inside a loop. In this section, you will learn how to nest loops in Python.

Let's go straight to coding our sample program for this section. Open IDLE again, then run a new file. On the editor window, enter the following:

count = 10
x = 0

while x < count:
    y = 0
    while y < 11:
    y = y + 1
x = x + 1

Save, then run the program.

```
count = 11
x = 0

while x < count:
    y = 0
    while y < 11:
        print (y)
        y = y + 1
    x = x + 1
```

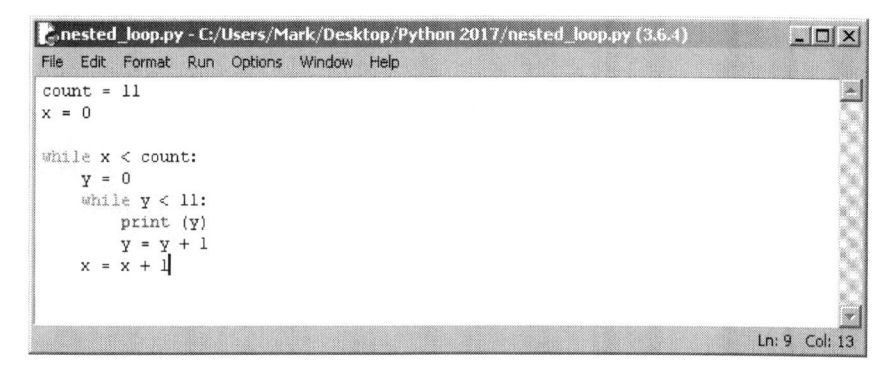

Figure 7.15. Sample program code showing nested loops, which, in this case, is a while loop inside another while loop.

As shown, the program displays the numbers 0-10 on your screen 10 times. Let's go back to the program and discuss each line, so that you will get a better idea of what it does.

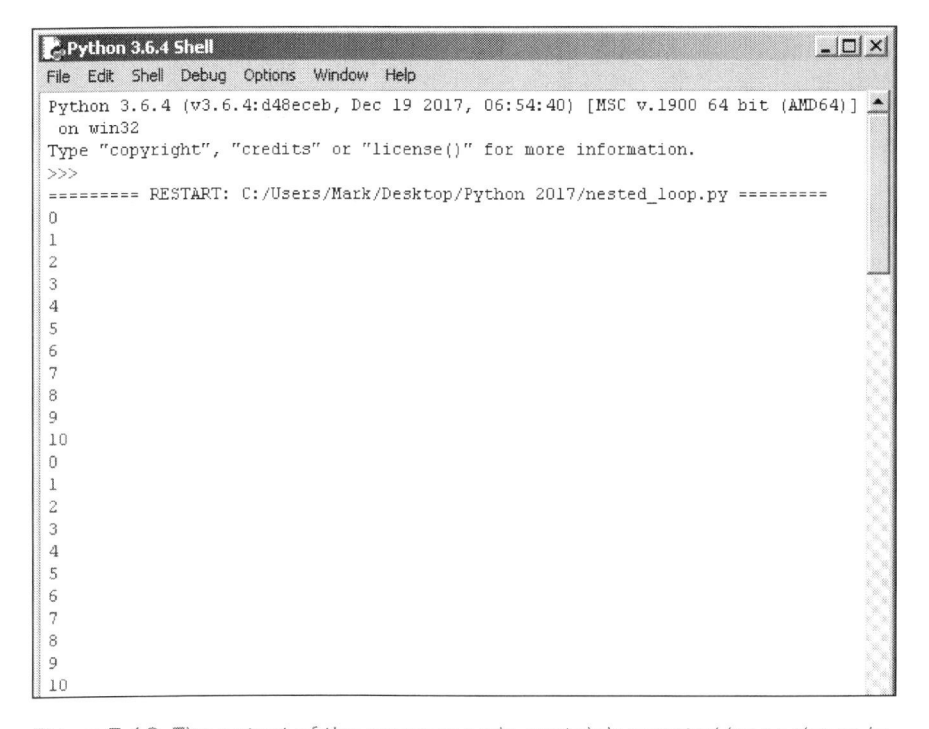

```
Python 3.6.4 Shell
File Edit Shell Debug Options Window Help
Python 3.6.4 (v3.6.4:d48eceb, Dec 19 2017, 06:54:40) [MSC v.1900 64 bit (AMD64)]
on win32
Type "copyright", "credits" or "license()" for more information.
>>>
========= RESTART: C:/Users/Mark/Desktop/Python 2017/nested_loop.py =========
0
1
2
3
4
5
6
7
8
9
10
0
1
2
3
4
5
6
7
8
9
10
```

Figure 7.16. The output of the program code containing nested loops shown in Fig. 7.15 displays 0-10 on your screen 10 times.

Lines 1 and 2 of the program sets the initial values of two variables, **count** and **x**.

Lines 3 and 4 shows the initial **while** loop, which states that while **x** **<count**, the value of **y = 0**.

On Line 5, the second while loop begins. First, it sets the condition **y < 11** (line 6), then prints **y**, before incrementing **y** by 1 (line 7). Once the while condition **y < 11** becomes false, the program exits the second while loop, then proceeds to increment **x** by 1 (line 8).

If you are still confused on the steps, go through the example again until it becomes clear. Stepping through each line is always good – it allows you to get a clearer picture of the code.

Let's try another example, this time using a **while** loop inside the **for** loop.

Add the following lines to your code.

```
name = ["Mark", "Fred", "Tom", "Craig", "Bobby", "Martha"]
for x in name:
  y = 0
  while y < 5:
   print (x)
   y = y + 1
```

Let's save, then run our program.

```
count = 11
x = 0

while x < count:
    y = 0
    while y < 11:
        print (y)
        y = y + 1
    x = x + 1

name = ["Mark", "Fred", "Tom", "Craig", "Bobby", "Martha"]

for x in name:
    y = 0
    while y < 5:
        print (x)
        y = y + 1
```

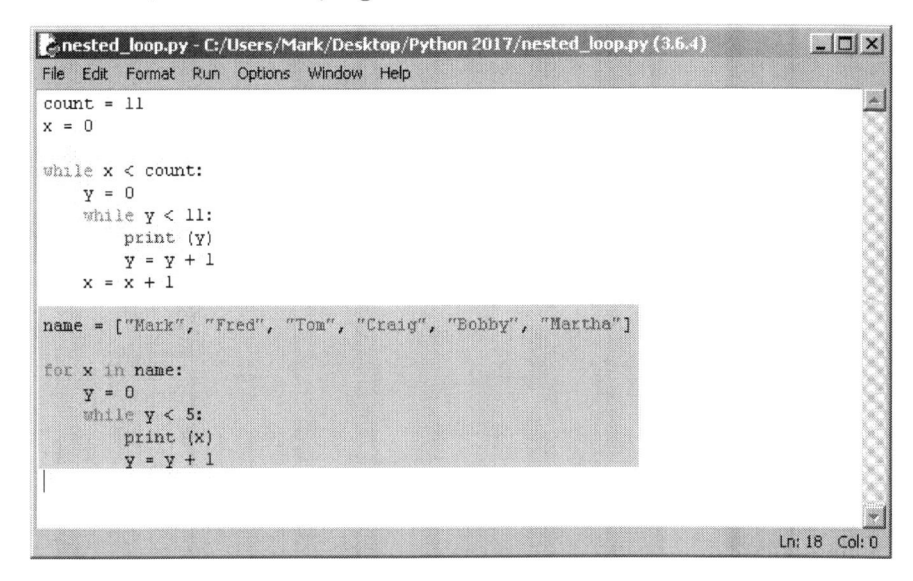

Figure 7.17. The program code showing the use of a **for** loop iterating through a list and a **while** loop within the **for** loop. The program exits the **while** loop once y < 5 becomes false, then continues on to the next name on the list via the **for** loop.

This time, the **for** loop iterates through the names on the list (as discussed in the previous section, the **for** loop iterates through a list automatically), printing each name 5x while y < 5. Once the while condition y < 5 becomes false, the program exits the **while** loop, then goes on to the next name on the list, which it then prints another 5x. The program does this, until it finishes going through each name on the list.

```
Python 3.6.4 Shell
File Edit Shell Debug Options Window Help
Mark
Mark
Mark
Mark
Mark
Fred
Fred
Fred
Fred
Fred
Tom
Tom
Tom
Tom
Tom
Craig
Craig
Craig
Craig
Craig
Bobby
Bobby
Bobby
Bobby
Bobby
Martha
Martha
Martha
Martha
Martha
>>>
```

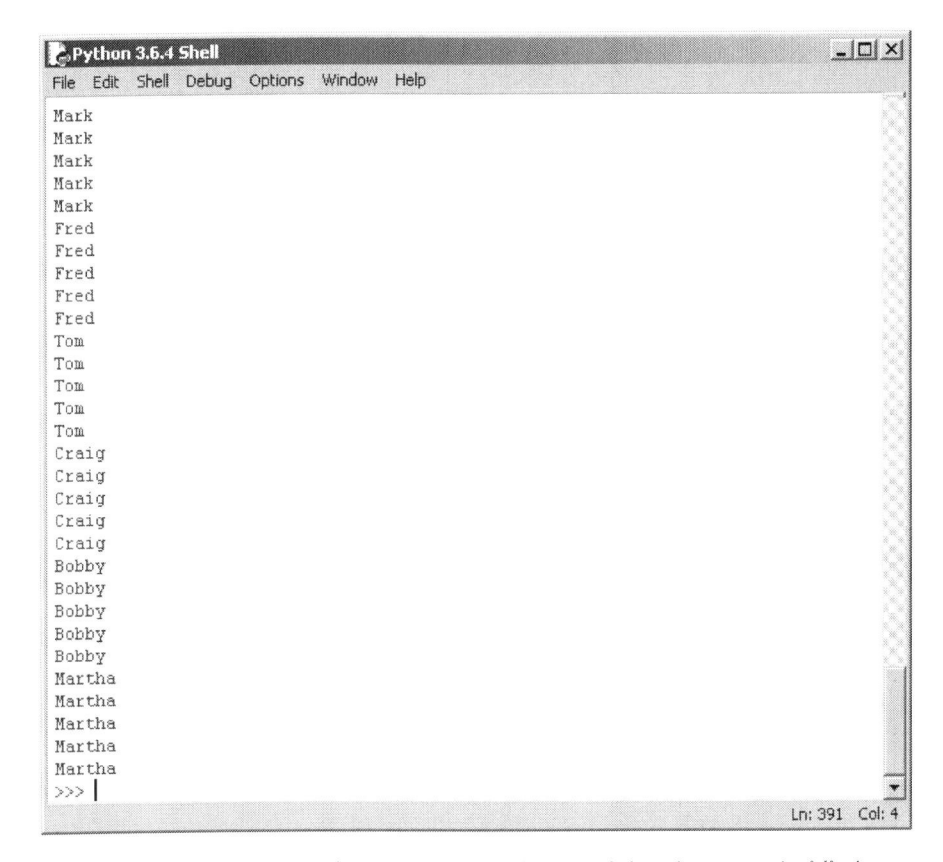

Figure 7.141. The output of our program code containing the nested **while** loop inside the **for** loop, as shown on Fig. 7.17.

That completes our discussion on **for** loops. We will cover **Break** and **Continue statements** next.

Break and Continue Statements

There might be circumstances when you need to break out of a **while** loop entirely, or skip an iteration within a **for** loop completely. This is where the **Break** and **Continue** statements come in.

Let's open another file on IDLE, then enter the following:

statement = "The quick brown fox jumped over the lazy dogs."
for letter in statement:
  print ("Current letter", letter)

Let's save the file before running the program.

As expected, the program will iterate through each letter in the string *statement*.

```
statement = "The quick brown fox jumped over the lazy dog."
for letter in statement:
    print ("Current letter", letter)
```

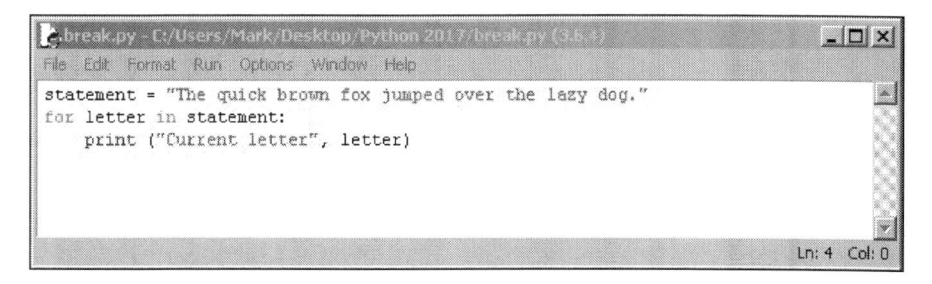

Figure 7.142. A simple for loop.

Note that you learned about this earlier in the **for** loop section of this chapter.

```
Python 3.6.4 (v3.6.4:d48eceb, Dec 19 2017, 06:54:40) [MSC v.1900 64 bit (AMD64)]
on win32
Type "copyright", "credits" or "license()" for more information.
>>>
============ RESTART: C:/Users/Mark/Desktop/Python 2017/break.py ============
Current letter T
Current letter h
Current letter e
Current letter
Current letter q
Current letter u
Current letter i
Current letter c
Current letter k
Current letter
```

Figure 7.20. The output of a for loop.

Now, let's modify the program by adding the following lines right after the print statement.

if letter == "e":
break

Save the program, then run. What do we get?

```
statement = "The quick brown box jumped over the lazy dogs."

for letter in statement:
    print ("Current letter", letter)
    if letter == "e":
        break
```

Figure 7.21. A sample break statement.

The program iterates through the statement and displays each letter up to the first letter e, after which it stops running. This is what happens when you put a **break** statement in your program.

```
============ RESTART: C:/Users/Mark/Desktop/Python 2017/break.py ============
Current letter T
Current letter h
Current letter e
>>>
```

Figure 7.22. Sample output of the program with the break statement shown on Fig. 7.21.

What if we want the program to stop, if it encounters the letter e? That is, we do not want the program to output any **e**. How do we handle this? Placing the **break** statement before the **print** statement in our program should address this.

for letter in statement:
　if letter == "e":
　　break
　print ("Current letter", letter)

This time, since the break statement comes first, when it encounters the letter e, it stops running. If you run the program again, you will see that it no longer prints the letter e.

Page 123

```
Python 3.6.4 Shell
File  Edit  Shell  Debug  Options  Window  Help
============ RESTART: C:/Users/Mark/Desktop/Python 2017/break.py ============
Current letter T
Current letter h
>>>
```

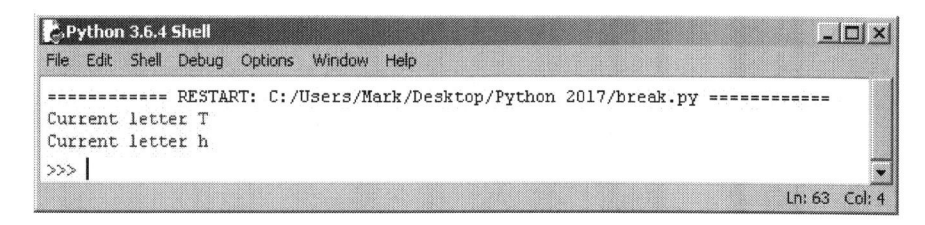

Figure 7.23. Output of our program with the break statement before the print statement.

Next, let's show an example of a **continue** statement.

Let's modify our program once more by adding the following lines to our program.

for letter in statement:
  if letter == "q":
    continue
  print ("Current letter", letter)

If you save and run the program, it will output the string without displaying the letter *q.* You can see the difference between **continue** and **break** statements. In a **continue** statement, the program *skips* the letter q, but continues to display the rest of the statement. In contrast, as we have shown previously, a **break** statement stops the program completely.

```
statement = "The quick brown fox jumped over the lazy dog."
for letter in statement:
    if letter == "e":
        break
    print ("Current letter", letter)

for letter in statement:
    if letter == "q":
        continue
    print("Current letter", letter)
```

```
============ RESTART: C:/Users/Mark/Desktop/Python 2017/break.py ============
Current letter T
Current letter h
Current letter e
Current letter
Current letter u
Current letter i
Current letter c
Current letter k
```

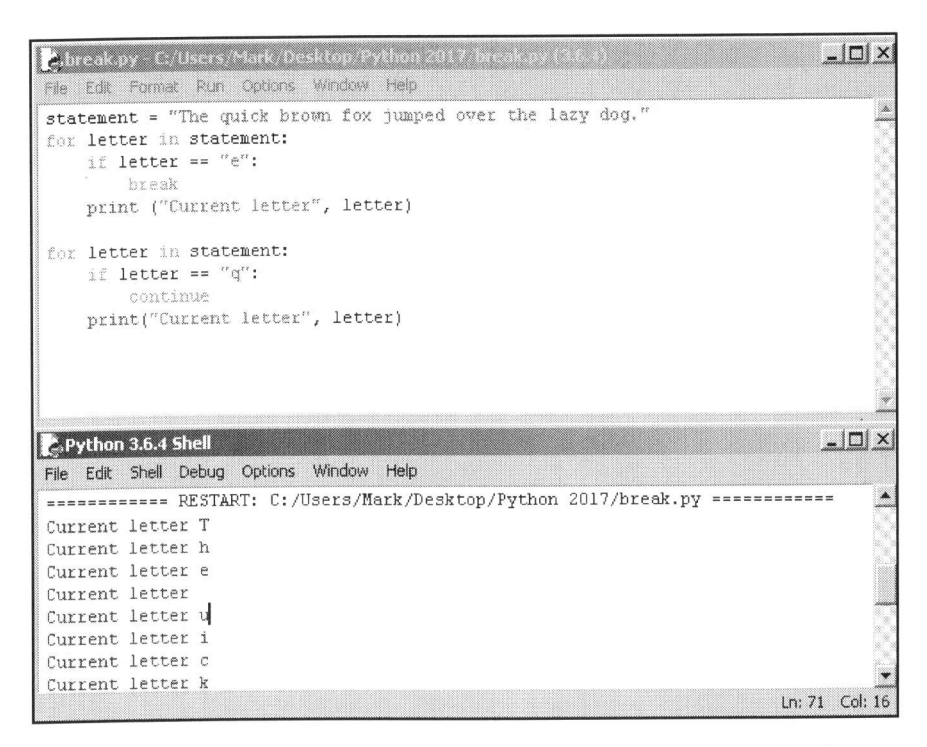

Figure 7.24. Output of our program with the continue statement. Notice that the program skips the letter *q*.

When writing loops, always check the indentation of your code. This is because anything that is lined up with a loop statement is covered under that statement. If you mistakenly indent a line of code in your program, it might bring up different results from the ones you intended the program to make.

This concludes our chapter on loops. You have learned about the different kinds of loops: the **while**, **for**, and **nested** loops, and you now also know how to use the **break** and **continue** statements. It is time for your coding exercise.

Coding Exercise: Loops

Unlike the exercises in the previous sections, the program you will create in this section actually does something useful.

Your objective is to create a simple interest calculator using loops. The program should compute the monthly interest on an investment over a

120-month term. The program output will be the month number, interest earned, and the new balance.

1. Create the following list variables:
- balance = 2250
- interestRate = .045
- term = 120

2. The program should have the following features:

a. Calculate the monthly interest earned by multiplying the balance by the interest rate divided by 12 (interest is given yearly, but calculated monthly).

b. Determine the new balance

c. Print the month number, interest earned and new balance to the console.

To make your program output neat, use the character entity \t to insert a tab between each output.

Your initial output should look as follows:

```
Python 3.6.4 Shell
File Edit Shell Debug Options Window Help
Python 3.6.4 (v3.6.4:d48eceb, Dec 19 2017, 06:54:40) [MSC v.1900 64 bit (AMD64)] on win32
Type "copyright", "credits" or "license()" for more information.
>>>
=========== RESTART: C:/Users/Mark/Desktop/Python 2017/loops_lab.py ===========
Month 1      Interest: $ 8.4375           Balance: $ 2258.4375
Month 2      Interest: $ 8.469140625      Balance: $ 2266.906640625
Month 3      Interest: $ 8.500899902343749 Balance: $ 2275.407540527344
Month 4      Interest: $ 8.53277827697754  Balance: $ 2283.9403188043216
Month 5      Interest: $ 8.564776195516206 Balance: $ 2292.5050949998376
Month 6      Interest: $ 8.59689410624939  Balance: $ 2301.101989106087
Month 7      Interest: $ 8.629132459147826 Balance: $ 2309.731121565235
Month 8      Interest: $ 8.661491705869631 Balance: $ 2318.3926132711044
Month 9      Interest: $ 8.69397229976664  Balance: $ 2327.086585570871
Month 10     Interest: $ 8.726574695890767 Balance: $ 2335.8131602667618
Month 11     Interest: $ 8.759299351000356 Balance: $ 2344.572459617762
Month 12     Interest: $ 8.792146723566608 Balance: $ 2353.3646063413285
                                                               Ln: 125 Col: 4
```

Figure 7.25. Initial output of the coding exercise.

Note that the initial results for both interest and balance are too precise. Since currency is rounded off at two digits, make sure that your code does the same by inserting %.2f at the end of the Interest and Balance parts of the print statement. %.2f outputs a floating point number with two trailing spaces. This results in a much cleaner output (see example below).

```
========== RESTART: C:/Users/Mark/Desktop/Python 2017/loops_lab.py ==========
Month 1      Interest: $ 8.44      Balance: $ 2258.44
Month 2      Interest: $ 8.47      Balance: $ 2266.91
Month 3      Interest: $ 8.50      Balance: $ 2275.41
Month 4      Interest: $ 8.53      Balance: $ 2283.94
Month 5      Interest: $ 8.56      Balance: $ 2292.51
Month 6      Interest: $ 8.60      Balance: $ 2301.10
Month 7      Interest: $ 8.63      Balance: $ 2309.73
Month 8      Interest: $ 8.66      Balance: $ 2318.39
Month 9      Interest: $ 8.69      Balance: $ 2327.09
Month 10     Interest: $ 8.73      Balance: $ 2335.81
Month 11     Interest: $ 8.76      Balance: $ 2344.57
Month 12     Interest: $ 8.79      Balance: $ 2353.36
Month 13     Interest: $ 8.83      Balance: $ 2362.19
Month 14     Interest: $ 8.86      Balance: $ 2371.05
Month 15     Interest: $ 8.89      Balance: $ 2379.94
Month 16     Interest: $ 8.92      Balance: $ 2388.86
```

Figure 7.26. Notice the much cleaner output, as the result of the use of %2f in the program.

A screenshot of the initial program is shown below.

```
balance = 2250
interestRate = .045
term = 120

x = 1
while x < term+1:
    interest = balance * interestRate/12
    balance = balance + interest
    print ("Month", x, "\t Interest: $", interest, "\t Balance: $", balance)
    x = x + 1
```

Figure 7.27. This screenshot shows the actual code of the initial version of the program.

The final program with a couple of %.2f inserted into the print statement is shown below.

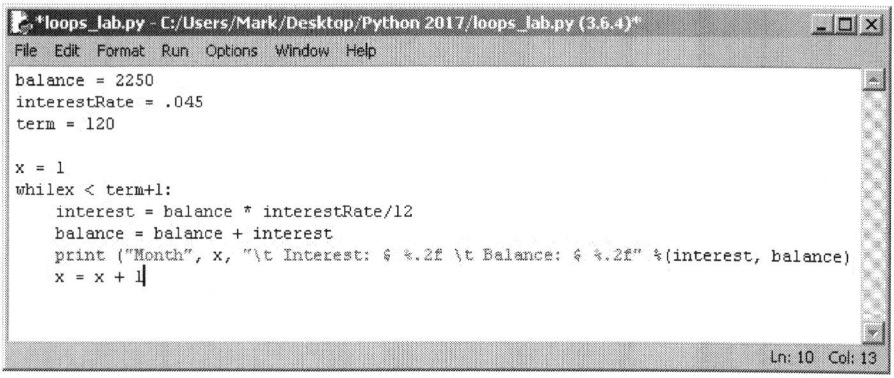

```
balance = 2250
interestRate = .045
term = 120

x = 1
while x < term+1:
    interest = balance * interestRate/12
    balance = balance + interest
    print ("Month", x, "\t Interest: $ %.2f \t Balance: $ %.2f" %(interest, balance)
    x = x + 1
```

Figure 7.28. Actual code of the program. Note the two instances of %.2f on the second to the last line of code.

Chapter 8 – Math Functions

In this chapter, you will learn about Python's powerful math functions. They are a strong suit of the language, and a major reason why data analysts prefer using Python over other programming languages.

The sheer number of functions in Python's extensive Math library makes it impossible to cover all of them in this book. However, you will learn the essential and more important ones in order to demonstrate what you can do with them. These functions are relatively easy to learn. You do not have to be math wizard to learn how to use them. You are close to finishing the book.

You will first learn about casting functions, followed by the more advanced math functions and then finally learn about randomization functions.

Casting functions are used to convert a variable type to another, such as using int(). This will allow you to convert a floating-point number to an integer.

The mathematical functions covered in the book are used for solving advanced equations and complex calculations.

Randomization functions, as their name suggests, allow random number generation or selection of a random number from a group of numbers. These functions are useful in programs where random numbers are required.

Chapter 8 ends with a coding exercise that will test your knowledge about math functions in Python.

Casting Functions

These functions are used for 'casting' a variable from one type to another. For example, when you have a floating-point number, but you need an integer, you use this function to get your desired number.

You will learn about the use of casting functions in Python in this section.

The first casting function we will discuss allows a floating-point number to be expressed as an integer and is expressed as int ().

You will then learn about expressing an integer as a floating-point number through the casting function float ().

You will also learn about displaying complex numbers, or very large real or imaginary numbers, in complex notation.

We will use our IDLE's shell window to demonstrate what we can do with these functions.

Run IDLE, then on the shell window, enter the following floating-point number:

X = 35.666666

On the next line, enter the following:

print (x)

The print statement prints the value of **x** on the next line.

Next, let's express **x** as an *int* by entering the following:

x = int (x)

Let's print the number again:

print (x)

The integer value of x, 35, is then printed.

As you can see, our original floating-point number has been converted to an integer, thanks to the casting function int ().

Note that the casting function does not round up the number (you will see a 36 instead of a 35, if you rounded up). The function just chops off the decimal point and everything to the right of it.

Let's continue with our example.

Enter the following on the shell window:

print (int (0.123423523))

When you press enter on your keyboard, you will see that only 0 is displayed on your screen. The casting function works for any floating-point number.

Now, let's see how this works for an integer that we want to express as a floating-point number.

Let's say we want to print an integer whose value is 50. Let's enter these on our shell window.

y = 50
print (y)

The value of y, which is 50, gets printed to the screen.

The following line of code will print this int as a floating-point number.

print (float (y))

The print statement and the casting function float (), displays the following output.

50.0

As you can see, although the value remains 50, we've now expressed our original int as a float.

Casting functions can be useful when doing integer or floating-point math, as you will see below.

Let's go back to our shell window, and check the values of x and y.

print (x)

will display 35, and

print (y)

will display 50.

Let's convert y to a floating-point number. Remember that we casted **y** as an integer previously, when we used it with a print statement. However, that does not mean that we've already converted y from an integer to a float. Using the float () function with the print statement simply meant that we displayed an integer variable as a float.

To convert **y** from an int to a float, enter the following on the shell window:

y = float (y)

If you print y, print(y), you'll see that we have now successfully converted it to a float.

Let's multiply x and y and see what the result will be.

print (x * y)

We now get 1750.0, a floating-point number.

Since y is a float, the product will also be a float.

To display our product as an integer, we can use the casting function when we multiply our variables.

print (x * int (y))

The product is now an integer, 1750, when printed to the screen.

We will next briefly discuss complex numbers. If you remember, we discussed complex number variables in Chapter 4 of this book. Complex, or scientific, numbers refer to numbers that are neither integers nor floating-point numbers. These are usually very large numbers.

Python allows complex numbers to be displayed in complex notation using the following format:

complex (complex number)

You may check this out on your shell window, by entering an arbitrary large number inside a parenthesis, as shown in the lines of code highlighted in yellow in Fig. 8.1.

You cannot convert complex numbers into an integer or a floating-point number.

That is the end of our casting function discussion. We will discuss the actual mathematical functions available for use in our programs in the next section.

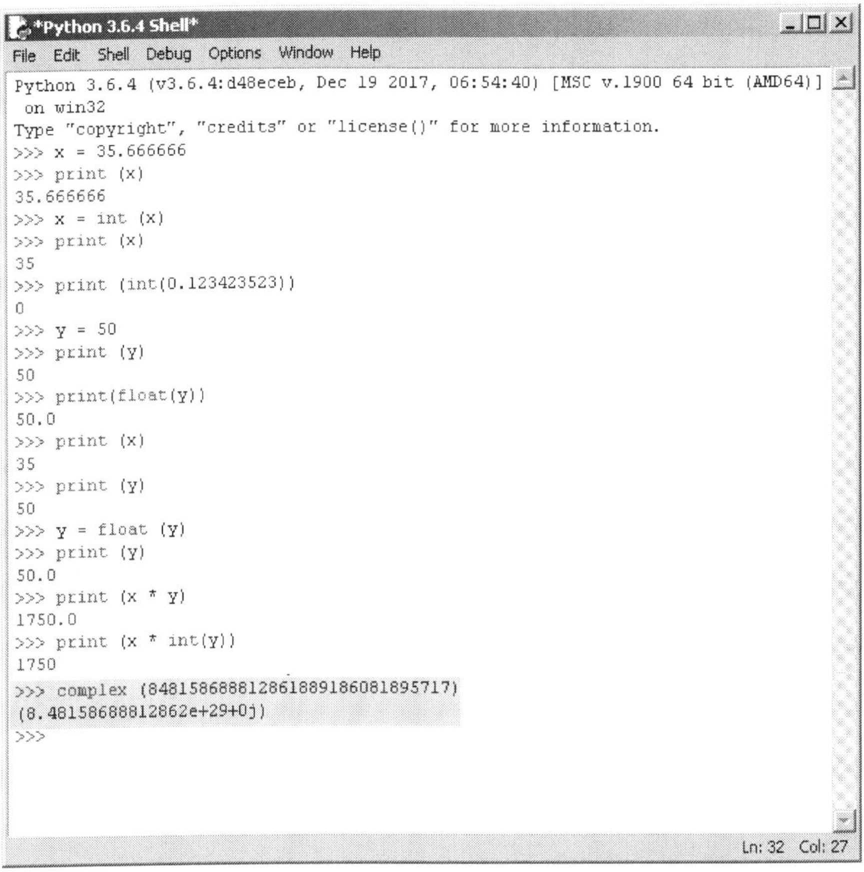

```
*Python 3.6.4 Shell*
File Edit Shell Debug Options Window Help
Python 3.6.4 (v3.6.4:d48eceb, Dec 19 2017, 06:54:40) [MSC v.1900 64 bit (AMD64)]
on win32
Type "copyright", "credits" or "license()" for more information.
>>> x = 35.666666
>>> print (x)
35.666666
>>> x = int (x)
>>> print (x)
35
>>> print (int(0.123423523))
0
>>> y = 50
>>> print (y)
50
>>> print(float(y))
50.0
>>> print (x)
35
>>> print (y)
50
>>> y = float (y)
>>> print (y)
50.0
>>> print (x * y)
1750.0
>>> print (x * int(y))
1750
>>> complex (848158688812861889186081895717)
(8.48158688812862e+29+0j)
>>>
```

Figure 8.43 Screenshot of the IDLE shell window showing how casting functions are used, as discussed in this section. The lines highlighted in yellow show how to display a complex number using that number's complex notation.

Mathematical Functions

This section provides a glimpse of the mathematical functions that we can use in our Python programs.

Go ahead and run IDLE and open a new file. Save the file using any name, such as, math_functions.py.

On your editor window, you must first import Python's math library by entering the following:

import math

Note that you use the **import** keyword, if you want to use any of Python's built-in function libraries for use in your programs.

Let's start with absolute value. Go ahead and create the following two values:

value1 = 89.6
value2 = 176

Let's subtract value2 from value1 and display the difference:

print (value1-value2)

At this point, let's save, then run our program.

As you can see, our difference for the subtraction operation gives us a negative value.

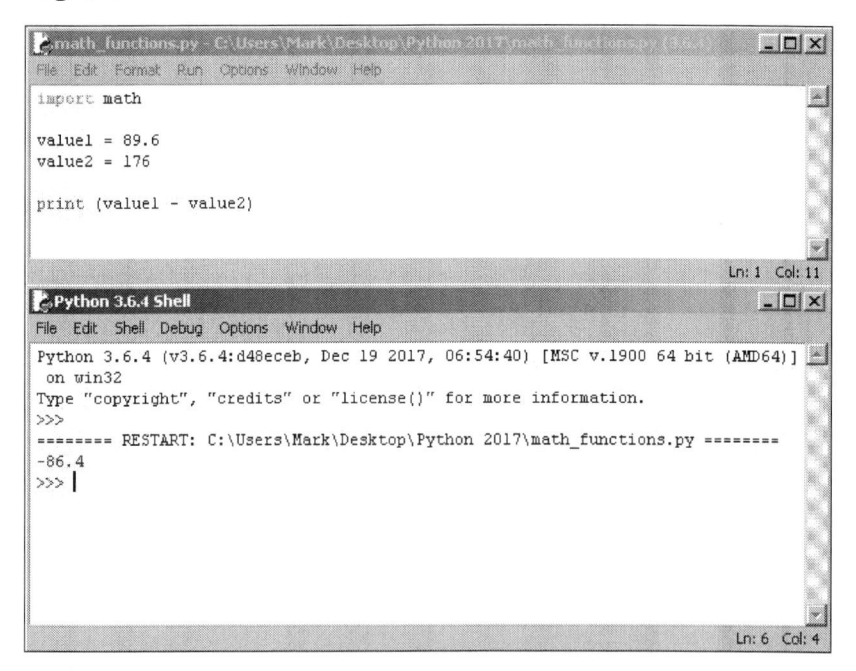

Figure8.44. Initially, the difference in the subtraction operation from our sample program is a negative value.

Let's say we want to display the absolute value instead, when subtracting value2 from value1. To do this, we use the **absolute value** function in our print statement:

print (abs (value1 – value2))

If we save and run the file again, we will see that the program now displays the absolute value of the difference.

```
import math

value1 = 89.6
value2 = 176

print (abs(value1 - value2))
```

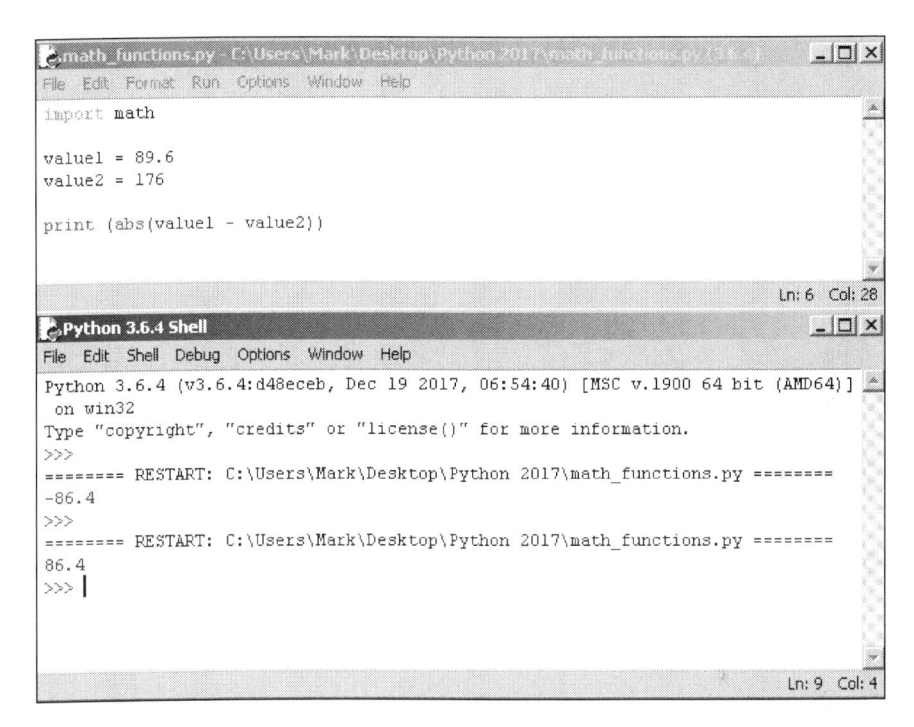

```
Python 3.6.4 (v3.6.4:d48eceb, Dec 19 2017, 06:54:40) [MSC v.1900 64 bit (AMD64)] on win32
Type "copyright", "credits" or "license()" for more information.
>>>
======== RESTART: C:\Users\Mark\Desktop\Python 2017\math_functions.py ========
-86.4
>>>
======== RESTART: C:\Users\Mark\Desktop\Python 2017\math_functions.py ========
86.4
>>>
```

Figure8.45. Using the absolute value function, our sample program now displays the difference as a positive value.

Next, we want to round up, then round down value1. To do this, enter the following lines on the editor window:

print (math.ceil (value1))
print (math.floor(value1))

Saving, then running the program displays the rounded-up and rounded-down values of value1.

To have our program display a number, such as 3, raised to a certain power, such as 4, we can use the following line:

print (pow (3,4))

Page 135

This is the same as the following line:

print (3**4)

Enter both lines in your program, then check if they have the same output.

```
math_functions.py - C:\Users\Mark\Desktop\Python 2017\math_functions.py (3.6.4)
File  Edit  Format  Run  Options  Window  Help
import math

value1 = 89.6
value2 = 176

print (abs(value1 - value2))
print (math.ceil (value1))
print (math.floor (value1))
print (pow (3,4))
print (3**4)
```

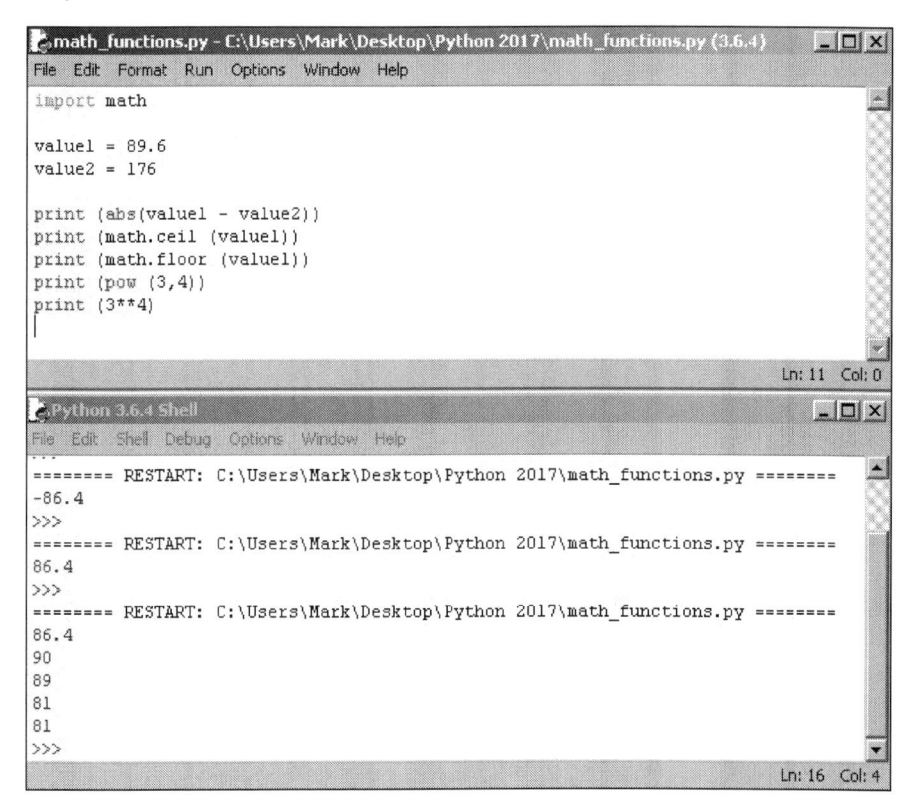

```
Python 3.6.4 Shell
File  Edit  Shell  Debug  Options  Window  Help
======== RESTART: C:\Users\Mark\Desktop\Python 2017\math_functions.py ========
-86.4
>>>
======== RESTART: C:\Users\Mark\Desktop\Python 2017\math_functions.py ========
86.4
>>>
======== RESTART: C:\Users\Mark\Desktop\Python 2017\math_functions.py ========
86.4
90
89
81
81
>>>
```

Figure 8.46. The **math.ceil** and **math.floor** functions round up and round down variables, while **pow (x, y)** raises int **x** by int **y**.

These are samples of the many mathematical operations you can perform in your Python programs. There are many more. Take the time to discover them for yourselves, since, as we've mentioned before, they are a major reason why Python is popular for use in mathematical programs.

That wraps up our short introduction to mathematical functions in Python. You will next learn about randomization functions.

Random Functions

Almost every program that is a game or a simulation has some element of randomness to it. Python has a robust library for introducing randomness into your programs.

Open and run IDLE, open a new file, then save it using any name you prefer, such as random.

The first thing you need to do is import the **random** library.

import random

Now, create a list of names. Use any names that come to mind, such as names of family members, friends, etc..

Then, add the following line of code to your program.

print (random.choice (names))

Save, then run the program several times. What do you see?

As you will note, your program randomly selects and displays a name from your list. You can use this for tuples as well.

```
import random

names = ["Fred", "Mary", "Thomas", "Kevin", "Mike", "June"]

print(random.choice (names))
```

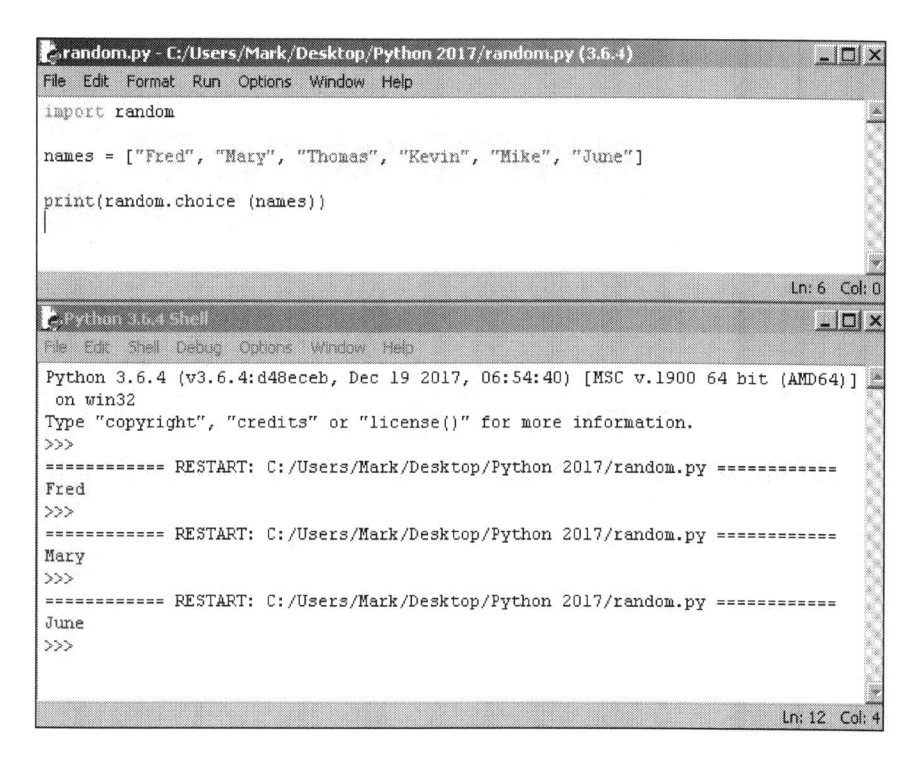

```
Python 3.6.4 (v3.6.4:d48eceb, Dec 19 2017, 06:54:40) [MSC v.1900 64 bit (AMD64)]
 on win32
Type "copyright", "credits" or "license()" for more information.
>>>
============ RESTART: C:/Users/Mark/Desktop/Python 2017/random.py ============
Fred
>>>
============ RESTART: C:/Users/Mark/Desktop/Python 2017/random.py ============
Mary
>>>
============ RESTART: C:/Users/Mark/Desktop/Python 2017/random.py ============
June
>>>
```

Figure 8.47. This screenshot shows our sample program randomly displaying names from our list.

In other programming languages, generating random numbers often means using a combination of a random function and some mathematics. This is not true with Python. For example, let's add the following lines of code to our program.

print (random.randrange (1, 1000))

Save, then run the program again. You can see that a random number in the range 1-1000 is displayed every time you run the program.

Note that the range of numbers is not limited such as starting from 0 and ending in 1,000,000.

If you're coming from another programming language, you will know that this is not as easy as in Python.

The randrange function even allows you to add more randomness to the process through a step parameter. For example, you may edit the previous print statement containing the randrange function using the following example:

print (random.randrange (1, 1000, 10)

This line means that the function will run through the parameters 10 times, before finally displaying a random number.

```
import random

names = ["Fred", "Mary", "Thomas", "Kevin", "Mike", "June"]
print(random.choice (names))

print (random.randrange(1,1000, 10))
```

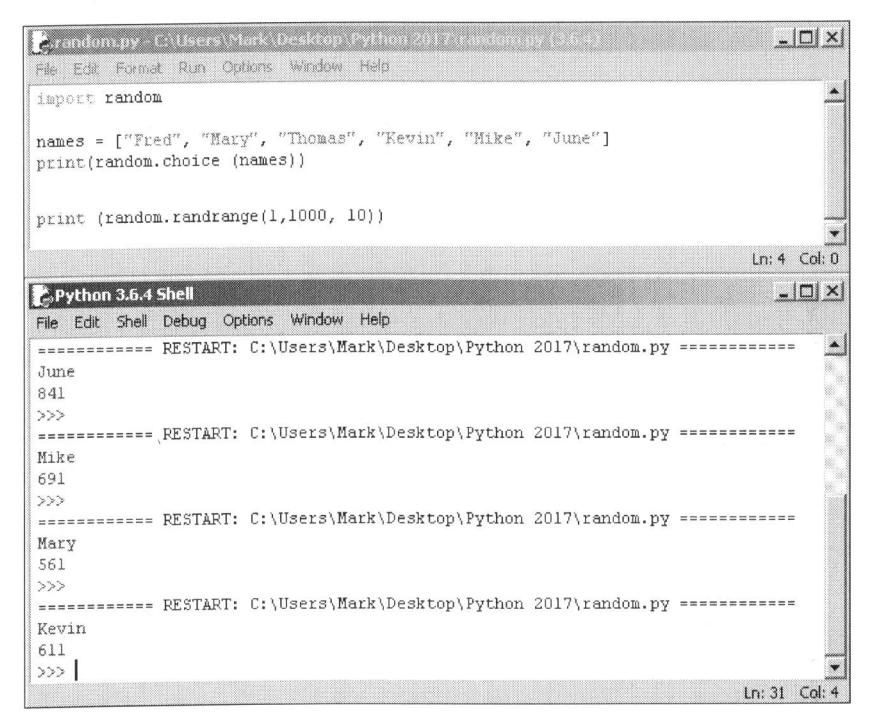

```
============ RESTART: C:\Users\Mark\Desktop\Python 2017\random.py ============
June
841
>>>
============ RESTART: C:\Users\Mark\Desktop\Python 2017\random.py ============
Mike
691
>>>
============ RESTART: C:\Users\Mark\Desktop\Python 2017\random.py ============
Mary
561
>>>
============ RESTART: C:\Users\Mark\Desktop\Python 2017\random.py ============
Kevin
611
>>>
```

Figure 8.48. Our sample program showing random names from our list and random numbers between 1 and 1,000.

We will comment out our randrange function from our sample program and go back to our earlier list of names. Next, add the following lines to the program.

random.shuffle (names)
print (names)

Run the program after saving it first. As you can see, the program now shuffles the names on our list, reassigns the indices, then displays a different-ordered list, each time you run the program.

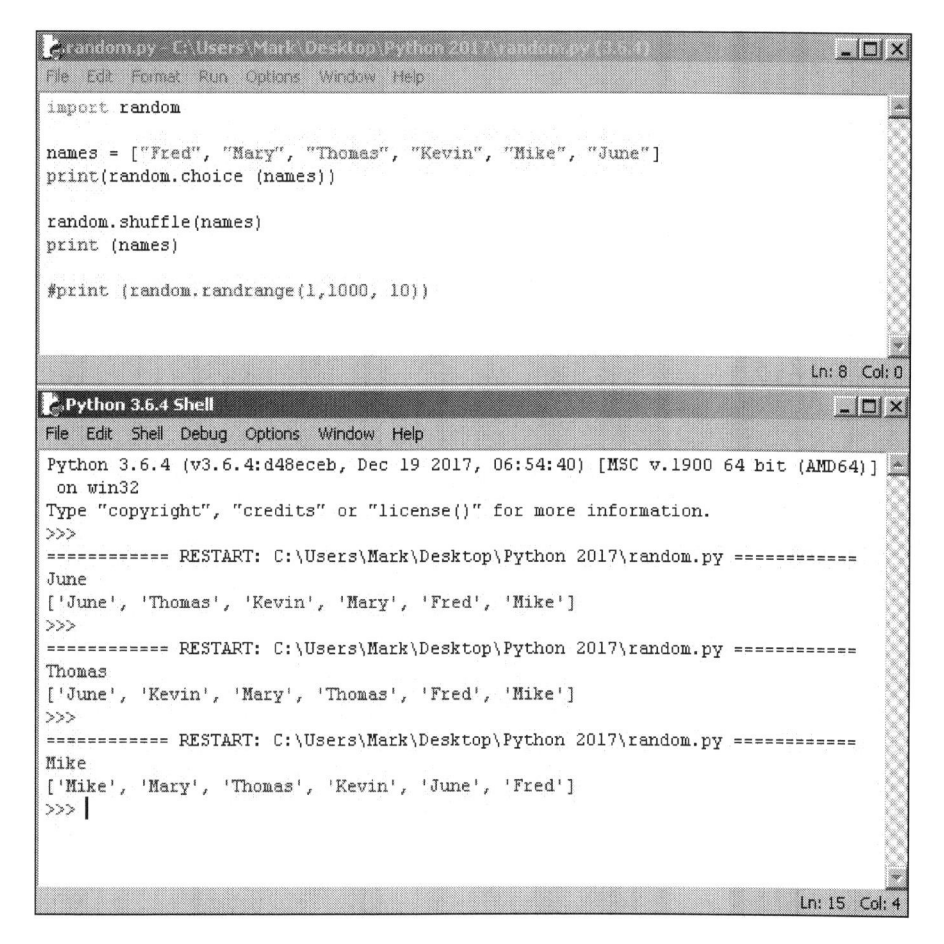

Figure 8.49. The **shuffle** function reorders the names in our list and displays a different-ordered list every time our sample program runs.

That is the end of this section and the chapter on math functions. It's now time for your coding exercise.

Coding Exercise: Math Functions

In this exercise, you'll be working with some of the math functions that are available within Python 3.0. You may use either interactive mode or write and save a code file to complete these exercises.

Step 1: To determine the hypotenuse of a right-angle triangle, the following formula is used:

Square Root((side1*side1) + (side2*side2))

However, Python has a math function that will determine the hypotenuse, given a length of side a and side b of the triangle. Using the list of Python math functions in the online documentation available at https://docs.python.org/3/library/math.html, determine the length of the hypotenuse the triangle shown below:

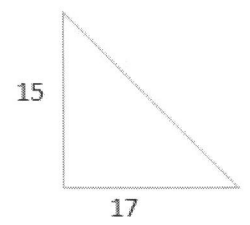

Figure 50.8 Compute for the hypotenuse of the triangle.

Step 2: Using the appropriate Python function, convert the following values from degrees to radians and radians to degrees:
- 180 Degrees
- 2 Radians
- 270 Degrees
- 5 Radians

For this part of the exercise, you'll need to write and save a formal Python script.

Step 3: Click File –> New File on your IDLE editor to create a blank document. Save this document as math_lab.py.

Write a program that uses a while loop to generate 100 random numbers between 1 and 10. Your code should appear like the code below:

```
import random

x = 0
while x < 100:
    number = random.randrange(1,10)
    print(number)
    x = x + 1
```

Figure 8.51. Program using Python's random function

Step 4: After the program prints out all the random number output, the sum of all the random numbers generated and the average of all the random numbers generated. It then outputs the average of all the random numbers generated. Your output in the IDLE window should appear something like this:

```
2
6
8
The sum is: 539
The average is: 5.39
>>>
```

Figure 8.52. Output of summing and averaging generated random numbers

Chapter 9 – String Functions

In this chapter, you will learn about Python's string functions. String processing plays an important role in any programming language.

Given the large number of string functions available to Python programmers, we will only cover some of them in this book. However, we will cover the most important functions. The related functions have been grouped together to make it easier for you to learn them. With these functions, you will appreciate why Python is a favorite among programmers for processing large amounts of data.

It will be your responsibility to learn more about these functions to see what you do with them. Once you become familiar with them, you can experiment with the other string functions on your own. Many programmers will tell you that constant practice is very important to your coding journey.

The first functions you will learn about are the string processing functions, including capitalize(), center(), and count() functions.

The next three functions you will learn about are find(), isalpha(), and isdigit(). These functions will allow you to search for specific characters within a string and identify them as letters or numbers.

Finally, the last three functions that will be discussed are join(), len(), and split(). These three functions will let you join two separate strings as one, identify the length of a string, and split a string into two or more strings.

This chapter ends with a coding exercise that will test your knowledge about string functions in Python.

The capitalize (), center (), and count () functions

In this section, you will learn about the following three (3) essential string processing functions:
1. capitalize()
2. center()
3. count()

The first function, capitalize(), makes the first letter in any given string a capital letter; the second one centers the string within a given number of characters, and count () returns the number of a given letter contained within a string.

Let's start with the first function. Open IDLE, then click **File>New File** or press **Ctrl+N**. Enter the following on the editor:

message = "welcome to Python!" (in this string, the 'w' in welcome is not a capital letter)

print(str.capitalize(message))

Save the file as strings1.py, then run the program. The following message is displayed on the shell window.

Welcome to python!

As you can see, the use of capitalize converted 'w', the first letter in the string *message* to a capital letter. The capital 'p' in Python becomes a small letter.

What will happen if there are two separate strings in a message? Let's look at an example to see how our two strings will behave.

Going back to our existing program, let's add another sentence after the first one in *message*.

message = "welcome to Python! Thanks for taking my class!"

Retain the print method as-is, then run the program again. The following is then displayed on the shell window:

Welcome to python! thanks for taking my class!

Take a closer look at our output. What do you see? Yes, that's right, the first letter in the second sentence becomes a small letter.

To ensure that both first letters in the two sentences end up capitalized and that already capitalized letters are not converted to small letters, you can use the following for strings with two or more sentences.

print(message [:1].upper + message[1:]

In this line of code, the first letter of the first string in *message* is capitalized, all capitalized letters are not converted to small letters, and the second string is treated as-is (without any changes).

Note: To retain the changes, you can also define *message* as:

message = message [:1].upper + message[1:]

Afterwards, you can just print *message*.

Let's now go to the next string function, center().

Add the following line to our strings1.py program file.

print(message.center(80))

Press **F5** to run the program. When prompted, click **Yes** on the confirmation message. The program then runs and outputs the *message* string, after counting 80 empty spaces.

If you want to display the string between * so that the output will be like the following:

*****************Welcome to Python! Thanks for taking my class!*******************

Just modify the code a bit:

print(message.center(80, '*'))

That is all for the center() function. The last function is count, which will count the number of times a specific character appears in a string.

Let's add another line of code to our program, by counting the number of times 's' appears in our *message* string.

print(message.count('s'))

Saving, then running the program displays an integer, or the number of times the character appears in the string:

3

The count() function can take a beginning and ending parameter that will limit the function to the characters between the parameters. For example:

Page 145

print(message.count('s', 5, 15))

This will count the number of times 's' appears between characters 5 and 15 of the string, which is 0, in this case.

```
message = "welcome to Python! Thanks for taking my class!"

print(str.capitalize(message))
print(message[:1].upper() + message[1:])

#To make the changes stick
message = message[:1].upper() + message[1:]
print(message)

print(message.center(80))
print(message.center(80, '*'))

print(message.count('s'))
print(message.count('s', 5, 15))
```

```
============ RESTART: C:\Users\Mark\Desktop\Python 2017\strings1.py ============
Welcome to python! thanks for taking my class!
Welcome to Python! Thanks for taking my class!
Welcome to Python! Thanks for taking my class!
               Welcome to Python! Thanks for taking my class!
*****************Welcome to Python! Thanks for taking my class!*****************
3
0
>>>
```

Figure 9.53. The code and output for the first three string functions discussed in this section.

That is all for our first three string functions. In the next section, we will discuss another three string functions related to finding a specific character and determining the type of character found within the string, i.e. is it a letter or a number?

The find (), isalpha (), and isdigit () functions

The next three functions you will learn about are:
1. find()
2. isalpha()

Page 146

3. isdigit()

The find() function, as its name suggests, finds a substring within a string. Let's open IDLE again, and click **File>New File**, or press **Ctrl+N**.

Enter the following on the editor window:

message = "Welcome to Python! Thanks for taking my class!"
print(message.find('for'))

In line 2, we use *find ()* to look for the occurrence of 'for' in the *message* string.

Save the file, then run it. The output will be 26, which refers to the location of 'for' in the string, or its index.

Next, let's try to find a phrase that is not in the string. Let's add the following line to our program.

print(message.find('xx'))

If you run and save the program again, you will see that it will return a -1 value, meaning that it cannot find the substring within the string.

From this example, we know that we can use find() to test for the presence of a substring within a string.

We will add an if-else statement to our program:

if message.find('xx') == -1:
   print("Not found in message")

Saving and running the program, then displays the following on your screen:

Not found in message

Now go to the isalpha() function, which is used to determine if a specific string is alphabetic or not. If yes, the function will return true, otherwise it will return false.

Let's try an example by adding another print method to our program.

print(message.isalpha())

If we save, then run the program, you will see that the output will be false. Why? Because *message* is not entirely alphabetic – there are a couple of exclamation marks within that string.

Let's add another string to our program, this time comprised entirely of letters.

message2="mark"

This time, if we print message2 using the following line of code:

print(message2.isalpha())

The program will return true.

The above principle applies to the isdigit() function as well – if the string is composed of digits only, the function will return true; if not, the function will return false.

We will try this out by adding another string to our program before saving it again.

message3= "768345345"

This time, since message3 is composed entirely of digits, then you'll get a True when you run the program.

```
message = "Welcome to Python! Thanks for taking my class!"
message2 = "mark"
message3 = "768345345"

print(message.find('for'))
print(message.find('xx'))
if message.find('xx') == -1:
    print("Not found in message")

print(message.isalpha())
print(message2.isalpha())
print(message3.isdigit())
```

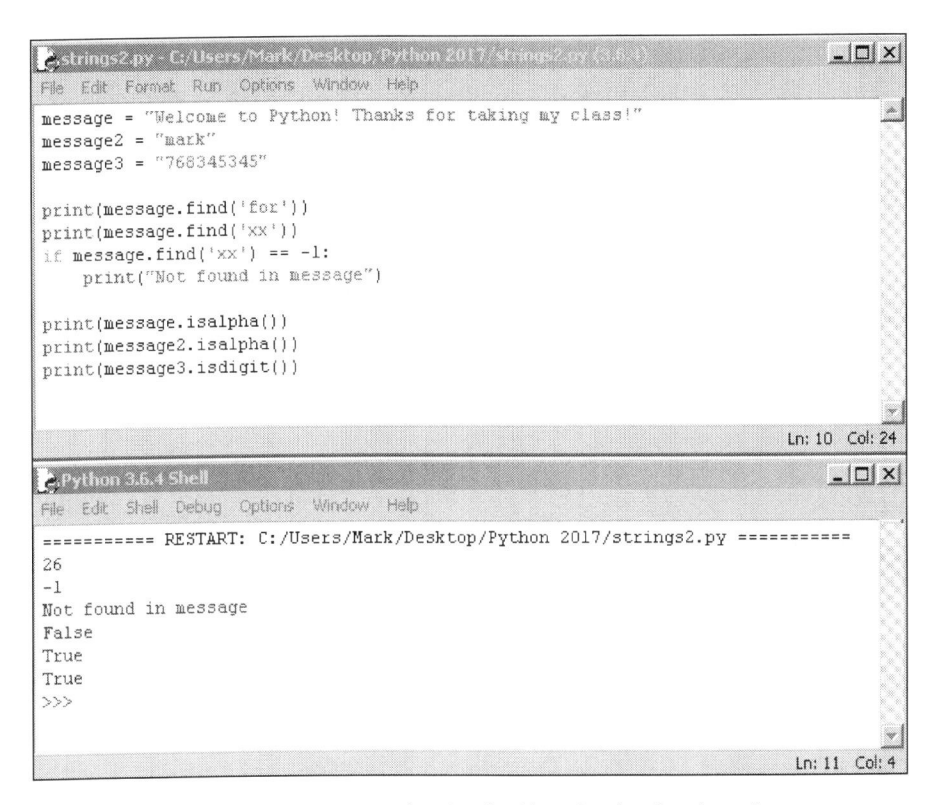

```
=========== RESTART: C:/Users/Mark/Desktop/Python 2017/strings2.py ===========
26
-1
Not found in message
False
True
True
>>>
```

Figure 9.54. The code and output for the 2nd batch of string functions discussed in this section.

That concludes our discussion on this batch of string functions. Let's go on to our next batch of functions.

The join (), len (), and split () functions

The last three of the string functions you will learn in this chapter are:
1. join()
2. len()
3. split()

These three are powerful and useful functions to know at this stage of your training in becoming a Python programmer.

Open IDLE, then click **File>New File**, or press **CTRL+N** on your keyboard.

On the editor window, enter the following:

```
name = ["Mark", "Adam", "Fred", "Wendy", "Peter", "Marsha"]
j = "|"
print(j.join(name))
```

Save, then run the program. The output will be as follows:

Mark|Adam|Fred|Wendy|Peter|Marsha

As you can see, the join() function in our program generated a string joining the names in our list, with each name separated by the pipe delimiter we defined in j. The delimiter can be anything – you may replace the | with a comma, semi-colon, or any other punctuation mark.

Now, let's go to the len() function. On your editor window, enter the following:

```
message = "Join me for the party tonight"
print(len(message))
```

Saving and running the program, will display the following number on the shell window:

29

In this case, the output is the number of characters in the *message* string. What the len() function does, is to count the number of characters in the string, or to determine its length.

Let's edit our program one last time. On the editor window, enter the following:

```
teams = "Yankees, Mets, Jets, Giants, Knicks, Nets"
print(teams.split(","))
```

After saving, then running the program, the output will be as follows:

['Yankees, 'Mets', 'Jets', 'Giants', 'Knicks', 'Nets']

In this case, the split() function generates a list names, with each name enclosed in single quotation marks and separated by a comma.

```
name = ["Mark", "Adam", "Fred", "Wendy", "Peter", "Marsha"]
j = "|"
message = "Join me for the party tonight"
teams = "Yankees, Mets, Jets, Giants, Knicks, Nets"

print (j.join(name))
print (len(message))
print (teams.split(","))
```

```
=========== RESTART: C:/Users/Mark/Desktop/Python 2017/strings3.py ===========
Mark|Adam|Fred|Wendy|Peter|Marsha
29
['Yankees', ' Mets', ' Jets', ' Giants', ' Knicks', ' Nets']
>>>
```

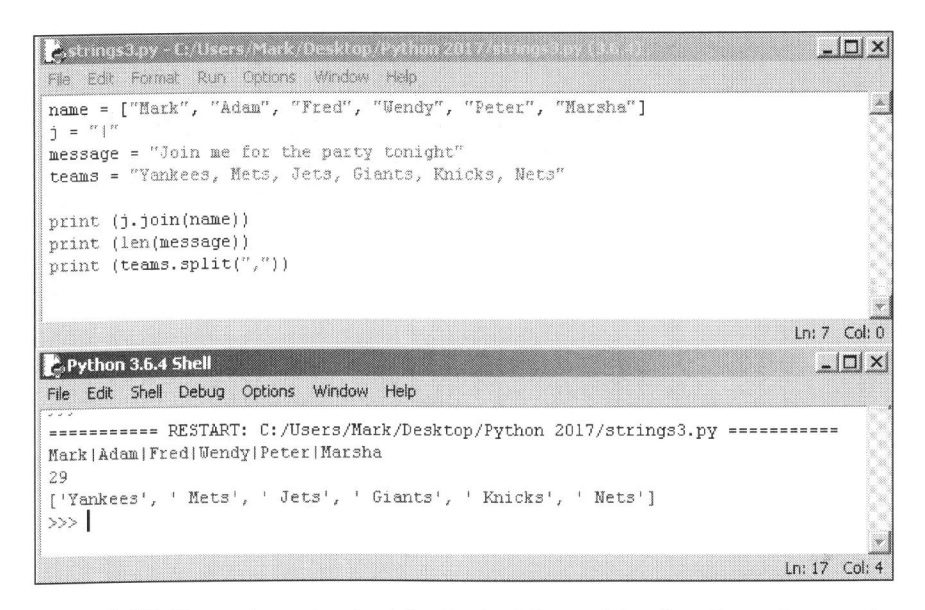

Figure 9.55. The code and output for the last three string functions discussed in this section.

That is the end of our discussion on string functions. We recommend learning more about string processing functions on your own. We will now proceed to the coding exercise for this chapter.

Coding Exercise: String Functions

This exercise will allow you to apply what you have learned about string functions in this chapter.
1. Create a new script in your Python editor and save it as strings_lab.py.
2. Enter the lines of code shown in Fig. xx in your program file. Save, then run the program.

```
poem = "With rue my heart is laden\n"
poem += "For golden friends I had\n"
poem += "For many a rose-lipped maiden\n"
poem += "And many a light foot lad\n"
poem += "By brooks too broad for leaping\n"
poem += "The light oot boys are laid\n"
poem += "The rose lipped girls are sleeping\n"
poem += "In fields where roses fade\n"
print(poem)
```

Figure 9.56. This will be your main program input for the coding exercise.

3. Using a loop, output each line and character number of the string. For example, line 2, character 2 is a 'o'. The initial part of your output should look something like Fig. xx.

```
Python 3.6.4 Shell
File Edit Shell Debug Options Window Help

With rue my heart is laden
For golden friends I had
For many a rose-lipped maiden
And many a light foot lad
By brooks too broad for leaping
The light oot boys are laid
The rose lipped girls are sleeping
In fields where roses fade

Line: 1 Char: 0 W
Line: 1 Char: 1 i
Line: 1 Char: 2 t
Line: 1 Char: 3 h
Line: 1 Char: 4
Line: 1 Char: 5 r
Line: 1 Char: 6 u
Line: 1 Char: 7 e
Line: 1 Char: 8
Line: 1 Char: 9 m
Line: 1 Char: 10 y
Line: 1 Char: 11
Line: 1 Char: 12 h
Line: 1 Char: 13 e
Line: 1 Char: 14 a
Line: 1 Char: 15 r
Line: 1 Char: 16 t
Line: 1 Char: 17
Line: 1 Char: 18 i
Line: 1 Char: 19 s
Line: 1 Char: 20
Line: 1 Char: 21 l
Line: 1 Char: 22 a
Line: 1 Char: 23 d
Line: 1 Char: 24 e
Line: 1 Char: 25 n
Line: 2 Char: 27 F
Line: 2 Char: 28 o
Line: 2 Char: 29 r
Line: 2 Char: 30
Line: 2 Char: 31 g

Ln: 301  Col: 0
```

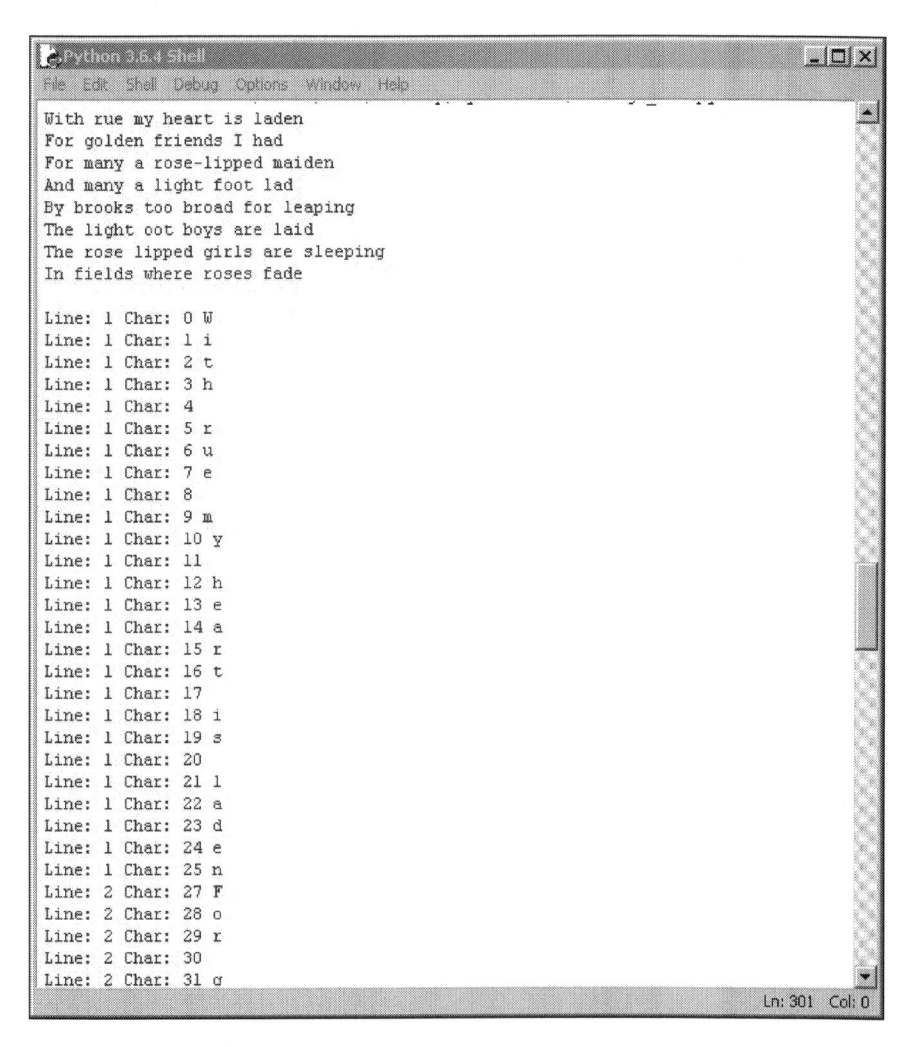

Figure 9.57. Initial program output showing the numbers per line and character in the poem.

4. Modify your code, so that the word "Capital" is printed to the right of each capital letter in your output. Your output should look something like the one in Fig. xx.

```
Line: 1 Char: 0 W Capital
Line: 1 Char: 1 i
Line: 1 Char: 2 t
Line: 1 Char: 3 h
Line: 1 Char: 4
Line: 1 Char: 5 r
Line: 1 Char: 6 u
Line: 1 Char: 7 e
Line: 1 Char: 8
Line: 1 Char: 9 m
Line: 1 Char: 10 y
Line: 1 Char: 11
Line: 1 Char: 12 h
```

Figure 9.58. The modified program output that identifies the capitalized letters in the poem.

The code used to create the expected result for this exercise is shown in Fig. xx. Your code may vary.

```
poem = "With rue my heart is laden\n"
poem += "For golden friends I had\n"
poem += "For many a rose-lipped maiden\n"
poem += "And many a light foot lad\n"
poem += "By brooks too broad for leaping\n"
poem += "The light oot boys are laid\n"
poem += "The rose lipped girls are sleeping\n"
poem += "In fields where roses fade\n"
print(poem)
char = 0
line = 1
while char < len(poem):
    if (poem[char] != "\n"):
        currentChar = poem[char]
        if (currentChar.isupper() == True):
            print("Line:", line, "Char:", char, currentChar, "Capital")
        else:
            print("Line:", line, "Char:", char, currentChar)
        char = char+1
    else:
        line = line+1
        char = char+1
```

Figure 9.59. Sample code for our program. Your program may vary from this one.

Chapter 10 – Tuples and Dictionaries

In this chapter, you will learn about data structures and specifically tuples and dictionaries in Python.

You will learn how to create tuples and access the values included in them. This chapter will also include information about functions that are available in tuples.

It will also discuss dictionaries – declaring a dictionary, accessing and editing values found in dictionaries and then sampling the various functions available in dictionaries.

At the end of the chapter, you will have your now-familiar coding exercise that will allow you to put into practice what you have learned about tuples and dictionaries.

Creating Tuples

In this section, you will learn about creating tuples. They are a familiar data structure in Python. Data structures allow you to hold data. Data in tuples can be strings, floating-point numbers, and integers, among other types. Tuples are lists of immutable, or unchangeable values. Data in tuples are immutable – they cannot be changed in any way.

Let's start by creating our first tuple. Open IDLE, then click **File>New File** or press **Ctrl+N**. Enter the following on the editor:

subjects = ("English", "Algebra", "Biology", "Physics", "Computer Science", "Physical Education")
gpas = (3.12, 2.34, 4.0, 3.11, 3.9, 4.55)
addresses = ("123 Main Street" ,)

These lines show that the data in the *subjects* tuple are composed entirely of strings, while those in the gpas tuple are composed entirely of floating-point numbers.

The addresses tuple is a mixture of strings and integers. It contains only a single value, with a comma after that value. You will learn more about why we defined the addresses tuple this way, in the next section under this chapter.

Note that string data in tuples are enclosed in quotation marks. In contrast, the floating-point numbers in our gpas tuple do not have these marks. The latter will also be true, if you use integers in your tuple.

Let's finalize our program by adding a couple of print statements:

print(subjects)
print(gpas)

As you can see from Fig. 10.1, the program outputs the data in the same sequence that they are found in the tuples (this accounts for why tuples are also sequences). As mentioned before, tuples are immutable – they cannot be changed.

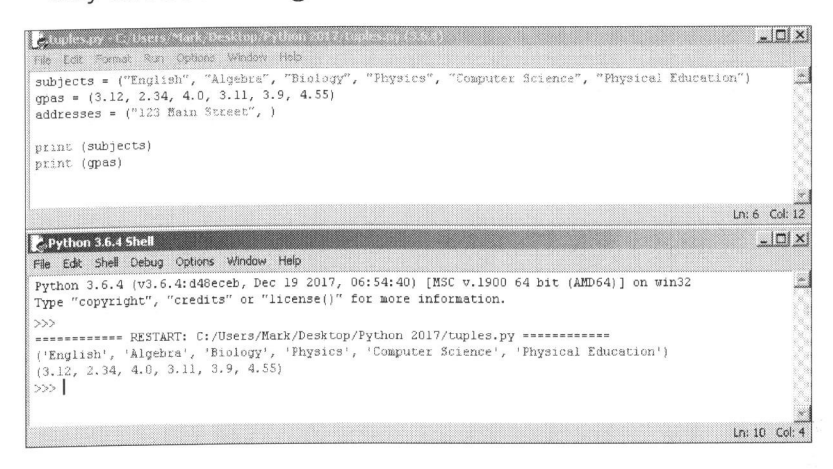

Figure 10.60. Code and output for the sample program in this section.

Now that you have learned about creating tuples, it is time to learn how to access the data found in your tuples.

Accessing Values in Tuples

As mentioned in the previous section, tuples are simply lists of immutable data. Tuples are excellent for storing data that do not change, e.g. in a game, the size of a game board can be stored in a tuple.

We will now learn about accessing the individual values in a tuple. Open IDLE, then click **File>New File** or press **Ctrl+N**, then enter the following on the editor:

```
family = ("Joan", "Rick", "Brett", "Kerri", "Rose", "Stacy")
print(family)
print(family[0])
print(family[5])
```

In line 1, we have a tuple of family members, which we then print in line 2.

Printing specific values from a tuple

In lines 3 and 4, we access the family member using the index number from the tuple, or the order in which the family member's name is found in the tuple. That means that, for the print statement in line 3, that family member is Joan; for the print statement in line 4, Stacy is the family member in the 5th index.

Saving and running the program generates the output that is shown in Fig. 10.2.

Looping through a Tuple

Let's loop through the tuple by adding code that will output the names of the family members in our tuple.

```
x = 0
while x < 6:
    print(family[x])
    x = x + 1
```

Save, then run the program again, and you will see that each name in the *family* tuple is printed on separate lines by the program.

```
family.py - C:/Users/Mark/Desktop/Python 2017/family.py (3.6.4)
File Edit Format Run Options Window Help
family = ("Joan", "Rick", "Brett", "Kerri", "Rose", "Stacy")
print(family)
print(family[0])
print(family[5])

#Looping through the Tuple
x = 0
while x < 6:
    print(family[x])
    x=x+1
```

```
Python 3.6.4 Shell
File Edit Shell Debug Options Window Help
============ RESTART: C:/Users/Mark/Desktop/Python 2017/family.py ============
('Joan', 'Rick', 'Brett', 'Kerri', 'Rose', 'Stacy')
Joan
Stacy
Joan
Rick
Brett
Kerri
Rose
Stacy
>>>
```

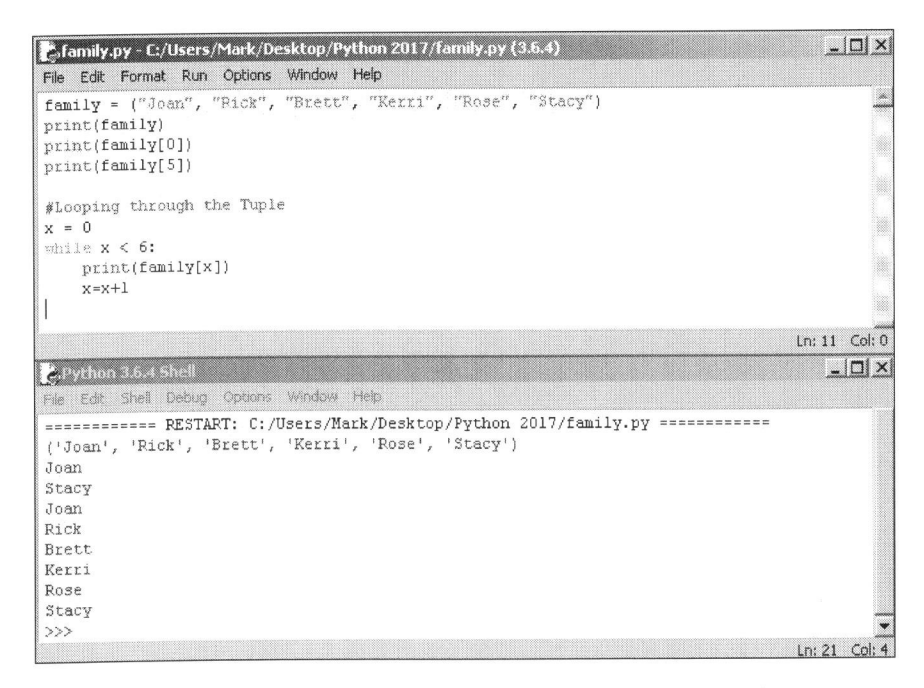

Figure 10.61. Code and output for the sample program in this section.

Note that, in the line *while x < 6*, changing the number to one that is greater than the total number of records in the tuple will result in a program error.

In addition, as mentioned previously, any change to the tuple will also result in an error. For example, if you add the following line to the program:

family[1] = "Ricky"

an error will also be displayed when you save, then run the program, since this line attempts to change the value of one of the values found in the tuple.

You have now learned how to access the individual values in a tuple. It is now time to learn about various tuple functions you can use in your Python programs.

Tuple Functions

In this section, you will learn about lists, which are different from tuples. This is because they contain data that can be changed. In short, lists are mutable, or changeable.

After a quick discussion on lists, you will learn about the various functions you can use on tuples.

What are lists?

Lists will b e discussed first. Open IDLE, then click **File>New File**, or press **Ctrl+N** on your keyboard. On the editor window, enter the following:

bands = ["Journey", "REO Speedwagon", "Kansas", "Heart", "Scandal", "Pink Floyd"]
print(bands)

Unlike tuples, data in a list are enclosed in brackets. In the case of tuples, data are enclosed in a parenthesis.

Just like in the tuple, after saving and running the program, you will see that our code displays the members of the *bands* list.

```
bands = ["Journey", "REO Speedwagon", "Kansas", "Heart", "Scandal", "Pink Floyd"]
print(bands)

print(bands[0])
print(bands[1:3])
bands[1]="Foreigner"
print(bands)
```

```
============ RESTART: C:/Users/Mark/Desktop/Python 2017/bands.py ============
['Journey', 'REO Speedwagon', 'Kansas', 'Heart', 'Scandal', 'Pink Floyd']
Journey
['REO Speedwagon', 'Kansas']
['Journey', 'Foreigner', 'Kansas', 'Heart', 'Scandal', 'Pink Floyd']
>>>
```

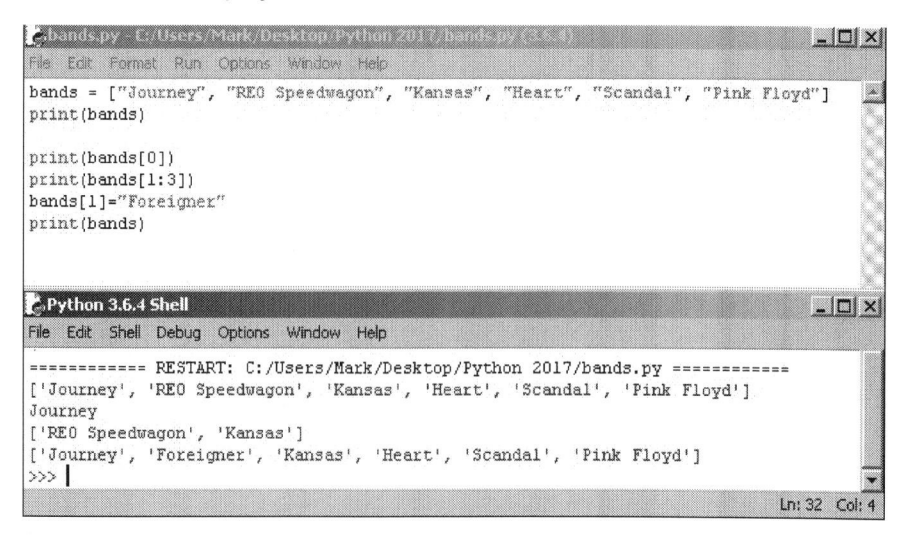

Figure 10.62. Code and output for the sample list program in this section.

To see how the modifications to the program code below work, refer to Fig. 10.3 above.

To print an individual band in the list, enclose the index number of the band in brackets in a print statement.

print(bands[0])

To print a range of names in the list, enclose the index number of the first value to be printed, add a colon and then the other index number. This is the index number for the value after the actual one you want printed. For example, if you want to print the values in indices 1 and 2, your print statement would be as follows:

print(bands[1:3])

To change the value of a name in the list, enclosed the index of the value to be changed in brackets, then the name of the name to be inserted in place of the original value. Thus:

bands[1] ="Foreigner"
print(bands)

Now that you know what lists are, let's look at some of the functions that we can use with tuples.

The len() Function

Open a new file on IDLE, then enter the following on the editor window:

computers =("IBM PC", "Apple Mac", "Compaq", "Gateway", "HP", "Toshiba")
print(len(computers))

If you save, then run the program, the answer, 6, will be displayed on the shell window. If you had been reading this book chapter-by-chapter, you will remember that len() was discussed in our chapter on string functions (see Chapter 9).

Using the len() Function to Loop through a Tuple

As shown above, the len() function can be used to determine the length, or the number of members, of our *computers* tuple. You can use the returned length to loop through the members of the tuple.

Enter the following loop that will return the members of the tuple:

```
X=0
while x < len(computers):
    print(computers[x])
    x=x+1
```

Running the program again after saving, iterates through the members of the tuple.

The min() and max() Functions

You can use the min() and max() functions to return the minimum and maximum values in a tuple. Let's try to show this using an example.

Add the following lines to your code:

```
scores = (10500, 11000, 12000, 15000, 9000, 950)
print ("Min:" min(scores))
print ("Max:" max(scores))
```

This will then return the values of the min and max values, or 950 and 15000, respectively, in our scores tuple.

Converting a List to a Tuple

Lastly, you can convert a list to a tuple.

To demonstrate, let's define a *websites* list with our program.

websites = ["Yahoo", "Google", "Alta Vista", "Dog Pile", "Cnn"]

To change this to a tuple, add the following line to your code:

websites = tuple(websites)

Note that the program will proceed as-is, with the conversion after saving and running it again.

To check if the list was really converted to a tuple, try to change the value of a member of the tuple. For example, enter the following:

websites[0] = "Bing"

In this case, saving, then running the program would result in an error, since data in a tuple cannot be changed.

```
computers=("IBM PC", "Apple Mac", "Compaq", "Gateway", "HP", "Toshiba")
websites=["Yahoo!", "Google", "Alta Vista", "Dog Pile", "Cnn"]

print(len(computers))        #The len() function

x=0
while x<len(computers):      #Looping through a tuple
    print(computers[x])
    x=x+1

scores = (10500, 11000, 12000, 15000, 9000, 950)
print("Min:", min(scores))   #The min() function
print("Max:", max(scores))   #The max() function

websites[0]="Bing"           #Replacing a list element with another value
print(websites)

websites=tuple(websites)     #Converting a list to a tuple
websites[0]="Bing"           #Replacing a tuple element results in an error
```

```
HP
Toshiba
Min: 950
Max: 15000
['Bing', 'Google', 'Alta Vista', 'Dog Pile', 'Cnn']
Traceback (most recent call last):
  File "C:\Users\Mark\Desktop\Python 2017\computers.py", line 19, in <module>
    websites[0]="Bing"
TypeError: 'tuple' object does not support item assignment
>>>
```

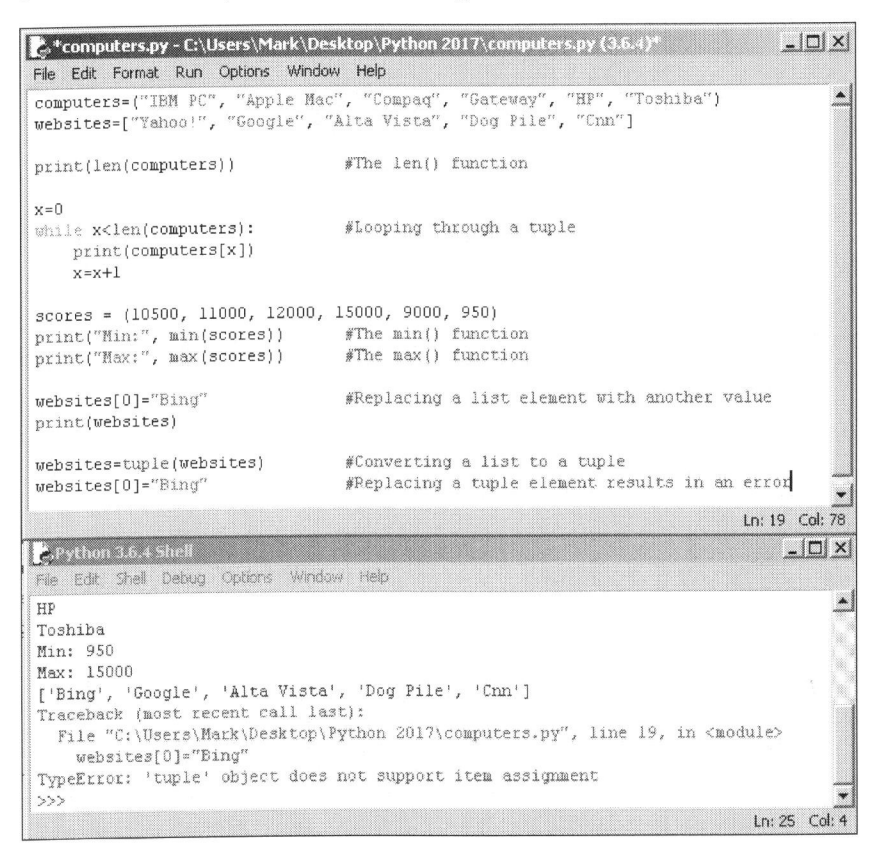

Figure 10.63. Code and output for the sample program in this section.

That wraps up our discussion on functions we can use on our tuples. Let's discuss dictionaries next.

Declaring a Dictionary

Dictionaries comprise elements related to each other. Each element has a key and associated value, with a colon between the key and its value. The elements are separated by commas.

Page 161

For example, we may have an *employee* dictionary with a couple of keys, one named *name*, with a corresponding value of *Mark Lassoff*, and the other SSN, with the employee's social security number as the corresponding value.

For examples of dictionaries and how they are outputted, check out Fig.10.4 below. Go ahead and write the program on IDLE, as you will use this in the next two sections of this chapter, where you will learn about accessing values in and using functions with dictionaries.

```
employee = {"Name":"Mark Lassoff",
            "SSN":"000-00-0000",
            "Position":"Founder",
            "Salary":"$10",
            "Department":"Instruction"}
player = {"Name": "Bill Smith","Team":"Yankees","Position":"Pitcher"}

print(employee)
print(player)
```

```
========== RESTART: C:/Users/Mark/Desktop/Python 2017/dictionary.py ==========
{'Name': 'Mark Lassoff', 'SSN': '000-00-0000', 'Position': 'Founder', 'Salary': '$10', 'Department': 'Instruction'}
{'Name': 'Bill Smith', 'Team': 'Yankees', 'Position': 'Pitcher'}
>>>
```

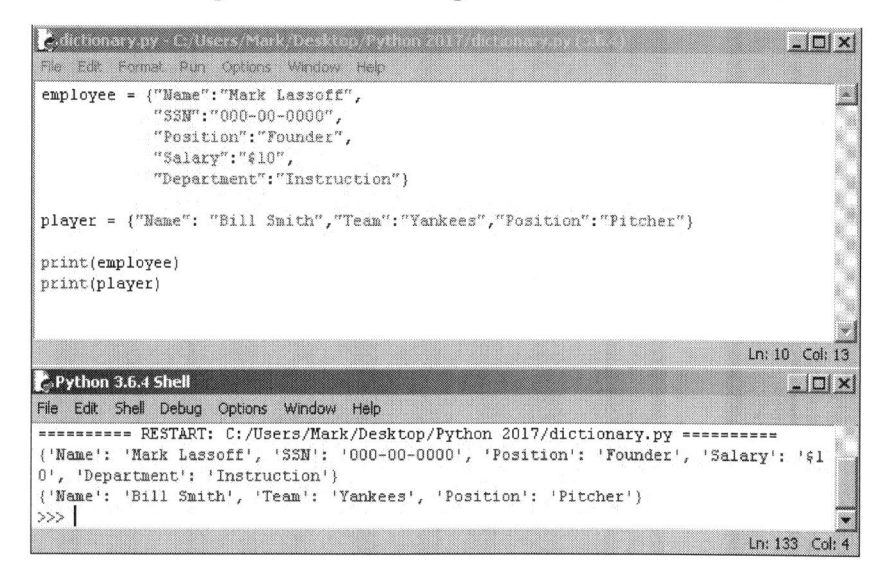

Figure10.64. Sample dictionaries and their output when printed. Note the keys and their values in each of the dictionaries. Dictionaries are printed the same way as any data structure in Python.

Accessing and Editing Values in Dictionaries

Now that you are more familiar with dictionaries, it is time to learn how to access and edit values of data in dictionaries.

Let's go back to the sample program in the previous section. Before proceeding, save the program using a different file name. This is because you will also be using the same program when you start learning about using functions with dictionaries in the next section.

Printing specific values from a dictionary

You would print a dictionary the same way as any Python data structure.

To print a specific value in a dictionary, refer to the key name. For example:

print(employee["Name"])
print(player["Position"])

Note that the key names should always be the same exact value as that in the dictionary. Otherwise, you will get an error. For example, if the key name is capitalized, then it should also be capitalized here.

Changing the elements in a dictionary

You may also change the elements in a dictionary. For example:

player["Position"] = "Catcher"

This replaces the current *Pitcher* value of the *Position* key in the dictionary with *Catcher*. To test this, we can print the value again, highlighting the change in the process.

print("Change:", player["Position"])

Note that the value for the *position* key has now been changed from *Pitcher* to *Catcher*.

You may also print the *player* dictionary again to verify.

Deleting an element in a dictionary

You may also delete an element from a dictionary. For example:

del employee["Salary"]

If you print the *employee* dictionary again, you will see this time that the *Salary* key and its corresponding value is no longer a part of the output.

```
employee = {"Name":"Mark Lassoff",
            "SSN":"000-00-0000",
            "Position":"Founder",
            "Salary":"$10",
            "Department":"Instruction"}

player = {"Name": "Bill Smith","Team":"Yankees","Position":"Pitcher"}

print(employee)
print(player)

print(employee["Name"])
print(player["Position"])

player["Position"]="Catcher"
print("Change:", player["Position"])
print(player)

del employee["Salary"]
print(employee)
```

```
========== RESTART: C:/Users/Mark/Desktop/Python 2017/dictionary2.py ==========
{'Name': 'Mark Lassoff', 'SSN': '000-00-0000', 'Position': 'Founder', 'Salary': '$10', 'Department': 'Instruction'}
{'Name': 'Bill Smith', 'Team': 'Yankees', 'Position': 'Pitcher'}
Mark Lassoff
Pitcher
Change: Catcher
{'Name': 'Bill Smith', 'Team': 'Yankees', 'Position': 'Catcher'}
{'Name': 'Mark Lassoff', 'SSN': '000-00-0000', 'Position': 'Founder', 'Department': 'Instruction'}
>>>
```

Figure 10.65. Code and output for the examples on accessing and editing values in a dictionary. Note that elements that were changed or deleted in the examples are highlighted.

This concludes our discussion on accessing and editing values in a dictionary. In the next section, where you will learn about functions that can be used in dictionaries.

Dictionary Functions

In this section, you will learn about the use of certain functions in dictionaries.

We will return to the sample program in the Declaring a Dictionary section of this chapter. Follow along with the examples below, to learn more about using functions with dictionaries.

The len() Function

Just like with tuples, you can use the len() function to get the number of elements in a dictionary.

print (len(employees))

prints the number of elements. Note that the elements refer to the key-value pairs. In the case of our sample program, the number returned would be 5.

The str() Function

You can also convert a dictionary to a string. For example:

print(str(employee)) converts the dictionary to a string, enclosed in curly brackets.

The clear() Function

This function clears the dictionary of its elements. Thus:

player.clear()
print(player)

displays an empty dictionary, enclosed in curly brackets.

The get function

You can also retrieve specific values from a dictionary using this function. For example:

print(employee.get("SSN"))

returns the employee's social security number.

The items function

Using this function, you can list the individual items in the dictionary in separate sets.

print(employee.items())

The values function

This returns the values of each key in the dictionary.

print(employee.values())

The keys function

This returns the individual keys in the dictionary.

print(employee.keys())

Getting the Elements and Key-Value Pairs in a Dictionary

You can also loop through the keys in a dictionary using the following function:

for c in employee:
    print(c)

This will return each key in the dictionary on separate lines.

To loop through the key-value pairs in a dictionary, use the following function:

for k,v in employee.items:
    print(k,v)

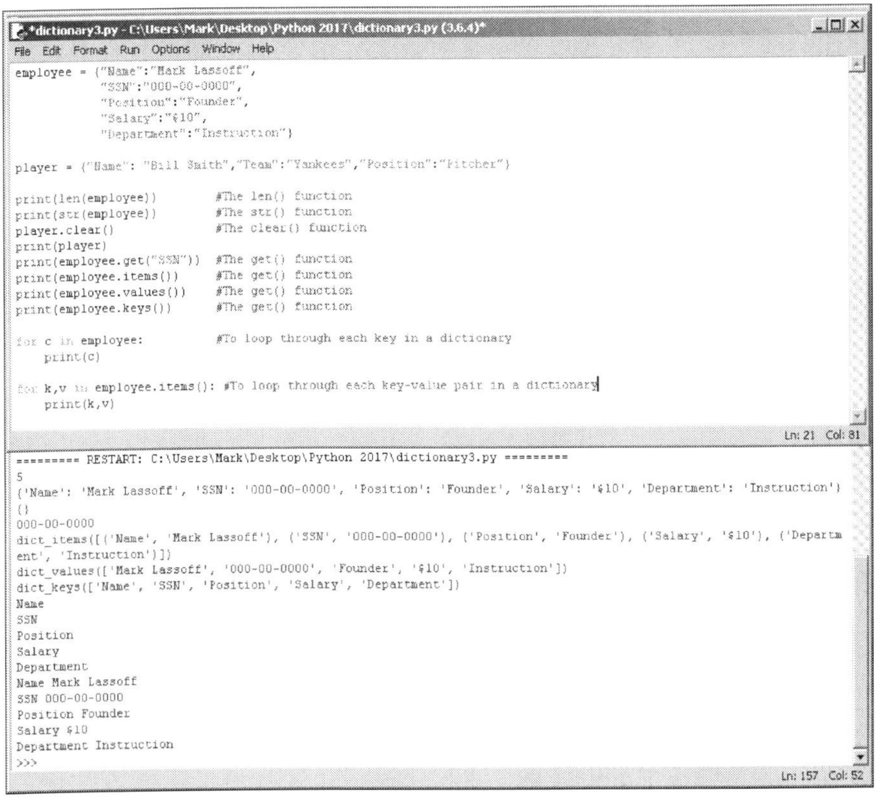

Figure 10.66. Code and output for the examples in this section.

That wraps up our discussion on using certain functions on dictionaries.

In this chapter, you have learned about creating tuples and dictionaries, accessing the values in these data structures, then working with them using various functions. You have also learned about creating and accessing values in lists. It's now time for your coding exercise.

Coding Exercise: String Functions

This lab exercise will allow you to work with tuples, lists, and dictionaries.

1. Create a new script in your Python editor, Save it using any name you want. Enter the following initial code into the script and test.

```
gpas = (3.14, 3.45, 3.98, 2.55, 3.24, 2.27)
gpas[1] = 2.25
```

Figure 10.67. The initial program input.

2. Execute the code and note the error that appears in the Python shell window. Did you expect this error?

```
Python 3.6.4 Shell                                                    _ □ ×
File Edit Shell Debug Options Window Help
Python 3.6.4 (v3.6.4:d48eceb, Dec 19 2017, 06:54:40) [MSC v.1900 64 bit (AMD64)]
on win32
Type "copyright", "credits" or "license()" for more information.
>>>
========== RESTART: C:/Users/Mark/Desktop/Python 2017/tuples_lab.py ==========
Traceback (most recent call last):
  File "C:/Users/Mark/Desktop/Python 2017/tuples_lab.py", line 2, in <module>
    gpas[1] = 2.25
TypeError: 'tuple' object does not support item assignment
>>>
                                                              Ln: 9  Col: 4
```

Figure 10.68. The error raised when running the program using the initial input in Step 1.

3. Use a for loop to loop through each element in the gpas tuple and output the average gpa stored in the tuple. Comment out or delete the line of code that is causing the TypeError output in Step 2.

Try to complete this on your own, before examining the code below.

```
gpas = (3.14, 3.45, 3.98, 2.55, 3.24, 2.27)
#gpas[1] = 2.25

x=0
total=0
while x < len(gpas):
    total = total + gpas[x]
    x = x + 1

average = total / len(gpas)

print("The average GPA is: ", average)
```

Figure 69.10. Try to create your own program given the requirements outlined in Steps 1-3, before looking at the program code we created for the exercise. Your program may vary.

4. Instead of a tuple, store the same data in a dictionary, so that each GPA value is identified by a string key containing the name of the person who achieved the GPA.

Bob:	3.14
Mark:	3.45
Melissa:	3.98
Travis:	2.55
DeeDee:	3.24
Ian:	2.27

5. Using the dictionary that you just created, calculate, and then output the average, as well as the names of the persons who achieved the highest and lowest GPA.

Chapter 11 – Time and Date

In this chapter, you will learn about the use of times and dates in Python programming.

We will first discuss how Python handles time in a time tuple. You will then look at Python's Calendar object, before finally talking about the use of the Time and Calendar functions in Python.

The last part of this chapter includes another coding exercise to apply the concepts that you have learned in the chapter.

The Time Tuple

In the previous chapter, we discussed tuples. In this section, you will learn about the Time tuple, which we will use later in the chapter. We will output the time tuple, so that you will know what it looks like.

Let's start by running IDLE, then opening the editor window by either clicking **File>New File** on the IDLE menu or pressing **Ctrl+N** on your keyboard.

On the editor window, the first step is to import the Time function.

import time

localtime=time.localtime(time.time())
print(localtime)

Save, then run the program. The time tuple will be the output of this program (see Fig. 11.1).

```
import time

localtime=time.localtime(time.time())
print(localtime)
```

```
Python 3.6.4 (v3.6.4:d48eceb, Dec 19 2017, 06:54:40) [MSC v.1900 64 bit (AMD64)]
on win32
Type "copyright", "credits" or "license()" for more information.
>>>
========== RESTART: C:/Users/Mark/Desktop/Python 2017/time_tuple.py ==========
time.struct_time(tm_year=2018, tm_mon=3, tm_mday=31, tm_hour=16, tm_min=34, tm_s
ec=32, tm_wday=5, tm_yday=90, tm_isdst=0)
>>>
```

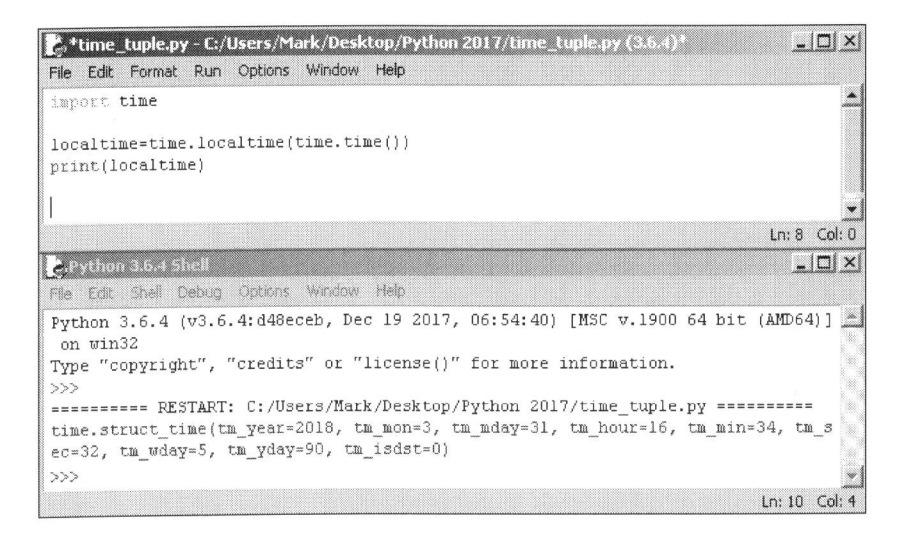

Figure 11.70. The time tuple is the output of the code shown on the editor window at the top.

Returning to our discussion in Chapter 10 regarding the characteristics of a tuple, you will remember that we can work with each member of the tuple, if needed.

To display the output in a human-readable format, add the following lines at the bottom:

formattedtime=time.asctime(time.localtime(time.time()))
print(formattedtime)

This time, the output is much more readable than the original raw time tuple.

Page 171

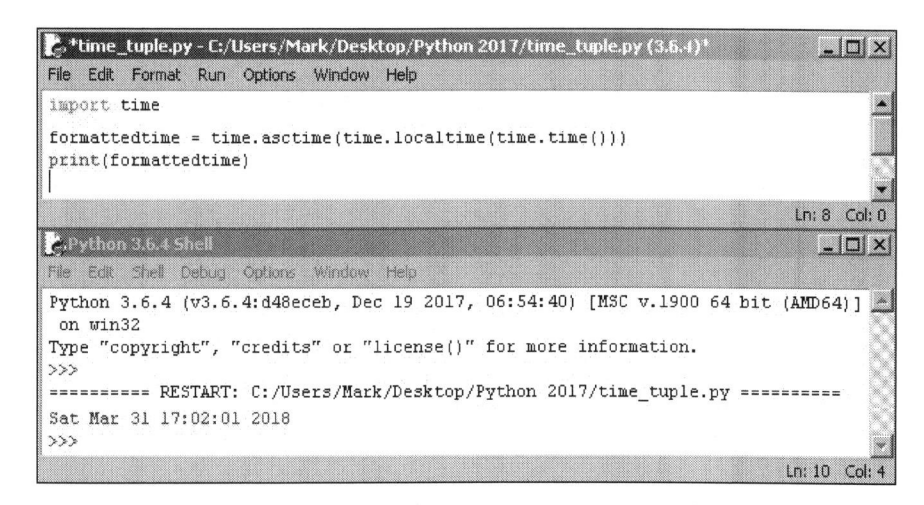

Figure 11.71. Properly-formatted time and date output from the sample program shown on the editor window at the top.

Let's dissect the time tuple some more, starting with the innermost section of the right-hand code segment shown on line 2 in Fig. 11.2. Let's use the IDLE shell window to do this.

time.time()

The output will be the number of seconds beginning on January 1, 1970.

Working outward, let's enter the next section.

time.localtime(time.time())

This time, the output is the time tuple.

Finally, let's enter the complete, right-hand side.

time.asctime(time.localtime(time.time()))

This time, the output is now more human-readable and less primitive.

```
============ RESTART: C:\Users\Mark\Desktop\Python 2017\time_tuple.py ============
time.struct_time(tm_year=2018, tm_mon=3, tm_mday=31, tm_hour=20, tm_min=52, tm_s
ec=18, tm_wday=5, tm_yday=90, tm_isdst=0)
Sat Mar 31 20:52:18 2018
>>> time.time()
1522500746.144918
>>> time.localtime(time.time())
time.struct_time(tm_year=2018, tm_mon=3, tm_mday=31, tm_hour=20, tm_min=53, tm_s
ec=22, tm_wday=5, tm_yday=90, tm_isdst=0)
>>> time.asctime(time.localtime(time.time()))
'Sat Mar 31 20:54:06 2018'
>>>
```

Figure 11.72. The time functions used in the sample program for this section, highlighted and run from the shell window. Note the differences in output.

Next, let's discuss the Calendar function.

The Calendar

Python can generate a formatted calendar for any month-year combination, as you will see in this section.

Let's again create another program using IDLE.

Similar to the Time function, we also need to import the Calendar function to work with the Calendar object in our Python program.

Enter the following:

import calendar
cal=calendar.month(2017, 2)
print(cal)

Note that line 2 shows the year and month enclosed in parentheses.

In addition, when saving the program, you should not name the program as **calendar**. This is because it will generate an error, since it will overwrite Python's built-in calendar function. This is the same for all your other programs where you import, or call, functions. The programs must not have the same name as the function being called. Otherwise, you will have trouble compiling your program.

For the output, see Fig. 11.4 below.

```
import calendar

cal = calendar.month(2009,10)
print(cal)
```

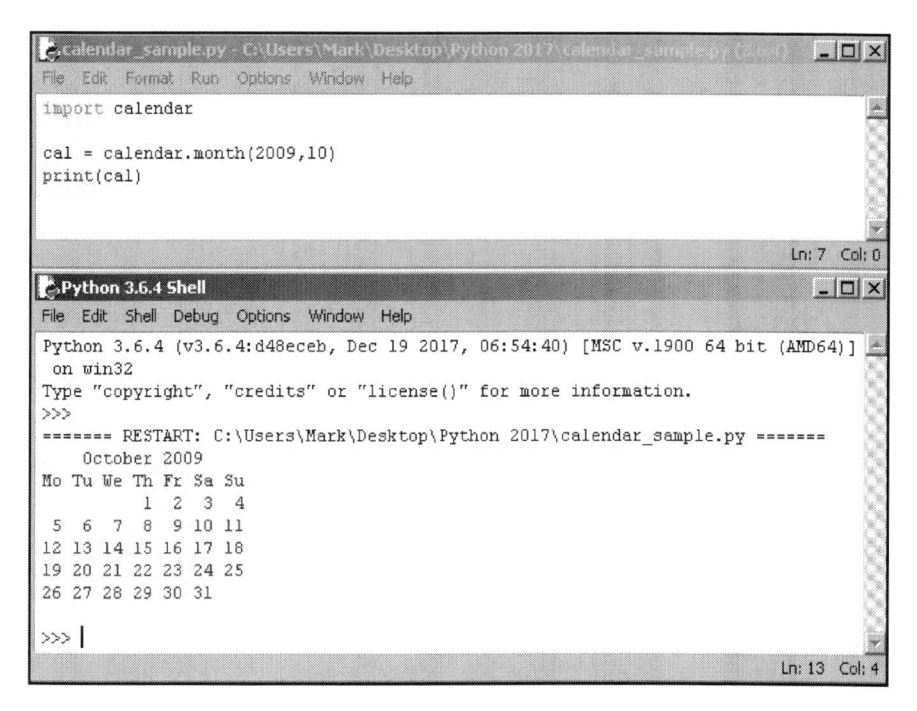

```
Python 3.6.4 (v3.6.4:d48eceb, Dec 19 2017, 06:54:40) [MSC v.1900 64 bit (AMD64)]
 on win32
Type "copyright", "credits" or "license()" for more information.
>>>
======= RESTART: C:\Users\Mark\Desktop\Python 2017\calendar_sample.py =======
    October 2009
Mo Tu We Th Fr Sa Su
          1  2  3  4
 5  6  7  8  9 10 11
12 13 14 15 16 17 18
19 20 21 22 23 24 25
26 27 28 29 30 31

>>>
```

Figure 11.73. Code and output for the sample program in this section.

We will discuss the various time and calendar functions that we can use in our Python programs next.

The Time and Calendar Functions

We will use the shell window when calling the different functions in this section. Thus, let's start IDLE.

On the shell window, we will import the time module first, before running the different time functions.

import time

Let's use the following as a guide for our different time and date functions.

We will first discuss the different methods we can use with the time function.

To show the UNIX epic time, which is the number of seconds starting from January 1, 1970, we use the aforementioned time.time() function.

time.time()

To show the time based on the clock of the PC running a program:

time.clock()

To show current GMT time:

time.gmtime(time.time))

We will now look at the methods we can use with our calendar function.

Let's import calendar first, before proceeding with our sample calls.

import calendar

To see the first weekday for the calendar:

calendar.firstweekday()

By default, this is set to 0, or Sunday.

To see if the current year is a leap year:

calendar.isleap(2018)

This will return *false,* since 2018 is not a leap year. If we enter the following instead:

calendar.isleap(2020)

This will return *true*, since 2020 is a leap year.

We will try to set the first weekday to Monday, instead of the default value of Sunday.

calendar.setfirstweekday(1)

We can try this example with an actual date to see if it works.

calendar.weekday(2018,4,2)

This will return 0, since April 2, 2018, falls on a Monday, or the first day of the week. If we enter the following:

calendar.weekday(2018,4,3)

It will return 1, since April 3, 2018, falls on a Tuesday, the day after the first day of the week.

```
Python 3.6.4 Shell
File Edit Shell Debug Options Window Help
Python 3.6.4 (v3.6.4:d48eceb, Dec 19 2017, 06:54:40) [MSC v.1900 64 bit (AMD64)]
on win32
Type "copyright", "credits" or "license()" for more information.
>>> import time
>>> time.time()
1522493762.825495
>>> time.clock()
1.1853453385109218e-06
>>> time.gmtime(time.time())
time.struct_time(tm_year=2018, tm_mon=3, tm_mday=31, tm_hour=10, tm_min=57, tm_s
ec=14, tm_wday=5, tm_yday=90, tm_isdst=0)
>>> import calendar
>>> calendar.firstweekday()
0
>>> calendar.isleap(2018)
False
>>> calendar.isleap(2020)
True
>>> calendar.setfirstweekday(1)
>>> calendar.weekday(2018,4,2)
0
>>> calendar.weekday(2018,4,3)
1
>>>
```

Figure 11.74. The various time and calendar functions and their output, as shown on IDLE's shell window.

To learn more about other time and calendar functions that you can use in your Python programs, go to the official Python documentation page at http://docs.python.org.

This is the end of our discussion on time and calendar. You will next be doing another coding exercise. This time it involves the time and calendar functions that were discussed in this section.

Coding Exercise: Functions

This coding exercise will allow you to work with time and dates in Python.
1. Using the Python date function and the appropriate arithmetic, generate the following with a Python program. Note that you should use your current date and time, instead of the same date and time shown on the example (see Fig. 11.6).

```
======== RESTART: C:/Users/Mark/Desktop/Python 2017/time_date_lab.py ========
Now it is  Sat Mar 31 19:44:25 2018
Tomorrow it will be  Sun Apr  1 19:44:25 2018
A year ago it was  Fri Mar 31 19:44:25 2017
In 100 hours it will be  Wed Apr  4 23:44:25 2018
>>>
```

Figure 11.75. Initial output of the Python program to be created for this exercise.

Remember that the following will generate a formatted current time statement.

time.asctime(time.localtime(time.time()))

Try to complete the exercise, before viewing the code shown in Fig.11.7

```
import time

now = time.time()
print ("Now it is ", time.asctime(time.localtime(now)))
print ("Tomorrow it will be ", time.asctime(time.localtime(now + (60*60*24))))
print ("A year ago it was ", time.asctime(time.localtime(now - (60*60*24*365))))
print ("In 100 hours it will be ", time.asctime(time.localtime(now + (60*60*100))))
```

Figure 11.76. Sample code for the Python program to be created for this exercise. Note that your program code may vary from this one.

2. At the top of your code, add a second import statement for the datetime module.

Create a new variable after the last print() statement that is called birthday. Use it to define your birthday with the following example for February 21, 1974, at 11:00 AM.

birthday=datetime.datetime(1974, 2, 21, 11, 00)

Add the following line of code below the definition of the birthday variable:

print("I was born on ", birthday.isoformat(" "))

Run your code and note the ISO format for your birthdate.

```
import time
import datetime

now = time.time()
print ("Now it is ", time.asctime(time.localtime(now)))
print ("Tomorrow it will be ", time.asctime(time.localtime(now + (60*60*24))))
print ("A year ago it was ", time.asctime(time.localtime(now - (60*60*24*365))))
print ("In 100 hours it will be ", time.asctime(time.localtime(now + (60*60*100))))

birthday = datetime.datetime(1974, 2, 21, 11, 00)
print("I was born on ", birthday.isoformat(" "))
```

```
======== RESTART: C:/Users/Mark/Desktop/Python 2017/time_date_lab.py ========
Now it is  Sat Mar 31 19:55:18 2018
Tomorrow it will be  Sun Apr  1 19:55:18 2018
A year ago it was  Fri Mar 31 19:55:18 2017
In 100 hours it will be  Wed Apr  4 23:55:18 2018
I was born on  1974-02-21 11:00:00
>>>
```

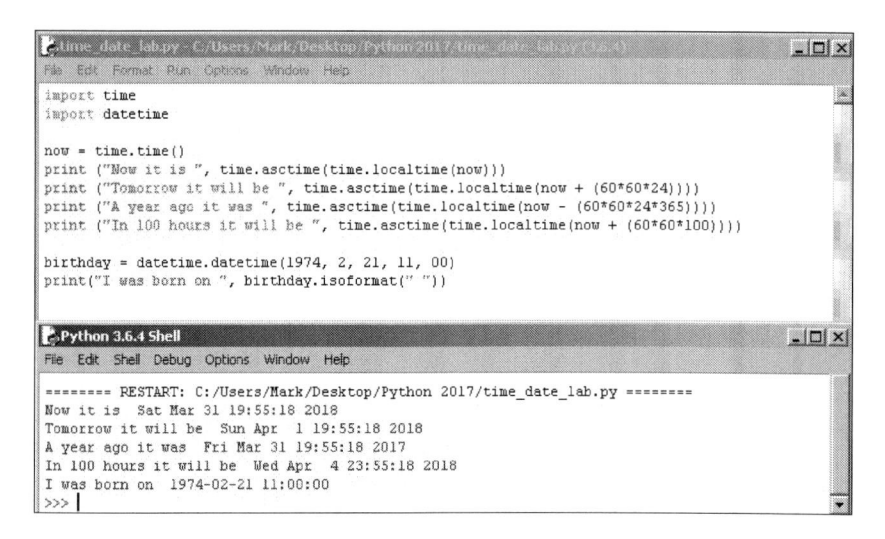

Figure 11.77. Sample output from the additional lines in Step 2 of this exercise. Note that birthdate is displayed using the standard ISO format.

Chapter 12 – Python Functions

If you had been going through this book chapter-by-chapter, you will know that we have been discussing Python functions since Chapter 1. You have learned how to use built-in Python functions in the earlier chapters of the book.

In this chapter, you will learn how to build custom, or your own, Python functions. After learning how to define and call a simple Python function, you will learn how to define required and keyword argument functions. This chapter covers setting up default function arguments and expecting return statements, which will make your functions useful. You will also learn how to create and consume Python modules.

The chapter will conclude with another coding exercise where you will create your own custom Python function.

Defining and Calling a Simple Function

As a beginning programmer, compartmentalization is an important concept that you can apply in your Python programs. What does compartmentalization mean? The simplest definition is that it allows you to reuse code somewhere else in the same program, or in another program.

Functions are how you implement compartmentalization in your Python programs. This is especially true in the case of similar procedures everywhere, such as setting up usernames and passwords and searching for the existence of a term, among others.

They make your work more efficient, since you do not have to start from scratch. As a result, compartmentalization and functions, speed up the entire development process and generate substantial savings.

In this section, you will learn how to define and call your own Python function. We will again use IDLE to do that. Once you have IDLE open, click either **File>New File** on the menu, or press **Ctrl+N** on your keyboard.

To define a function, use the ***def*** keyword. Let's try it now, by entering the following on the editor window:

```
def greetingEnglish(): #This function greets the user in the English
language
    print("Greetings and Salutations")
    return
```

When called, this simple function will display a greeting in English on your screen.

Let's add another function to our code.

```
def greetingSpanish(): #This function greets in Spanish
    print("Buenos Dias")
    return
```

Like our first function, the second function, when called, displays a greeting. However, this greeting is in Spanish.

We will now save the functions. Since you will be using the same code again later in this section, you may save the function as greetings.py.

Saving the functions did not display anything on the shell window. This is because functions do not run, unless they are called from within a program.

We will modify our greetings.py file by adding a couple of lines for calling our functions.

```
greetingEnglish()
greetingSpanish()
```

When you save and then run the program, the output is displayed on the shell window. This is because the two lines we added to the file are function calls.

Functions can be called an unlimited number of times from within a program. Therefore, if you add another greetingEnglish() function call to the bottom of your greetings.py file, running the program again will display the English greetings twice on the shell window.

```
#Function definition
def greetingEnglish():
    #This function greets the user in the English language
    print("Greetings and Salutations")
    return

def greetingSpanish():
    #This function greets the user in Spanish
    print("Buenos Dias")
    return

#Function calls
greetingEnglish()
greetingSpanish()
```

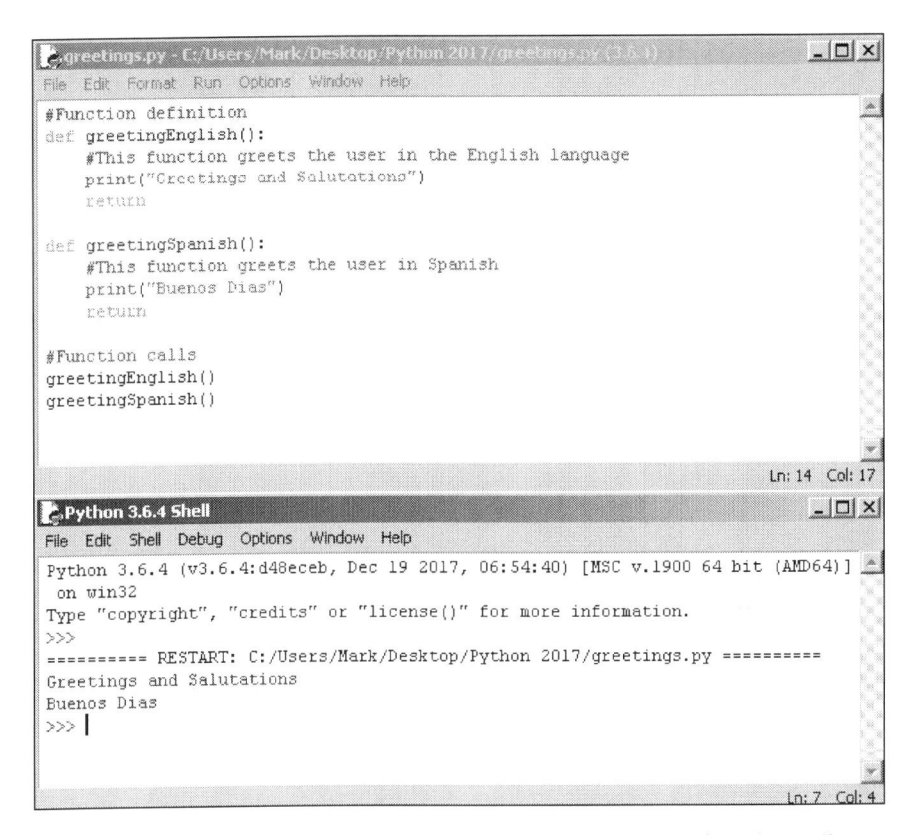

```
Python 3.6.4 (v3.6.4:d48eceb, Dec 19 2017, 06:54:40) [MSC v.1900 64 bit (AMD64)]
on win32
Type "copyright", "credits" or "license()" for more information.
>>>
========== RESTART: C:/Users/Mark/Desktop/Python 2017/greetings.py ==========
Greetings and Salutations
Buenos Dias
>>>
```

Figure 12.78. Code and output of the function definition and function call samples discussed in this section.

These examples are simple. However, functions in the real world may be more complicated and longer than these. Keep in mind that functions should perform 'singular' roles. You should not create a function that performs two different tasks. Otherwise, your functions will become overly complicated and make your programming work more difficult.

We have discussed defining and calling a simple function. In the next section, you will learn about required argument functions, which are more interesting than the simple function examples we have covered so far.

Required Argument Functions

In this section, you will learn more about required argument functions, which send an argument or arguments back to the function. The function call passes the argument back to the function.

If the function does not receive an expected argument back, an error results. Therefore, we refer to this type of function as a *required argument* function. If the required argument is missing, our program returns an error.

To illustrate, let's write a function with a single required argument first. We will then write another function with several required arguments.

def greetMe(str):
   print ("Welcome to the function", str)
   return

In our function definition, the required argument, **str**, is enclosed in a parenthesis.

We will add a couple of function calls at the bottom.

greetme("Kevin")
greetme("Brett")

In these function calls, **Kevin** and **Brett** correspond to the **str** argument expected by our function definition.

We will save the program as arguments.py.

If we run the program, the shell window displays the two separate function calls, one displaying **Kevin** and the other showing **Brett**.

Let's define another function, **calculateBattingAverage**, with several required arguments, namely **atBats**, **hits**, and **walks**. Let's add this function to our arguments.py file.

def calculateBattingAverage(atBats, hits, walks):
   battingAverage = hits/(atBats-walks)
   print(battingAverage)
   return

We will also add a couple of function calls.

calculateBattingAverage(200,54,12)
calculateBattingAverage(300,108,6)

When we save, then run the program, our function calls pass the arguments, *atBats*, *hits*, and *walks*, to the *calculateBattingAverage* function, which then computes the batting average based on the formula, *hits/(atBats-walks)*, before printing *battingAverage* to the screen.

Note that the arguments must be passed, which means they are required. If a function call does not return an argument, you will get an error when running the program.

In addition, the function calls must pass the arguments in the same order that they are defined in our function definition. In the first function call, for instance, 200 corresponds to *atBats*, 54 to *hits*, and 12 to *walks*. If the values are not passed in that same order, our *battingAverage* computation will be incorrect.

```
#Function definition

def greetMe(str):
    #This function greets the name passed in
    print("Welcome to the function", str)
    return

def calculateBattingAverage(atBats, hits, walks):
    #This function calculates batting average
    battingAverage = hits/(atBats-walks)
    print(battingAverage)
    return

#Function calls
greetMe("Kevin")
greetMe("Brett")
calculateBattingAverage(200,54,12)
calculateBattingAverage(300,108,6)
```

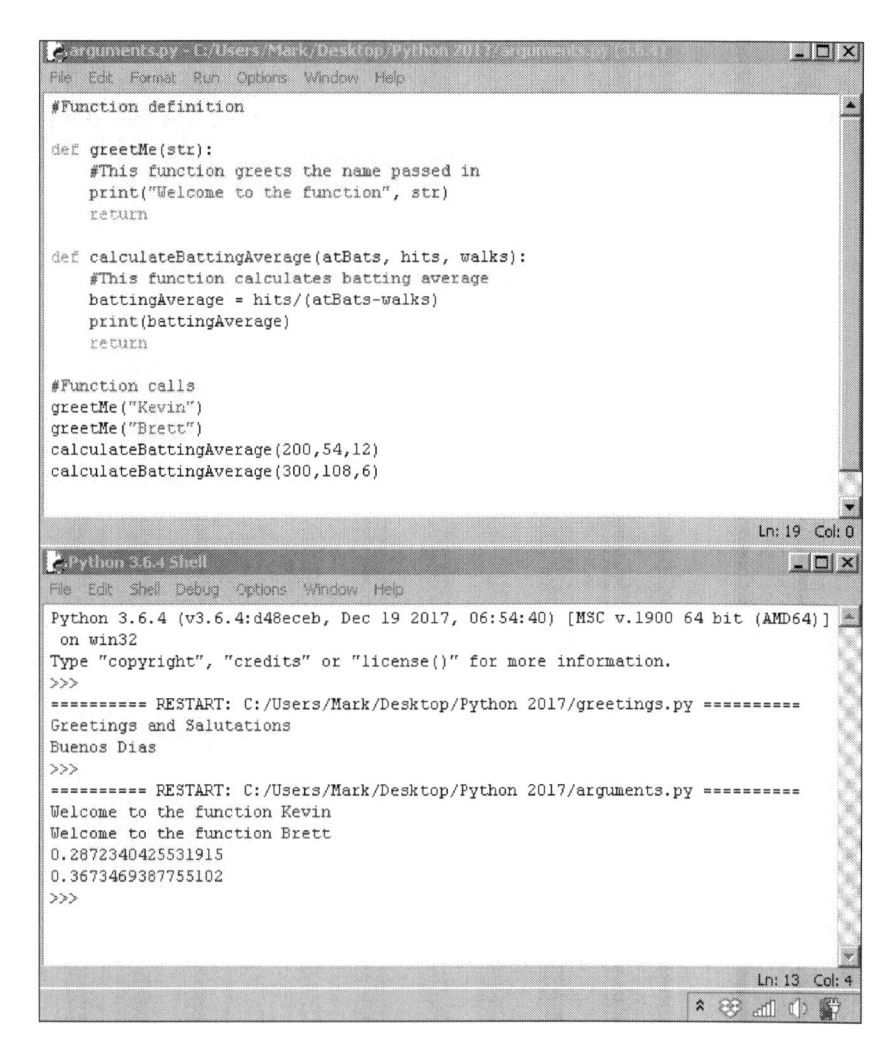

```
Python 3.6.4 (v3.6.4:d48eceb, Dec 19 2017, 06:54:40) [MSC v.1900 64 bit (AMD64)] on win32
Type "copyright", "credits" or "license()" for more information.
>>>
========== RESTART: C:/Users/Mark/Desktop/Python 2017/greetings.py ==========
Greetings and Salutations
Buenos Dias
>>>
========== RESTART: C:/Users/Mark/Desktop/Python 2017/arguments.py ==========
Welcome to the function Kevin
Welcome to the function Brett
0.2872340425531915
0.3673469387755102
>>>
```

Figure 12.79. Code and output of the required argument function examples discussed in this section.

That is the end of the discussion on required function arguments. We will now look at keyword argument functions. We will discuss another form of function that does away with the order of the arguments passed in our function calls.

Keyword Argument Functions

From the previous section, we emphasized that function arguments must be passed in the same order they are defined. Otherwise, an error or errors may result. This type of function does away with that requirement.

Let's run IDLE once again. Open the editor window and define another function.

def greetTwoPeople(person1, person2):
   #This function greets two people
   print("Greetings", person1)
   print("Hello, How are you?", person2)
   return

We will now add a function call. If we go by what we learned in the previous section, our function call would follow the following format:

greetTwoPeople("Mark", "Brett")

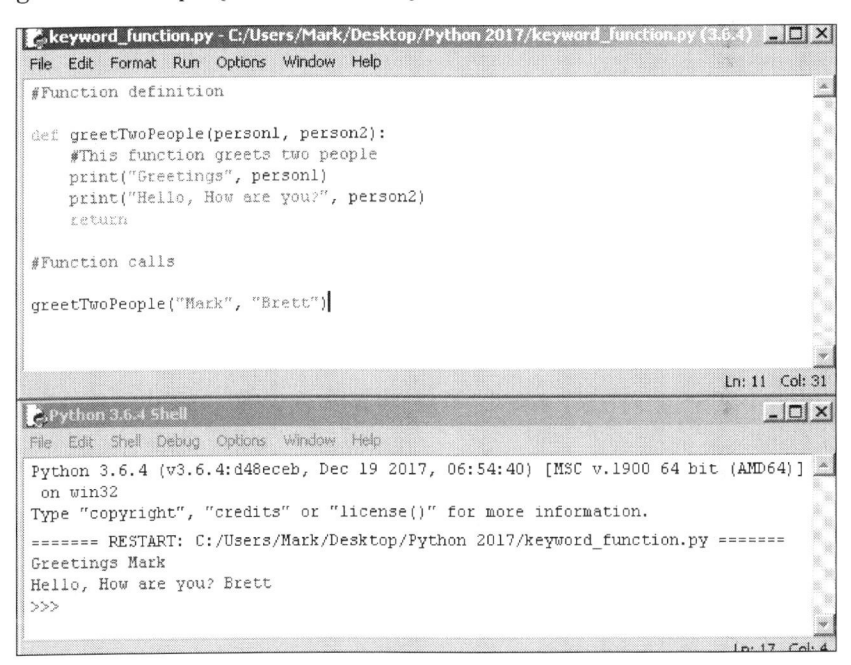

Figure 12.80. This is another example of the required argument function discussed in the previous section. There is a better alternative to this function, as shown in Fig. 12.4.

However, there is another way to do this. Using the keyword argument function, our call would have the following format:

greetTwoPeople(person1="Mark", person2="Brett")

In this function call, we are passing the argument together with the keyword, e.g. person1 = "Mark", instead of just the argument.

Using this format, the order in which the arguments are passed becomes irrelevant. Thus, the following:

greetTwoPeople(person2="Mark", person1="Brett")

will display the result shown in Fig. 12.4. instead.

```
#Function definition

def greetTwoPeople(person1, person2):
    #This function greets two people
    print("Greetings", person1)
    print("Hello, How are you?", person2)
    return

#Function calls

greetTwoPeople(person2="Mark", person1="Brett")
```

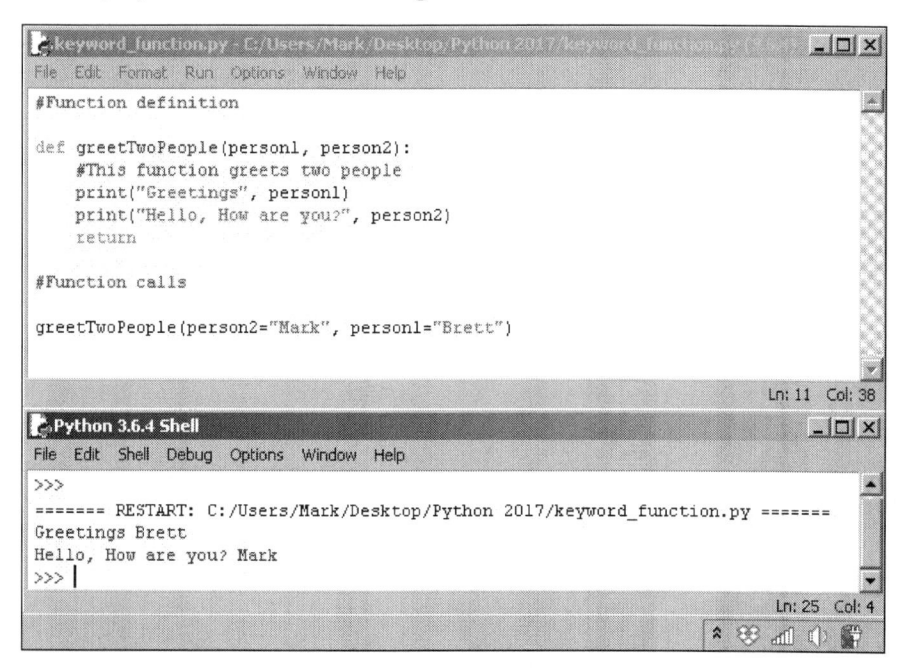

```
>>>
======= RESTART: C:/Users/Mark/Desktop/Python 2017/keyword_function.py =======
Greetings Brett
Hello, How are you? Mark
>>>
```

Figure 12.81. Order becomes irrelevant, if we passed the parameters together with the argument in the function call, as this example clearly shows.

We will try this with the calculateBattingAverage function that we defined in the previous section.

def calculateBa (atBats, hits, walks):
  ba = hits/(atBats-walks)
  print(ba)
  return

Let's add a function call.

calculateBa(walks=25, atBats=317, hits=67)

Our function call does not follow the specific order shown in the function definition. Instead, **walks** come first, followed by **atBats**, then **hits**. Because we are passing along the parameters together with the arguments, the order does not matter, and our **calculateBa** function is still able to compute the batting average.

```
#Function definition
def greetTwoPeople(person1, person2):
    #This function greets two people
    print("Greetings", person1)
    print("Hello, How are you?", person2)
    return

def calculateBa (atBats, hits, walks):
    ba = hits/(atBats-walks)
    print(ba)
    return

#Function calls

greetTwoPeople(person1="Mark", person2="Brett")
calculateBa(walks=25, atBats=317, hits=67)
```

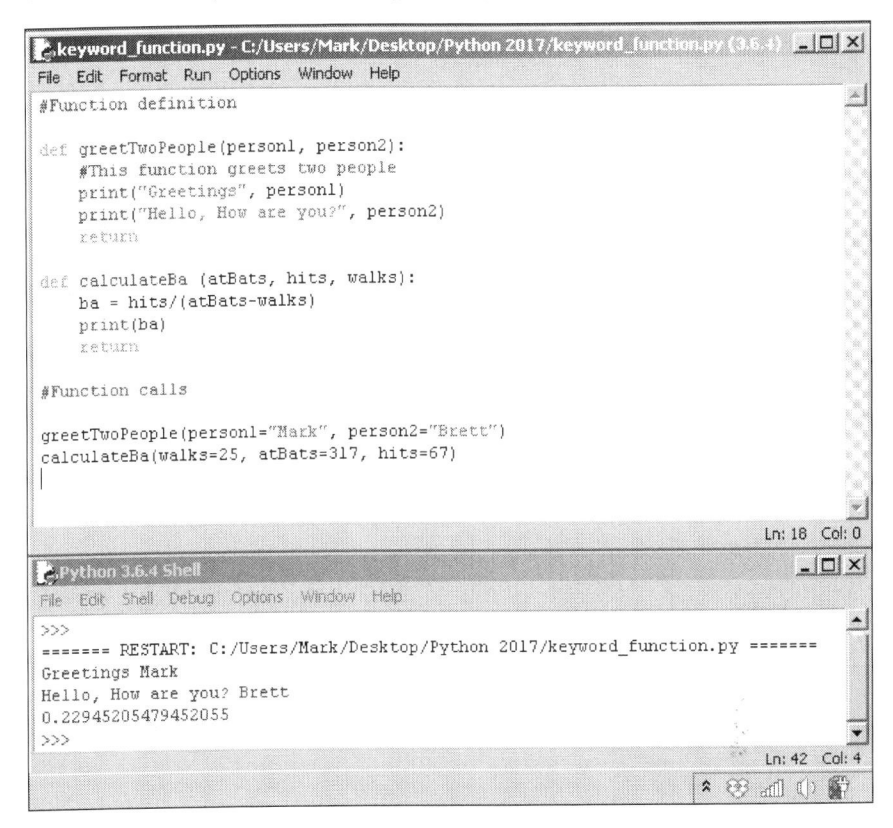

```
======= RESTART: C:/Users/Mark/Desktop/Python 2017/keyword_function.py =======
Greetings Mark
Hello, How are you? Brett
0.22945205479452055
>>>
```

Figure 12.82. As this example shows, if the function calls pass the parameters together with the arguments, the order in which the arguments are passed to the function are not relevant anymore and does not result in an error.

This is the end of our discussion on keyword argument functions. Let's go on to the next section.

Default Function Arguments

In the section on required arguments functions, it was emphasized that arguments are must be passed by function calls. Otherwise, there will be a program error. This section will discuss default function arguments, where function calls that do not pass an argument, will still be able to do so, and not bring up an error as a result.

To illustrate, let's open IDLE again, then define a function on the editor window.

```
def employeeInformation(name, ssn, position):
    print("Name:", name)
    print("Ssn:", ssn)
    print("Position:", position)
    return
```

Next, let's define a function call.

```
employeeInformation(name="Mark", ssn="000-00-000", position="founder")
```

Save the file as defaults.py, then run the program. As expected, the function call passes the arguments back to the function, and the function displays the arguments on the screen.

If we only pass arguments for the **name** and **position** parameters, we will get an error. This is because the function is also expecting an argument for the **ssn** parameter.

```
def employeeInformation(name="Mark Lassoff", ssn="000-00-000", position=""):
    print("Name:", name)
    print("Ssn:", ssn)
    print("Position:", position)
    return

def moreEmployee(name, other):
    print("Employee Info:")
    print("Name:", name)
    for var in other:
        print(var)
    return

employeeInformation(position="founder")
moreEmployee("Mark Lassoff", "Founder", "9-1-2009", "206")
```

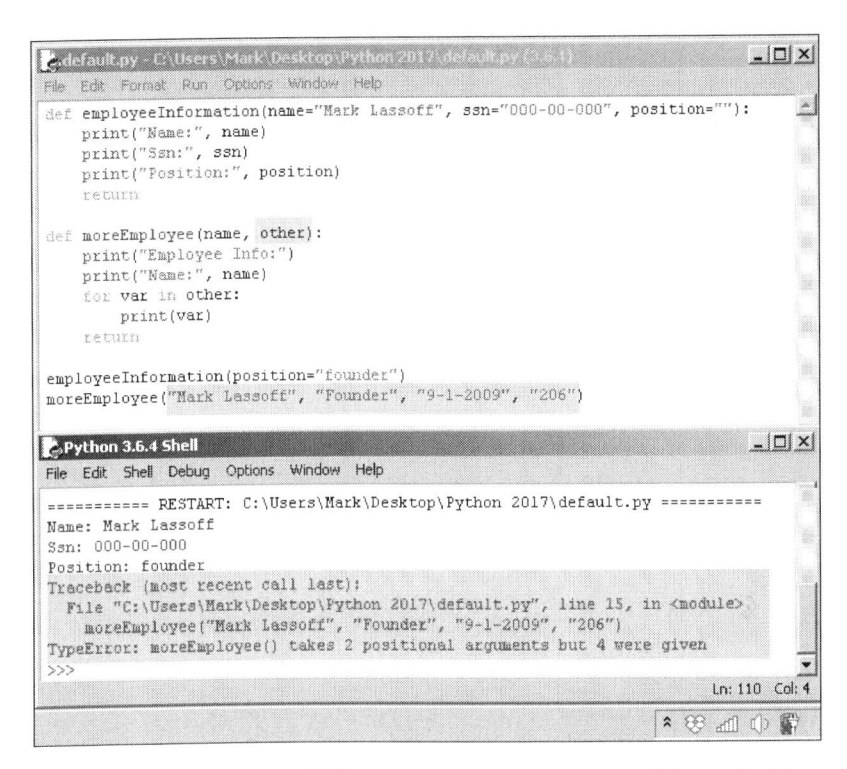

```
=========== RESTART: C:\Users\Mark\Desktop\Python 2017\default.py ===========
Name: Mark Lassoff
Ssn: 000-00-000
Position: founder
Traceback (most recent call last):
  File "C:\Users\Mark\Desktop\Python 2017\default.py", line 15, in <module>
    moreEmployee("Mark Lassoff", "Founder", "9-1-2009", "206")
TypeError: moreEmployee() takes 2 positional arguments but 4 were given
>>>
```

Figure 12.83. Errors result if more arguments are passed than what the function is expecting, as the highlighted areas in this screenshot shows.

We can avoid this limitation by setting default arguments for our parameters. How do we define default arguments? Let's edit our program to illustrate.

Let's edit our function definition by inserting default values for the function parameters.

def employeeInformation(name="Mark Lassoff", ssn="000-00-000", position=""):

Let's also edit our function call by removing the arguments.

employeeInformation()

If we save, then run the program again, the result will be as follows:

Name: Mark Lassoff
Ssn: 000-00-000

Position:

The program, therefore, runs without any error, even if we do not pass any arguments to it via the function call.

We can also pass an argument in our function call for the **position** parameter, if we want. Let's say:

employeeInformation(position="founder")

When we run the program, the result will be:

Name: Mark Lassoff
Ssn: 000-00-000
Position: founder

You should define default values for your functions, if possible. This will allow your programs to exit gracefully, instead of exiting with an error if there are problems in your arguments.

There is another situation where you may need to process a function with more arguments than was specified. Here is another example.

Let's add another function definition to our defaults.py file.

def moreEmployee(name, other):
  print("Employee Info:")
  print("Name:", name)

  for var in other:
    print(var)
  return

In this function definition, the **other** parameter takes all the other arguments that may be passed to it from a function call.

Let's also show the function call for the new function.

moreEmployee("Mark Lassoff", "Founder", "9-1-2009", "206")

If we save, then run the program, we will get an error that states the function is only expecting two (2) arguments. However, four have been given.

Let's modify line 1 of our function definition by putting an asterisk before the **other** parameter. Our modified line 1 is shown as follows:

def moreEmployee(name, *other):

This time, if we save, then run the program again, all the other arguments that we passed back to the function from the function call, are now included in the program output, as shown in Fig.12.x.

```
def employeeInformation(name="Mark Lassoff", ssn="000-00-000", position=""):
    print("Name:", name)
    print("Ssn:", ssn)
    print("Position:", position)
    return

def moreEmployee(name, *other):
    print("Employee Info:")
    print("Name:", name)
    for var in other:
        print(var)
    return

employeeInformation(position="founder")
moreEmployee("Mark Lassoff", "Founder", "9-1-2009", "206")
```

```
========== RESTART: C:/Users/Mark/Desktop/Python 2017/default.py ==========
Name: Mark Lassoff
Ssn: 000-00-000
Position: founder
Traceback (most recent call last):
  File "C:/Users/Mark/Desktop/Python 2017/default.py", line 15, in <module>
    moreEmployee("Mark Lassoff", "Founder", "9-1-2009", "206")
TypeError: moreEmployee() takes 2 positional arguments but 4 were given
>>>
========== RESTART: C:/Users/Mark/Desktop/Python 2017/default.py ==========
Name: Mark Lassoff
Ssn: 000-00-000
Position: founder
Employee Info:
Name: Mark Lassoff
Founder
9-1-2009
206
>>>
```

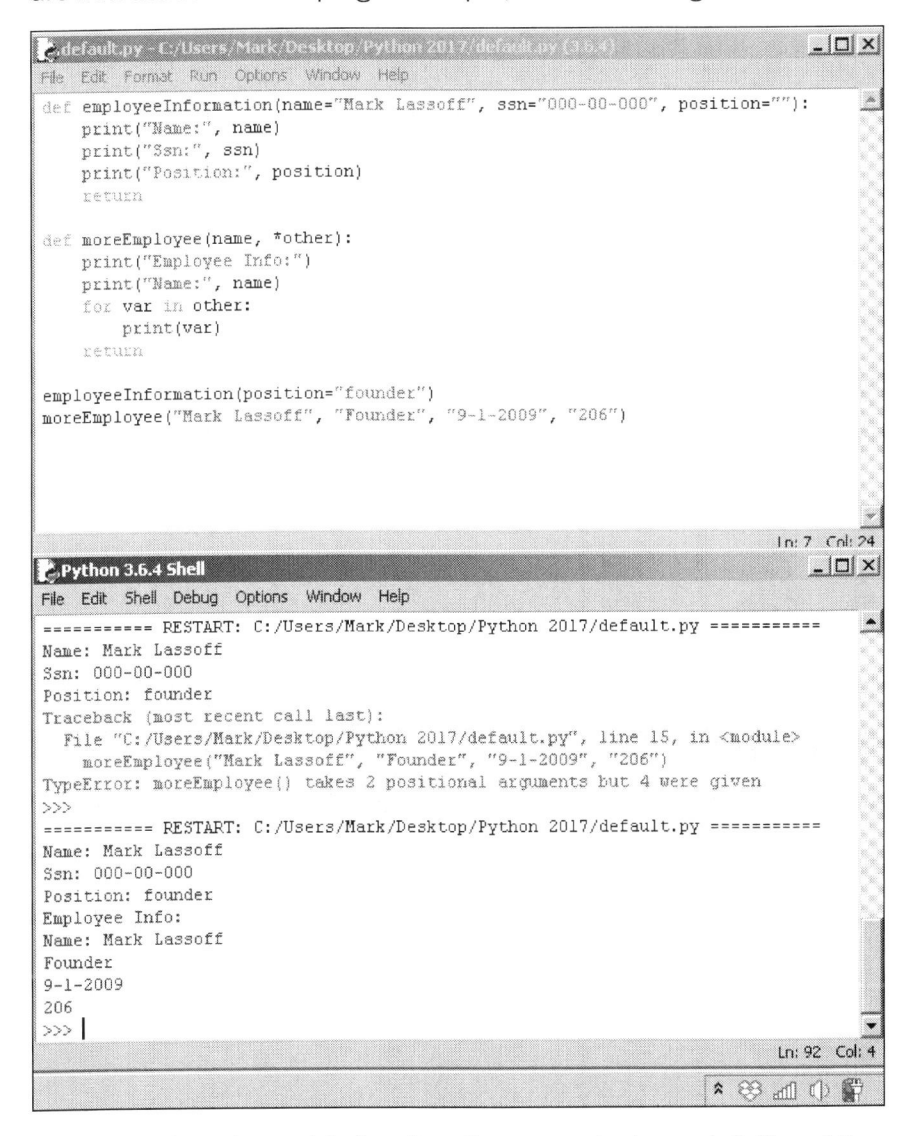

Figure 12.7. Inserting an * before the *other* parameter in our definition of the *moreEmployee* function eliminates the error and allows the function to handle the other values returned by the function call.

That is the end of our discussion on default function arguments. In the next section, you will learn more about the return statement, which we have been including from the start of our sample programs in this section.

Return Statement

Although you have encountered the return statement before, it is not just there for show. il plays an important part in functions, as we'll explain in this section.

To illustrate this, we will create another program. Open IDLE, then open the editor window, and enter the following function:

```
def calculateDogYears(humanYears):
    dogYears= humanYears * 7
    print("Dog Years:", dogYears)
    return
```

We will also add a function call, as we've been doing in the previous sections.

calculateDogYears(9.5)

Let's save the file as dog_years.py, before running the program.

As expected, when we run the program, it will display the equivalent human years for the given dog years.

```
def calculateDogYears(humanYears):
    dogYears= humanYears * 7
    print("Dog Years:", dogYears)
    return

calculateDogYears(9.5)
```

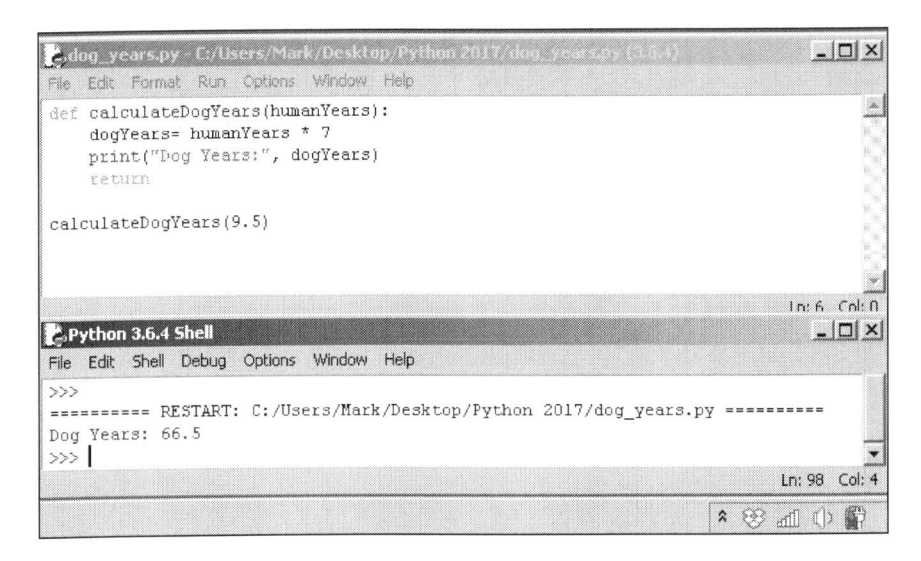

```
========== RESTART: C:/Users/Mark/Desktop/Python 2017/dog_years.py ==========
Dog Years: 66.5
>>>
```

Figure 12.8. The normal function, as discussed in the previous sections. Modifying the return statement, as shown in this section, will make the function truly portable.

We will now slightly modify the program to truly make it portable. We will make changes in the return statement and in the function call. The function definition will now look as follows:

def calculateDogYears(humanYears):
  dogYears= humanYears * 7
  return dogYears

Modify the function call as follows:

myDogYears = calculateDogYears(9.5)
print("Dog Years:", myDogYears)

The function becomes truly portable. We can call it from any other program. In this example, our function will return the value of dogYears back to the calling function.

To ensure that you understand this, let's try something simpler.

Let's modify our dog_years.py file by defining another function and inserting another function call for the new function.

Our new function is:

```
def addThese(a, b):
    return a + b
```

The additional function call is:

```
print("200 + 55 =", addThese(200,55))
```

The output of the modified dog_years.py file is shown in Fig. 12.9.

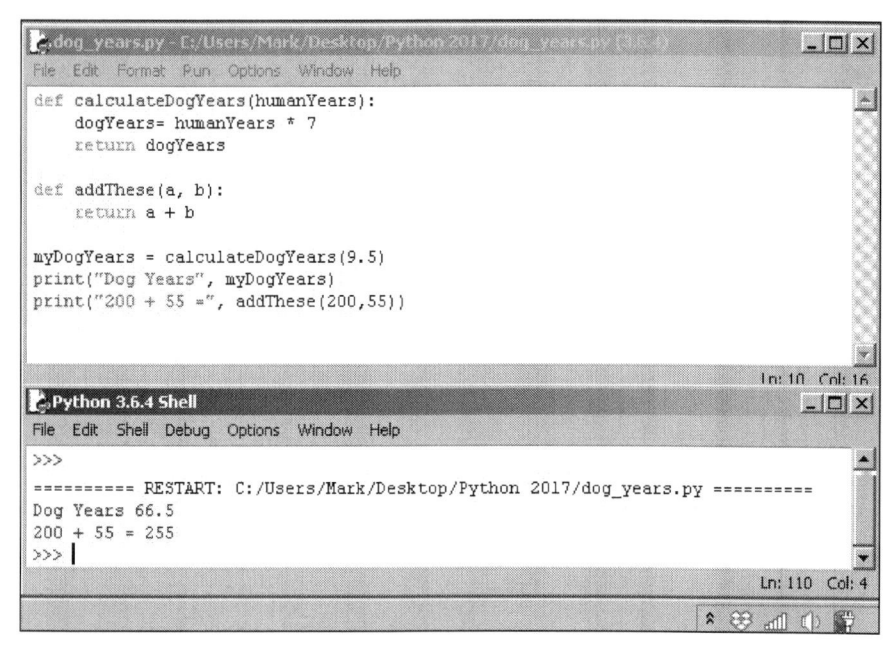

Figure 12.9. With the return statement modified to look like what is shown in this screenshot, the function becomes portable and can be called from any Python program.

Our function definitions are much more concise using the format with the modified return statement that we introduced in this section. You can put together several functions and place them in a method, which you can then call from your Python programs. We will show you how to do this in the next section. This is the end of our discussion on the return statement.

Creating and Consuming Python Modules

We have only used built-in Python modules, such as the date, time and calendar methods that were discussed in Chapter 11. In this section, you will learn how to create and use your own custom Python modules.

We will open IDLE, then the editor window, and define the functions that will compose our module.

def greetEnglish():
  return "Greetings!"

def greetSpanish():
  return "Buenos Dias"
def greetFrench():
  return "Bon Jour"
def greetHebrew():
  return "Shalom"

We will save the file as mymodule.py. You need to save modules in the same directory where all your other Python files are saved. Otherwise, you will encounter an error when you try to use the module in your programs.

```
def greetEnglish():
    return "Greetings!"

def greetSpanish():
    return "Buenos Dias"

def greetFrench():
    return "Bon Jour"

def greetHebrew():
    return "Shalom"
```

Figure 12.10. The code for the custom module sample discussed in this section.

Let's open another editor window and enter the following:

```
import myModule
print(myModule.greetEnglish())
print (myModule.greetFrench())
```

We will save this file as consumeModule.py. When we run it, it will call the functions in the module we created earlier, with the result shown in Fig. 12.10.

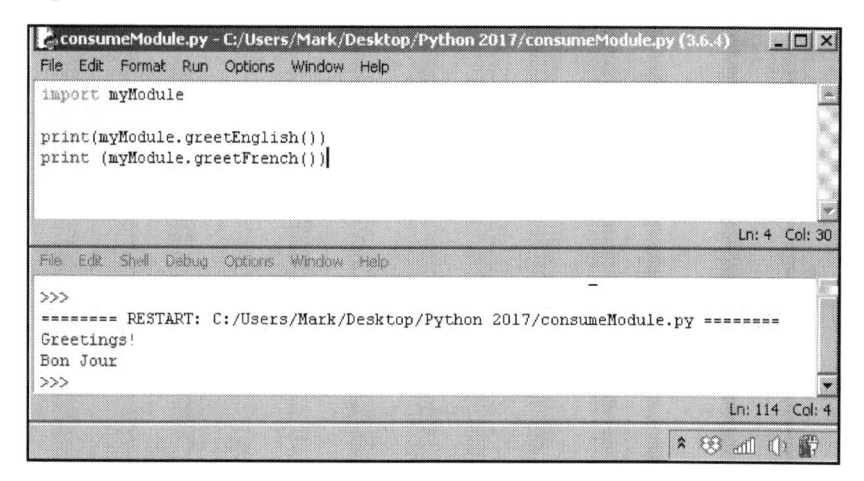

Figure 12.11. The program showing how to consume the sample custom module that is discussed in this section.

We have now learned how to create and consume our own custom module. Earlier in this chapter, you learned how to create and consume your own custom functions. You have also learned how to create the required argument and keyword argument functions. You have also learned how to set up default arguments for your functions, and how to use the return statement for your function calls. It's now time for your coding exercise.

Coding Exercise: Functions

This coding exercise will allow you to practice with functions. You will create three useful custom functions that can be reused in your Python programs.
1. The formula to convert Celsius to Fahrenheit is as follows:

*Fahrenheit = Celsius * 1.8 + 32*
Example: 32 = 0 * 1.8 + 32

Example: 212 = 100 * 1.8 + 32

The formula to convert Fahrenheit to Celsius is:

Celsius = (Fahrenheit – 32) / 1.8
Example: 100 = (212-32) / 1.8

2. Considering the equations above, write a function called fToC that returns the temperature in Celsius when it gets passed the temperature in Fahrenheit. The function call would look like this:

celsTemp = fToC(fahrTemp)

3. Considering the equations above, write a function called cToF that returns the temperature in Fahrenheit when it gets passed the temperature in Celsius. The function call would look like this:

fahrTemp = cToF(celsTemp)

4. Write a function that will convert either Celsius to Fahrenheit or vice-versa. The function should receive two parameters. The first parameter is the temperature to convert. The second parameter a Boolean indicating whether the value sent is Celsius or Fahrenheit.

5. Test your functions to make sure that they all work. This can be done by writing function calls to them and ensuring they return the expected values.

Chapter 13 – Input and Output

In this chapter, you will learn about file input and output, or file I/O, as it is more commonly known in programming.

This chapter will first teach you how to read keyboard input. To this point, your programs have all made use of hardcoded variables. You have not been prompted to enter values that your programs then take to arrive at another given value. In this chapter, you will learn to create a program that will allow you to read the values entered on a keyboard.

Next, you will learn about reading an external text file from your drive. You will take data from this file and pass it on to a program.

You will then segue into writing input to an external text file. If you can read from an external file, you should also be able to write to an external file. We will show you how to do this here.

The final part of this chapter will be your coding exercise, involving input and output operations.

Reading Keyboard Input

All the values you have worked with in your programs and even in your coding exercises are hardcoded. This I not very convenient. It is also not how things work in the real world, where programs deal with real values that are entered either via the keyboard or text files. In this section, you are going to learn how to read keyboard input.

As in earlier chapters, you will create an actual program to help you master the fundamentals of file input and output. Let's start by opening IDLE, then creating a new file.

On the editor, enter the following:

name = input("What is your name: ")

Save, then run the program.

On the shell window, that single line in our program asks us to enter our name.

Since our program still does not do anything with the input, when we press **Enter** after entering our name as the input, nothing happens. We will now add to our program, the lines that will take our keyboard input as a string.

print("Welcome to Python", name)

If we save, then run our program again, we now see that Python takes our keyboard input as a string.

Let's add a few more lines to our code. This time, let's ask for age.

age = input("How old are you?")
print("You are" , age, "years old")

Let's add another couple of lines that will let our program display the age, after a certain number of years have passed.

age = age+5
print("In five years you will be: ", age)

If we compile our program, then run it again, we get an error. If you trace back through the error, you will see that Python is expecting a string as input, not an integer. This is because input() *always* reads data from the keyboard as a string.

To resolve this error, you must cast age as an integer first. To do that, add the following line to the program. This line should be inserted prior to the line where you computed for the age after 5 years.

age = int(age)

Save, then run the program again. This time, no error is generated.

Let's add another example where we compute for the GPA, then perform a mathematical operation involving the GPA that is entered on the keyboard.

gpa = input("What is your GPA? ")
print("Your GPA is", gpa)
gpa = gpa+10

As you can see when you save and run the program, this will also generate an error. The solution is to cast GPA as a float, which will then automatically cast GPA as a string when you run a mathematical operation against it. The line where you cast GPA as a float, must be inserted right before the line where the mathematical operation is performed. The correct lines are seen below.

gpa = input("What is your GPA? ")
print("Your GPA is", gpa)
gpa = float(gpa)
gpa = gpa+10

NOTE: In Python 3, input() is the only built-in function for reading data from standard input. Python 2 had two functions – input() and raw_input().

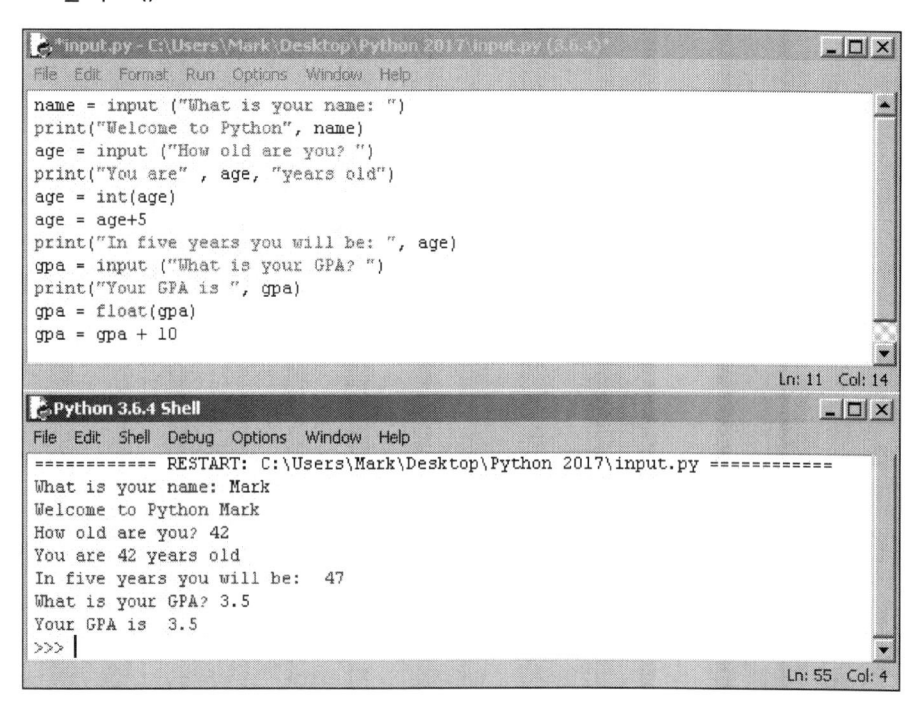

Figure 13.84. The code and output for the sample program in this section.

Reading an External Text File

In this section, you will learn about file input and output, or file I/O, where your program reads input from an external text file.

Let's start off by saving a list of employees in a text file. For example, we can have an employee.txt file containing the names of the following employees:

- Mark
- Kevin
- Wendy
- Chris
- Phil
- Bryan
- Stephen

Open IDLE, then open a new file.

On the editor window, enter the following:

myfile = open("employees.txt", "r") => here, **r** means reading, with the file pointer pointing to the beginning of the file
print (myfile.read())

This line opens our employee.txt file in reading mode, then returns the contents of the text file (see Fig. 13.2).

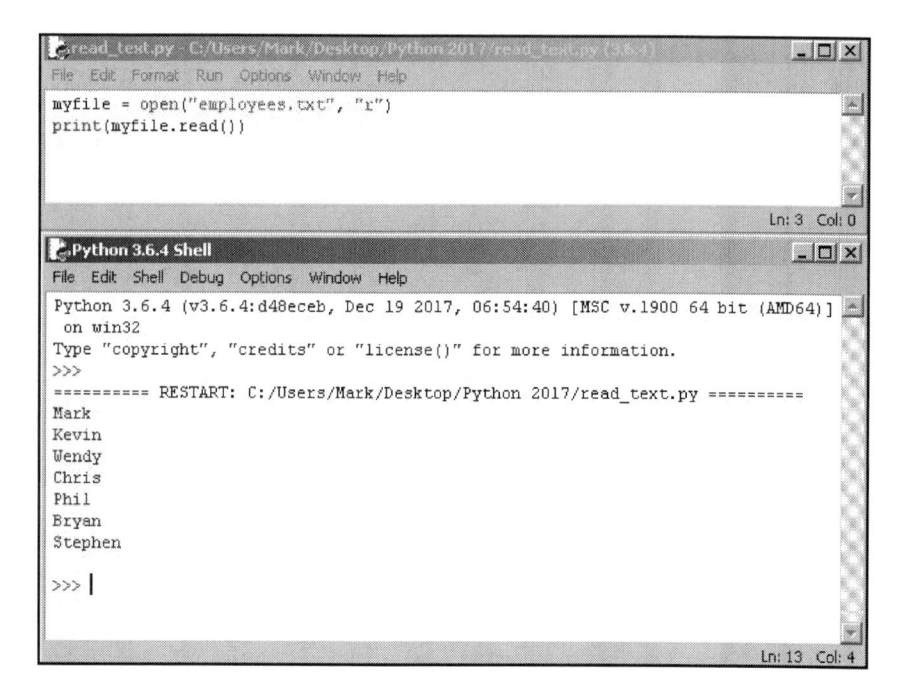

Figure 13.85. The read() function returns the contents of our text file.

We will now edit the line containing the print statement a bit:

print(myfile.read(15))

When you run the file again, this time it will read the first 15 characters inside the text file.

To read the text file line by line, we can use the readline method. To try this out, add the following line in your program:

print(myfile.readline())

This will print the character that comes after the first 15 characters in the program in another line (see Fig. 13.3).

```
myfile = open("employees.txt", "r")
print(myfile.read(15))
```

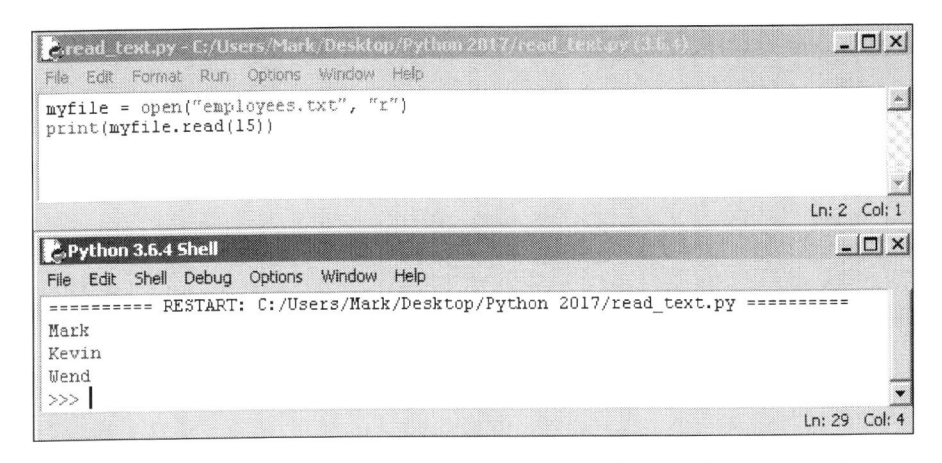

```
========== RESTART: C:/Users/Mark/Desktop/Python 2017/read_text.py ==========
Mark
Kevin
Wend
>>>
```

Figure 13.86. Our modified read() function returns the first 15 characters in the text file.

Let's add another print statement containing the same line as before.

print(myfile.readline())

The output is shown in Fig. 13.4.

```
myfile = open("employees.txt", "r")
print(myfile.read(15))
print(myfile.readline())
print (myfile.readline())
```

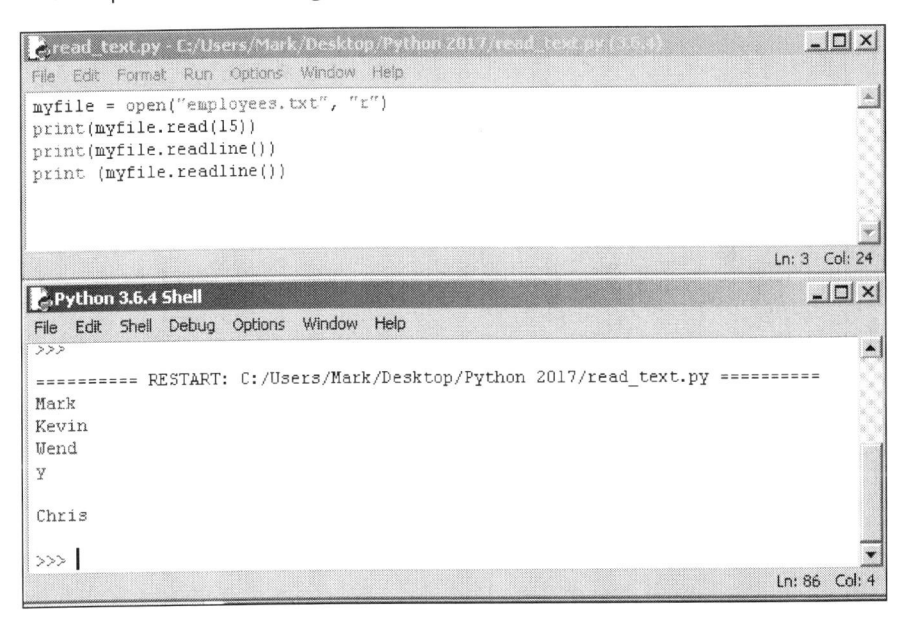

```
>>>
========== RESTART: C:/Users/Mark/Desktop/Python 2017/read_text.py ==========
Mark
Kevin
Wend
y

Chris

>>>
```

Figure 13.87. The readline() function goes through each line in our text file.

Next, let's comment out lines 2-4 of our program, then loop through the file by inserting the following lines in our program.

for line in myfile:

   print(line)

This will loop through the contents of our text file, as shown in Fig. 13.5

```
myfile = open("employees.txt", "r")
##print(myfile.read(15))
##print(myfile.readline())
##print (myfile.readline(15))
for line in myfile:
    print(line)
```

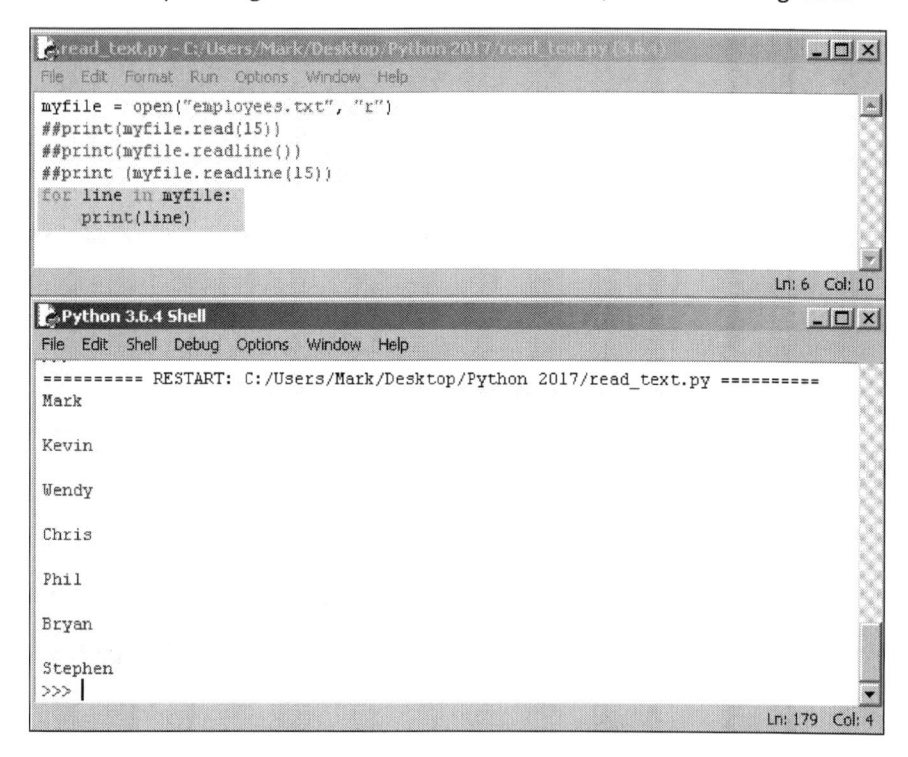

```
========== RESTART: C:/Users/Mark/Desktop/Python 2017/read_text.py ==========
Mark

Kevin

Wendy

Chris

Phil

Bryan

Stephen
>>>
```

Figure 13.88. The highlighted lines in our sample program loops through each line in our text file.

By looping through the contents of our text file, we can perform further processing on the file. For example, we can add a number before the name of each employee in our file (see Fig. 13.6).

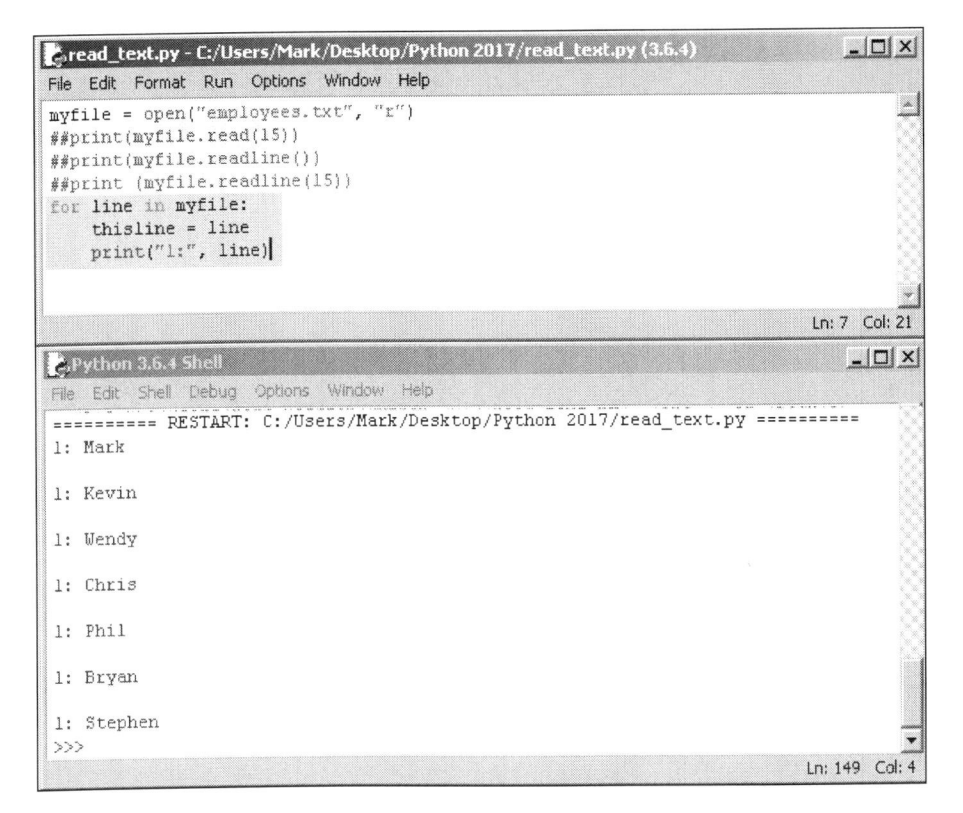

Figure 13.89. Looping through each line in our text file, allows further processing to be performed on the file's contents.

This concludes this section. In the next section, you will learn how to write to an external file.

Writing an External Text File

In the first two sections of this chapter, you learned about reading input from the keyboard and an external file.

Here, we will teach you how to output to an external text file. In this way, you can permanently store data in a file. This allows you to maintain state with your Python programs, making them more robust and complex in the process.

In this section, you will write a program that records names into a file.

Let's go ahead and open IDLE. We will open a new file, then save it as write.py.

On the editor window, the first step is to enter our file pointer.

file = open("namesList.txt", "w")

We will then define our variables.

name=""
listOfNames=""

Next, we will define a while loop that will ask us to enter names. Inside this loop is another loop, which will detect, if we enter a name with the value XXX, then add the names we have entered, except for XXX, to a list.

while (name != "XXX"):
  name = input("Name: ")

  if (name != "XXX"):
    listOfNames += name
    listOfNames += ","

We will then exit the loop by printing the list of names, before saving the names to our namesList.txt file.

print ("Saving ", listOfNames)
file.write(listOfNames)

We will then close the file.

file.close()

Let's test our program. If you entered the code above correctly, you will get the output shown in Fig. 13.7.

```
file = open("namesList.txt", "w")
name=""
listOfNames=""
while (name != "XXX"):
    name = input("Name: ")
    if (name != "XXX"):
        listOfNames += name
        listOfNames += ","
print ("Saving ", listOfNames)
file.write(listOfNames)
file.close()
```

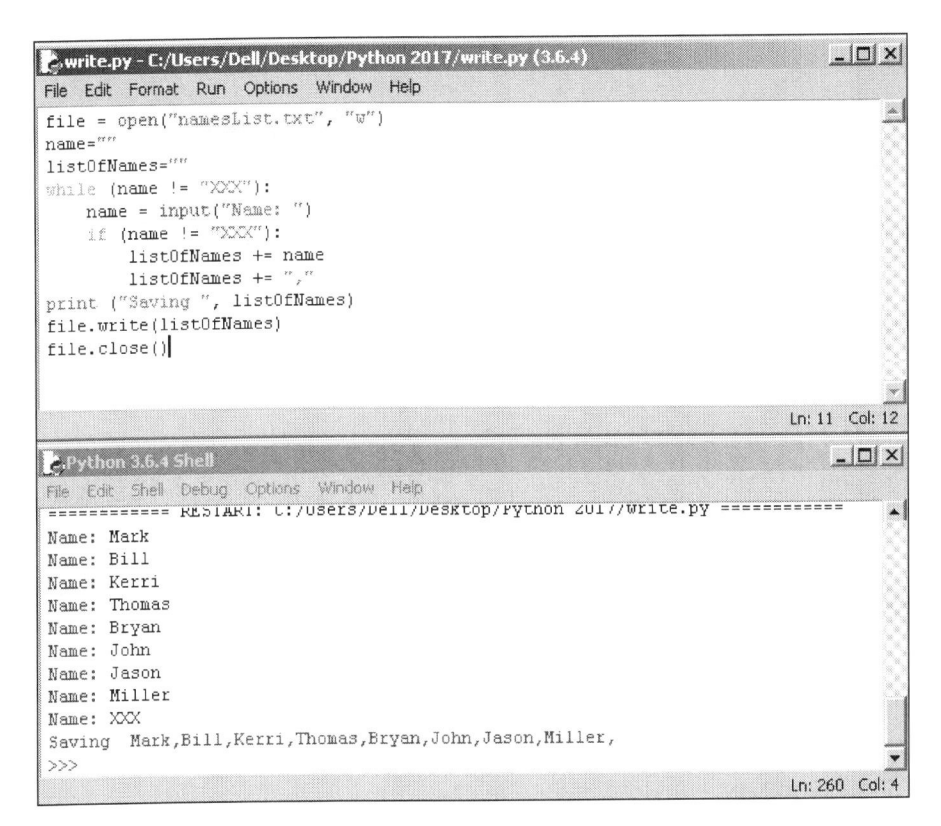

```
============ RESTART: C:/Users/Dell/Desktop/Python 2017/write.py ============
Name: Mark
Name: Bill
Name: Kerri
Name: Thomas
Name: Bryan
Name: John
Name: Jason
Name: Miller
Name: XXX
Saving  Mark,Bill,Kerri,Thomas,Bryan,John,Jason,Miller,
>>>
```

Figure 13.90. Sample code and output for this section. Check the namesList.txt file on your computer to see if you have done everything correctly.

You should also check your filesystem for namesList.txt. When you open the file, the names you entered should be listed inside the file.

You should run the program again and enter names, other than the ones you entered previously. If you check the namesList.txt file again, you will see that the file has been overwritten with the new names. This is because the file is being written over every time, courtesy of our file pointer:

file = open("namesList.txt", "w")

In the line of code above, "w" means *write*, where every time you run the program and enter a new list of names, the file gets overwritten with the new names. To change this behavior, replace the "w" with "a", or *append*, which will ensure that all new names are instead appended to the list (see Fig. 13.8).

```
file = open("namesList.txt", "a")
name=""
listOfNames=""
while (name != "XXX"):
    name = input("Name: ")
    if (name != "XXX"):
        listOfNames += name
        listOfNames += ","
print("Saving ", listOfNames)
file.write(listOfNames)
file.close()
```

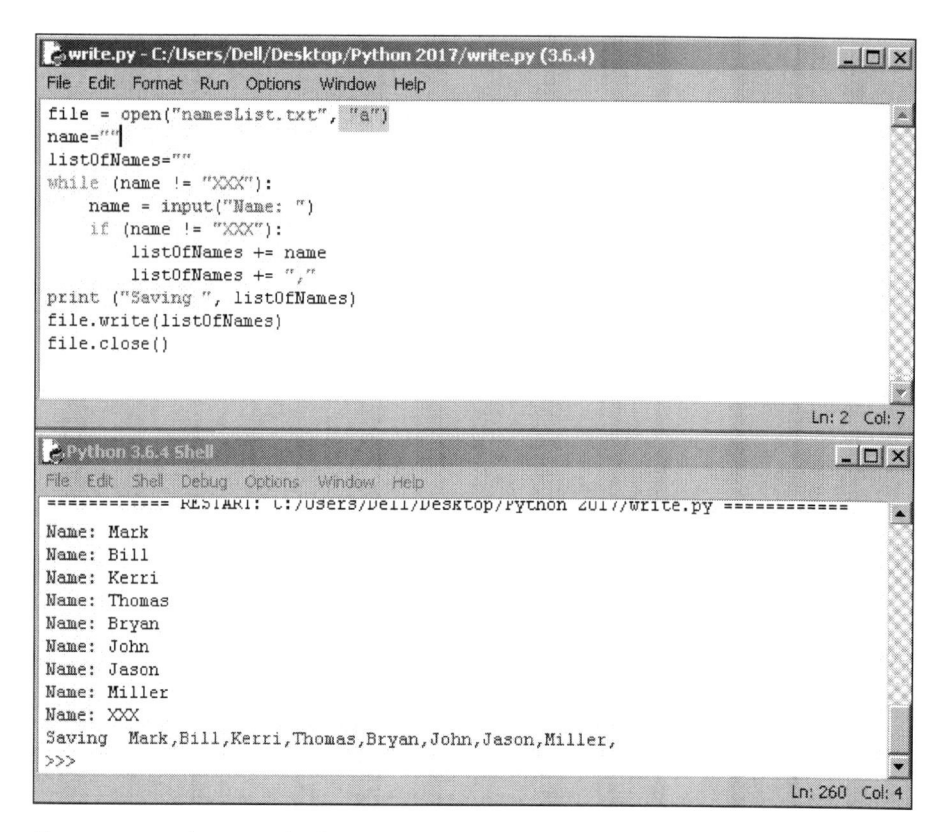

```
============ RESTART: C:/Users/Dell/Desktop/Python 2017/write.py ============
Name: Mark
Name: Bill
Name: Kerri
Name: Thomas
Name: Bryan
Name: John
Name: Jason
Name: Miller
Name: XXX
Saving  Mark,Bill,Kerri,Thomas,Bryan,John,Jason,Miller,
>>>
```

Figure 13.91. Changing the "w", or write mode, in the file pointer to "a", or append mode, ensures that all values you enter are included in the namesList.txt file. Write mode overwrites the file, each time you run the program and enter names. Append mode *appends* the new values you enter, each time you run the program with the old values already inside the namesList.txt file.

This wraps up this section. We've already discussed accepting keyboard input, reading from a text file, then writing to a text file in this chapter. We will now present our coding exercise.

Coding Exercise: File I/O

This coding exercise will allow you to practice the file I/O concepts that you learned in this chapter. You will work with external file data.

1. Load IDLE and choose **File>New File**, then save the file as file_io.py. Download the companies.csv file attached to this section. The data in this file is as follows:

7-Eleven   1964   Dallas
McDonald's   1955   Oak Brook
Dunkin'Donuts   1950   Canton
UPS Store   1980   San Diego
Wingstop. 1998 Dallas
ACE Hardware   1924   Oak Brook

2. Write a Python program, so that the CSV file is read in to the program and the information is printed to the command line. (*Hint: You can use the character entity \t to produce a tab and make your output as neat as possible.)*

3. After the companies are outputted, use an input() command to prompt the user for a company name, a year established, and a location. Store this data in three variables that are named appropriately.

4. Write the necessary code to store the data entered – company name, year established, and location – in the correct CSV format. Output a message to the user, indicating that the data has been stored.

5. Run the program and ensure that it works as expected. If there are errors or problems, debug your code until it is working properly.

Chapter 14 – More with Python

This is it. It is the final chapter in our Python for Beginners course.

In this section, you are going to learn about other concepts in Python programming that do not fit well in the earlier chapters of the book. However, they are still important to know. These are all cool skills that you need to learn, as you go about becoming a proficient Python programmer.

You will first learn about how to handle exceptions, which occur when a user does something unexpected, that causes a run-time error in your Python programs.

We'll then look at web server coding in Python. This includes how we run Python on a web server and use it to communicate with HTML to the end-user.

Finally, we'll look at processing form data with Python. When web forms are filled up, it is often processed using the Python programming language.

Handling Exceptions

Sometimes, when a Python program executes, a user introduces conditions that cause run-time errors. As a result, your program stops executing. These errors can often be anticipated as you write your programs, such as with network availability or unavailable files. As a good developer, you should anticipate these errors by knowing how to handle these exceptions in your code.

Let's look at an example of a try-catch exception.

Open IDLE and click **File>New File,** then enter the following on the editor window:

```
print("We have 10 pounds of apples.")
number = input("How many ways are we dividing the apples?")
number =int(numbers)
```

```
try:
    poundsEach = 10/number
    print("Each person gets", poundsEach, "pounds of apples.")
except ZeroDivisionError:
    print("You can't divide by zero. Try again.")
```

Let's save, then run our program.

When prompted to enter the number of ways to divide the apples, enter any number except 0. You will see that the program is able to compute how many apples each person gets. However, when you enter 0, since numbers cannot be divided by 0, you will be prompted to enter another number. This is shown in the output that is shown on the shell window in Fig. 14.1.

```
apples.py - C:/Users/Mark/Desktop/Python 2017/apples.py (3.6.4)
File Edit Format Run Options Window Help
print("We have 10 pounds of Apples.")
number = input ("How many ways are we dividing the apples?" )
number = int(number)
try:
    poundsEach = 10/number
    print("Each person gets", poundsEach, "pounds of apples.")
except ZeroDivisionError:
    print("You can't divide by zero. Try again")
                                                            Ln: 5  Col: 26
```

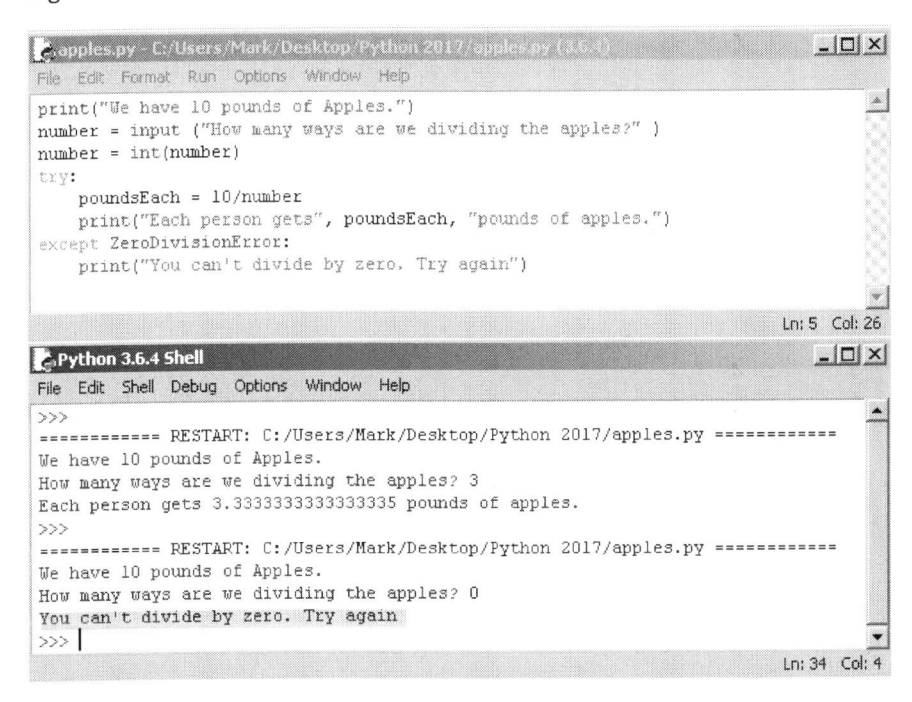

```
Python 3.6.4 Shell
File Edit Shell Debug Options Window Help
>>>
============ RESTART: C:/Users/Mark/Desktop/Python 2017/apples.py ============
We have 10 pounds of Apples.
How many ways are we dividing the apples? 3
Each person gets 3.3333333333333335 pounds of apples.
>>>
============ RESTART: C:/Users/Mark/Desktop/Python 2017/apples.py ============
We have 10 pounds of Apples.
How many ways are we dividing the apples? 0
You can't divide by zero. Try again
>>>
                                                            Ln: 34  Col: 4
```

Figure 14.92. The highlighted line shows how our program gracefully handles the condition, when a user enters 0 as program input.

What happens if your program does not include a try-catch exception? You can find out by commenting out the following lines from the program:

try:

except ZeroDvisionError:
   print("You can't divide by zero. Try again.")

If you save and run the program, and enter 0 again as an input, your program will now display an ugly-looking, non-descriptive error message and your program cannot handle the input (see Fig. 14.2).

```
print("We have 10 pounds of Apples.")
number = input ("How many ways are we dividing the apples?" )
number = int(number)
##try:
poundsEach = 10/number
print("Each person gets", poundsEach, "pounds of apples.")
##except ZeroDivisionError:
##    print("You can't divide by zero. Try again")
```

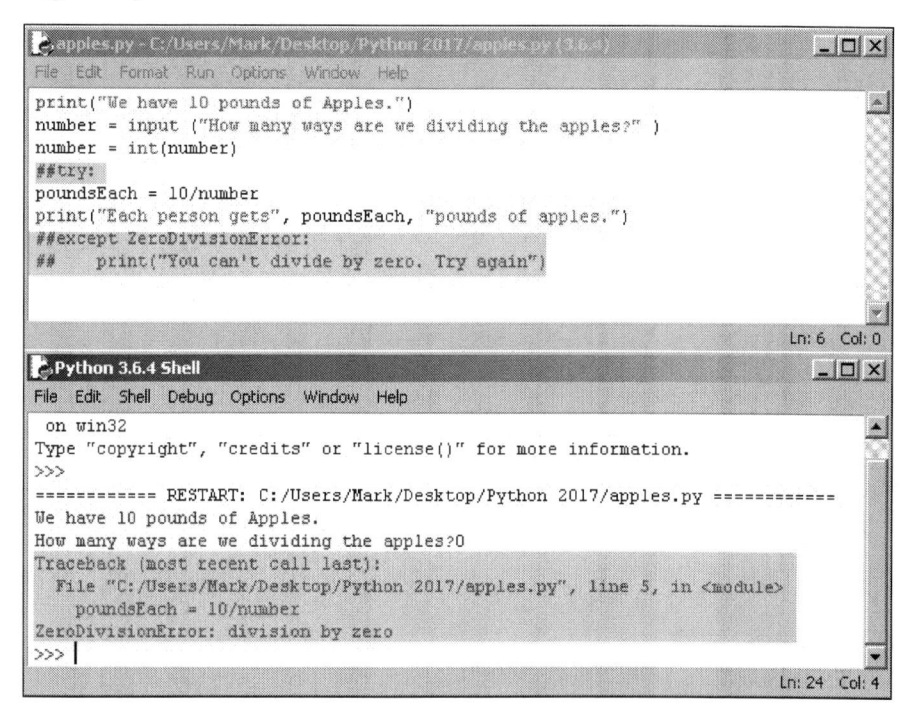

```
on win32
Type "copyright", "credits" or "license()" for more information.
>>>
============ RESTART: C:/Users/Mark/Desktop/Python 2017/apples.py ============
We have 10 pounds of Apples.
How many ways are we dividing the apples?0
Traceback (most recent call last):
  File "C:/Users/Mark/Desktop/Python 2017/apples.py", line 5, in <module>
    poundsEach = 10/number
ZeroDivisionError: division by zero
>>>
```

Figure 14.93. When we comment out the try-catch exception from our program (see the highlighted lines of code on the editor window), our program returns a non-descriptive and ugly-looking error instead. This is a stark contrast to the clean-looking error message we get with the try-catch exception in Fig. 14.1.

Let's try another example using the namesList.txt file that we coded earlier in Chapter 13.

Open another file on IDLE, then enter the following on the editor window:

try:

```
file = open("namesList.txt", "a")
file.write("EOF")
```

These lines open our namesList.txt file, then writes "EOF" at the end of the file.

Let's add an exception:

```
except IOError:
    print("IO Error")
    file.close()

else:
    print("EOF written successfully")
    file.close()
```

The exception catches, then prints *IO Error,* if the program can't write to namesList.txt file for any reason. If there is no error, the lines under the *else* statement take over – *EOF written successfully* is displayed, informing the user that *EOF* has been appended to our namesList.txt file.

Saving and running the program will have the output shown in Fig. 14.3, since we are able to insert *EOF* to our text file. However, if the file is not available, you will get an *IO Error* message printed on screen. You can check the actual namesList.txt file to see if there is indeed an *EOF* at the end of the file.

```
try:
    file = open("namesList.txt", "a")
    file.write ("EOF")
except IOError:
    print ("IO Error")
    file.close()
else:
    print("EOF written successfully")
    file.close()
```

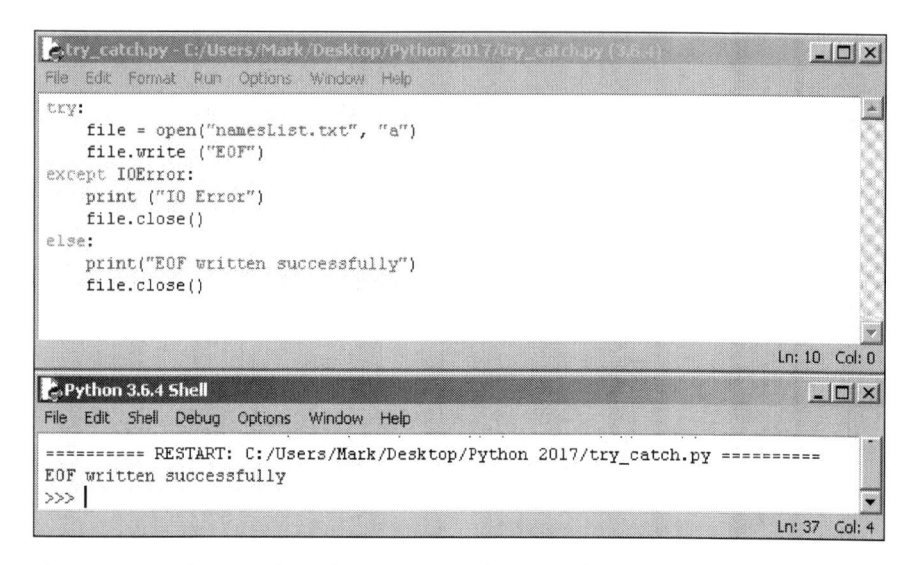

```
========== RESTART: C:/Users/Mark/Desktop/Python 2017/try_catch.py ==========
EOF written successfully
>>>
```

Figure 14.94. The sample code and output for the other try-catch exception example discussed in this section.

There are only two try-catch exception examples discussed in this section. However, there are many more that you will encounter as you go about becoming a more proficient Python programmer. To give your users a better idea of what is wrong with their input when they use your programs, you should ensure that your Python programs are able to handle exceptions.

In the next section, we will discuss web server coding with Python.

Web Server Coding with Python

Many people use Python for backend web code, or code that runs on a web server.

Python comes with its own web server. To run this server, open a command-line, if you're using Windows, or a terminal, if you're using Linux or MacOS, then enter the following command:

python -m http.server --bind localhost --cgi 8000

You can put Python files in the cgi-bin of the folder, where your Python web server is located. For example, say we have a hello.py file containing the following lines of code:

print("Content-Type: text/html\n")

print("<!doctype html><title>Hello</title><h2>hello world</h2>")

To run this simple HTML file, open your web browser, then enter the following on the URL bar:

http://localhost:8000/cgi-bin/hello.py

The web browser then runs the Python file (see Fig. 14.4).

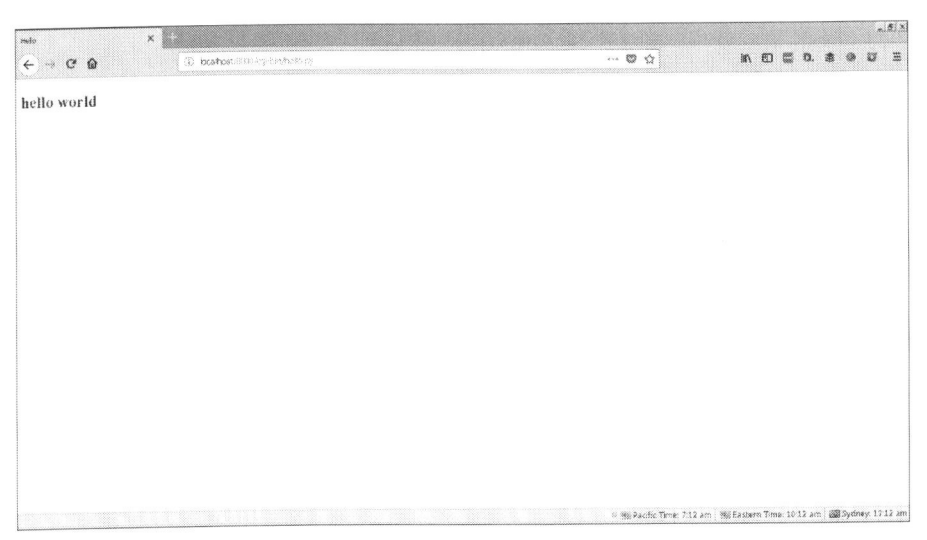

Figure 14.95. A Python file running on a web browser.

When you run the file, the command-line or terminal, whichever you are using, displays the info about the file you are running from the server (see Fig. 14.5).

Figure 14.96. The command-line displays info from the server about the running Python file.

Let's try another Python script. This one shows the Python environment variables on your system.

```
import os

print ("Content-type: text/html\r\n\r\n")
print ("<font size=+1>Environment</font><\br>")

for param in os.environ.keys():
   print("<b>%20s</b>: %s<\br>" % (param, os.environ[param]))
   print("<br/>")
```

Save this file as environ.py in your CGI-BIN, then run it from the browser by entering the following on the URL bar:

localhost:8000/cgi-bin/environ.py

We have one last example. This one shows us modifying the hello.py file using our ordinary text editor, instead of IDLE.

Open the hello.py file using your text editor, then enter the following:

```
print("Content-Type: text/html\n")
print("<!doctype html>")
print("<html>")
print("<head><title>Python Script</title></head>")
print("<body>")
print("<h1>Welcome to the world of Python on the Web!</h1>")
print("<p>We learned this in Python for Beginners (2017)</p>")
print("</body></html>")
```

Save the file, then run it from the browser:

localhost:8000/cgi-bin/hello.py

The output is shown in Fig. 14.6.

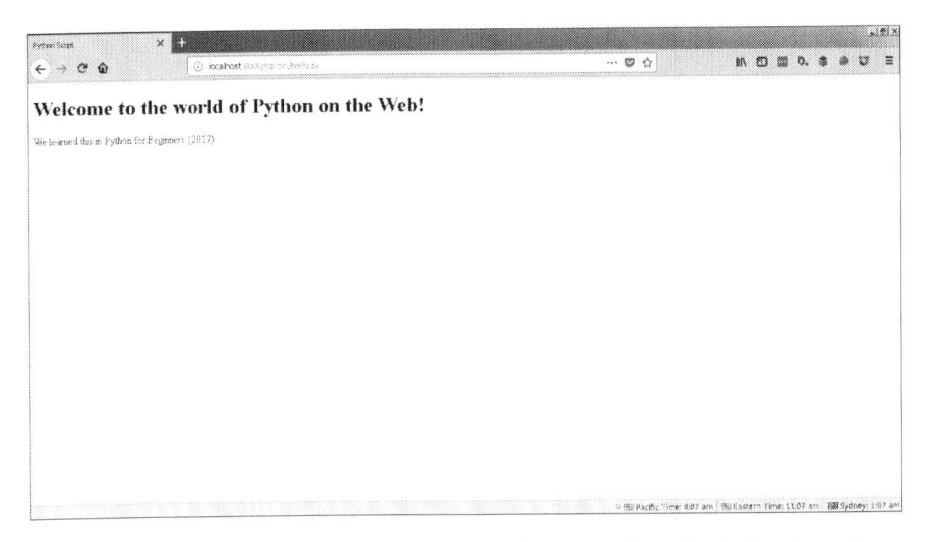

Figure 14.97. Running the hello.py file on a web server. If you look closely at the file itself, you can see that it includes HTML tags within each print statement.

That concludes our section on web server coding with Python. We now segue into processing HTML form data on the web with Python.

Processing Form Data with Python

In this section, you will learn how Python interacts with HTML to process form data.

First, let's create a name_form.html file for our form data.

```
<html>
<head>
<title>Form with Python</title>
<body>
<form method="get" action="http://localhost:8000/cgi-bin/form_process.py">
<label for="first">First Name</label>
<input type="text" id="first" name="first"/>
<label for="last">Last Name</label>
<input type="text" id="last" name="last"/>
<button type="submit">Submit to Python Script</button>
```

```
</form>
</body>
</html>
```

When run from the browser, this HTML file will appear like the one in Fig. 14.7.

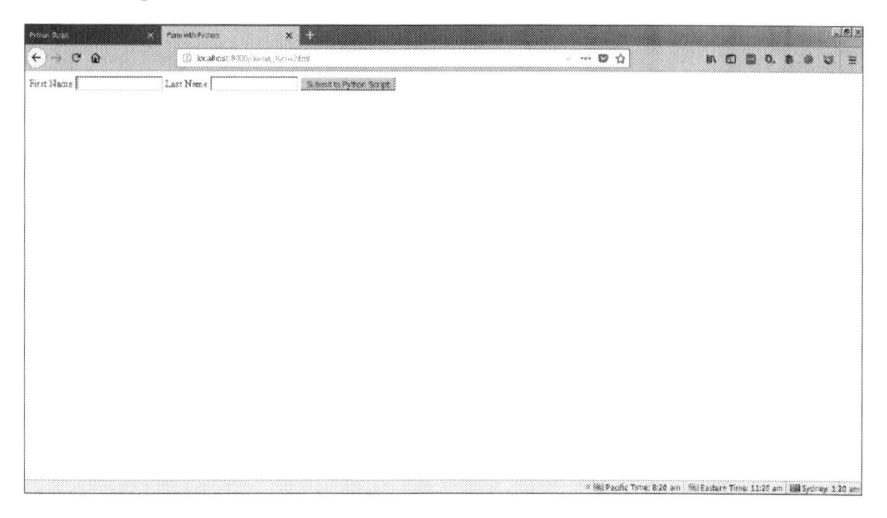

[Screenshot of browser window showing an HTML form with First Name and Last Name fields, and a "Submit to Python Script" button.]

Figure 14.98. Your HTML form will appear like this.

We will now code the Python program that will receive and process the data entered on the HTML form.

First, let's import the modules that will be needed to handle the CGI.

import cgi, cgitb

Next, we'll create the storage instance for the form data.

form = cgi.FieldStorage()

We will then enter the variables that will receive the values entered on the *first* and *last* fields in our HTML form.

first_name = form.getvalue('first')
last_name = form.getvalue('last')

Next, let's enter the HTML tags that will display the form values on the browser.

```
print("Content-type:text/html\r\n\r\n")
print("<html>")
print("<head>")
print("<title>Hello - Second CGI Program</title>")
print("</head>")
print("<body>")
print("<h2>Greetings %s %s</h2>" % (first_name, last_name)
print("</body>")
print("</html>")
```

Let's save our Python file as form_process.py.

We will now tie it all up together. Enter your first name and last name on the appropriate boxes on the browser, then click the **Submit to Python Script** button (see Fig. 14.8).

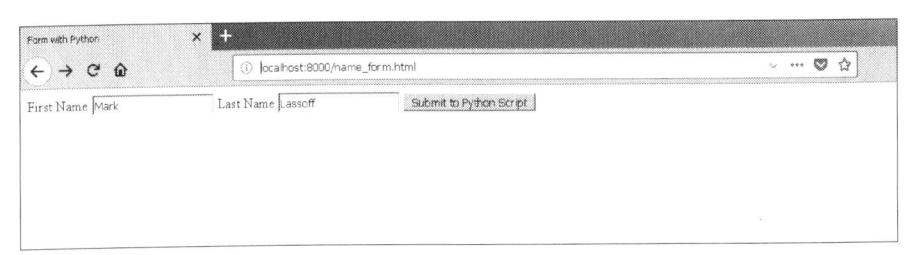

Figure 14.99. Enter your first and last names on the appropriate boxes on the HTML form, then click the **Submit to Python Script** button to pass the values on the boxes to the Python script for processing.

The first and last names are then passed to the Python script, which displays the passed values on the URL bar (see Fig. 14.9).

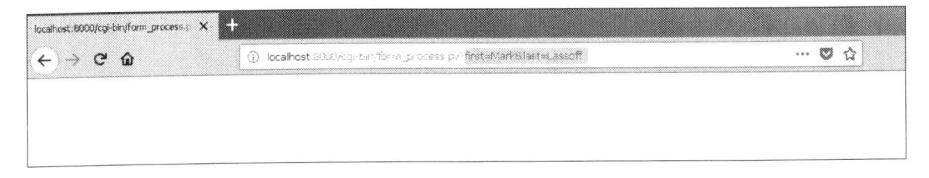

Figure 14.100. The Python script then processes the values passed from the HTML form and displays the *first* and *last* values on the URL bar, seen highlighted in this screen capture.

Wrap Up and Goodbye

That concludes this chapter, and the book.

If you went through the book chapter-by-chapter, you would have learned much at this stage. From using IDLE, you learned about the print() function, variable assignments and the different variable types, gone on to operators and loops, and tackled the different Python functions. You also gained knowledge about data structures, created your own functions, learned about file input and output and finally more advanced topics, such as exception handling and coding with web servers.

This is just the beginning. However, you should know by now that Python is a powerful programming language. Armed with the skills you have gained in this course, you should now be ready to take your programming career a step further.

Made in the USA
Columbia, SC
29 November 2018